Doing Therapy with Children and Adolescents with Asperger Syndrome

Doing Therapy with Children and Adolescents with Asperger Syndrome

Richard Bromfield

JOHN WILEY & SONS, INC.

Copyright © 2010 by John Wiley & Sons, Inc. All rights reserved.

Published by John Wiley & Sons, Inc., Hoboken, New Jersey.

Published simultaneously in Canada.

Library of Congress Cataloging-in-Publication Data:
Bromfield, Richard.
    Doing therapy with children and adolescents with Asperger syndrome / by Richard Bromfield.
        p. ; cm.
    Includes bibliographical references and index.
    ISBN 978-0-470-54025-1 (cloth : alk. paper)
    1. Asperger's syndrome in children—Treatment.   I. Title.
    [DNLM: 1. Adolescent. 2. Child. 3. Asperger Syndrome—therapy. 4. Asperger Syndrome—psychology. 5. Autistic Disorder—therapy. 6. Psychotherapy—methods.   WS 350.6 B868d 2010]
    RJ506.A9B76 2010
    618.92'858832—dc22

                                                                                        2009041457

Printed in the United States of America

10 9 8 7 6 5 4 3 2 1

For Lorraine, the best and sweetest aunt ever.

Contents

Preface   viii
Acknowledgments   xvii
Important Notes   xviii

1 ♦ What Asperger's Means for the Child   1

2 ♦ Meet the Parents   11

3 ♦ Beginning Therapy   19

4 ♦ Hypersensitivity   29

5 ♦ Anxiety   43

6 ♦ Communication   61

7 ♦ Intellect, Cognitive Style, and Creativity   77

8 ♦ Feelings and Depression   101

9 ♦ Social Difficulties   121

10 ♦ Theory of Mind and Other So-Called Impediments
      to Therapy   147

11 ♦ Connecting It All   169

      Appendix: Working with Parents   175
      References   187
          Author Index   201
          Subject Index   205
          About the Author   217

Preface

I clinically met my first children with Asperger's and High-Functioning Autism in 1981 at Camp Wediko here in New England. Like many college students before us, my newlywed wife and I had driven north to New Hampshire to spend an intensive summer learning more about the careers we were about to enter: she, special education, and myself, clinical psychology. She was assigned to Think City, the camp school, and I was a counselor for the Stallions, a group of teens who, I was told, didn't fit in with any of the other cabins or groups of children. "I think you'll find them interesting," the late and wonderful camp director said to me with a smile.

Within minutes of entering the cabin, I saw children who differed in ways immediate to my amateur eyes and ears. Unlike the other children I'd seen at Wediko and before, the Stallions didn't interact with one another. There was none of the chitchat, jostling, and testing of each other that one expects from teens thrown into a mix. Some of the boys were withdrawn and barely able to say their names. Some boys talked loud and nonstop, not noticing when other people spoke or weren't listening. A majority of the boys came from disadvantaged and stressed homes.

The rail-thin Dmitri recited the facts of his family's ancestry; he couldn't tell us the details of his own family. The stocky and smiling Eddie laced and relaced his sneakers as if his feet required 58 psi of pressure. Don, a lineman-sized teen from Boston's inner city, giggled in a soft and high voice. Distracted and mesmerized by his dancing fingers, the delicate-looking Hardy paid little attention to the rest of us. Harlem's wiry Carlos occupied himself as athletic boys are prone to do, balancing on one leg while tossing a baseball in one hand. These boys, and the rest of the Stallions, came in every size and color. Although at first glance they looked like 10 kinds of boys with 10 distinct issues, there was one thing they shared: a collective unease that was palpable. Never had I seen and felt a group of children so uncomfortable with themselves.

I had no idea how a real psychologist would have assessed and treated these boys. By the end of the summer, there was much my novice mind felt certain about. The boys were complex. And just as the camp's director promised, they were intriguing.

In major ways, these boys seemed unlike most of the campers at Wediko that summer. They had greater difficulty communicating. It felt as if we had a cabin of 10 boys from 10 planets who spoke 10 languages. I often found myself translating one boy's words into forms that the other boys or I could grasp. Oft times, we found that what on the surface appeared to be random words or behaviors actually spoke to the child's fear or anxiety.

Communicating in social and group settings was especially hard for these boys. They didn't sense the natural rhythms and beats, the give and take of conversation that the other children did. When our boys spoke out in wider camp settings, they were treated with rolling eyes, laughter, and teasing that could turn cruel. The average teen, no less the troubled ones at our camp, weren't interested in endless punning or a lecture on geology. All but one of the Stallions were uncoordinated and inept at sports, depriving them of any "street cred" that might have raised their social stature in the camp culture. I and my fellow counselors spent a good deal of our focus and efforts protecting these boys from the rejection and humiliation ever ready at the hands of other campers who had their own issues of esteem.

But as unique and out of the ordinary as these boys were, it was the sameness of their humanity that had then struck me. Dmitri's interest in rocks may have sounded excessive and compulsive to the rest of us, yet he wanted his interest shared and respected, as might any other boy telling a more measured and engaging story about his new dog or his exploits on the baseball field. However odd and preoccupying Eddie's perpetual re-adjusting of his laces and clothes looked, he dearly appreciated my noting just how impossible it was for him to get comfortable. Hardy liked that I gently helped him to focus when we spoke and that I didn't stare at his wiggling fingers or critique his fascination with his hands. One didn't have to be a psychologist or autism expert to notice that for all their awkwardness, these boys wanted friends, just as they sought—and could profoundly feel—kindness, generosity, acceptance, respect, affection, and, perhaps more than anything, understanding for who they were, warts and all.

Even then, I grasped that being the Stallions' counselor from dawn to late night, though arduous, was nothing compared to what those boys faced, surviving away from their families and neighborhoods in a strange wilderness of nature and peer culture. Even at this early stage of our professional careers, it was obvious to every counselor in our cabin that these boys—"The Mighty, Mighty Stallions"—faced developmental challenges far greater than did the typical children we knew outside of camp. Having Asperger's or High-Functioning Autism wasn't a pass that exempted these boys from any part of life and development. Our boys had the same psychological needs as did every nonautistic boy. Our boys had to grow life skills, competencies, esteems, identities, and so on, just as other children did. Their developmental difficulties and deficits—the ones I would soon learn had to do with autism—only made those psychological tasks harder to face and manage. As if not enough, the Stallions had additional problems. Dmitri had asthma and a neuromuscular disorder, Hardy had gender confusion, Eddie had learning problems, Don had been neglected, and Carlos had been abused. Even then, a veritable toddler in the world of mental health, I could see the disproportion and unfairness in the boys' developmental burdens.

A few weeks after leaving Wediko, I enrolled in a doctoral program in clinical psychology at the University of North Carolina. There, I soon learned officially what autism was about. The university was the home of Dr. Eric Schopler and TEACCH (Treatment and Education of Autistic and related Communication-handicapped Children), his innovative and maverick program for children with autism—a program that would come to be internationally recognized. When I told Dr. Schopler about Wediko and the Stallions, he smiled. He made clear his strong opinion that my enthusiasm was a product of a naive generosity of spirit, a phenomenon he'd said he witnessed in many beginning psychologists.

Dr. Schopler proceeded to straighten my thinking. He explained that I had projected my feelings onto my campers as if they (my words, now) were walking Rorschach inkblots. I had seen—imagined, Dr. Schopler would have corrected—in those boys what I'd wanted and needed to perceive. According to Dr. Schopler, my attributing feelings and thinking to those boys was as inaccurate and unfounded as believing my dog was distressed by the nightly news, or better yet, happy over the town's expanding its off-the-leash park hours.

Dr. Schopler's input was neither critical nor unkind. His motive was compassionate and well founded for the children with autism that he'd long studied and knew so well. His point was that by assuming these children had inner experiences that (he believed) they did not, my misplaced sympathy was burdening the children with irrelevant understanding, missing out on who they really were and what they really needed. To see them as I would see any other children implied that I would treat them as such, and Dr. Schopler knew from harsh reality that this would mean these children would go without the interventions that truly offered them help. In short, and by his view, my sensitive view of these children was paradoxically cruel and unresponsive to a population of children that already suffered too much.

As a young psychologist starting out, I was in a quandary, torn between the wisdom and insights of the world's expert and the reality I had observed in the presence of those boys. Perhaps, I wondered, he was right. Had my wish to connect with these children and my wish for them to connect with me blinded this therapist to the truth? Was I viewing the world of Asperger's and High-Functioning Autism through distorted or discolored glasses? I knew how Dr. Schopler would have answered those questions; I wasn't so sure myself. That my perceptions of these children might actually be born out of sentiment unnerved me. The last thing I wanted was to harm children and their families. And more so, if I could be so mistaken and misguided when it came to autism, what did that say about my general abilities and fitness to be a psychologist?

I didn't actually treat a child with autism until my fourth year of graduate school. I was an intern at the Massachusetts Mental Health Center, a training hospital that partnered between Harvard Medical School and the Commonwealth of Massachusetts to serve the Mission Hill area of Boston. I was assigned to Timothy, a 6-year-old boy recently discharged from the inpatient unit to the outpatient clinic. Over several years, Timothy had been diagnosed with Infantile Autism by several prominent child psychiatrists and clinics in Boston, including the developmental team at the famed Children's Hospital Medical Center. Timothy had been an unresponsive infant and toddler, showing all of the defining traits for Infantile Autism according to the *Diagnostic and Statistical Manual of Mental Disorders III* (*DSM III*; American Psychiatric Association [APA], 1980).

When I met Timothy, I met a boy who neatly fit the formal diagnostic criteria. He spun, made no eye contact, sniffed everything, reversed his pronouns, repeated most every phrase to a fading echo, was obsessed with television shows and trivia, and noticed when so much as a paper clip moved from my desk. His intellectual skills and development were initially tested at the borderline to low-average level. But what else did I find when I met and got to know this child?

I found a boy who hungered for a connection with me, his new therapist; a boy who, for all of his inability to show affection, painfully missed his previous therapist; a boy who wanted me to recognize his vulnerabilities and fears, especially those involving his being in therapy and with me. I found a boy who wanted me to respect his interpersonal anxieties and move at a pace he could tolerate—physically, emotionally, and psychologically—neither too close nor too far away; a boy who wanted me to accept him as he was and not to demand eye contact, affection, or any other conventional sign that I mattered to him; a boy who worked hard and tirelessly to get me to grasp what he tried to communicate and who let me know loud and clear when I got it and when I didn't. Despite his IQ testing, I found a boy who enjoyed playing with language, and in spite of what the literature said about autism and stunted play, I found a boy who immensely enjoyed his own kind of play. Most profoundly, I found a boy who ever sought my understanding and who, I soon learned, ever did his own version of beaming when it came, when I was able to deliver it. Even when I read and reread all that autism literature had discovered and pronounced, even when I questioned my own clinical vision, I couldn't dismiss the pervasive and obvious signs that Timothy shared the big human needs that I, my wife, and every other person I knew lived and breathed. And in case I haven't made it clear enough, as you will read in Chapter 10, I found a boy who could talk and play in psychotherapy and who could profit from a long-term therapeutic relationship.

Prior to my meeting Timothy, leading professionals in Boston had told his parents that he would never live independently, would never make it through school, would never ride a bicycle, would require residential schools as a child and a sheltered workplace as an adult, and so on. To make a long story short, Timothy not only made it through high school, but he also graduated from one of the country's leading engineering universities. With each successive testing, his intellectual functioning rose until leveling in the high-average to superior range. Timothy learned to ride a 10-speed bicycle very well and as a teenager used it to commute all over the city, from his home to Fenway Park (where he worked as a food vendor), to the Boston Public Library (where he read newspapers from around the world), to the YMCA (where he competed in a recreational league), and so forth. He also learned to drive a car and fly a plane. In his late twenties, Timothy now lives on his own in a home that he supports with a highly skilled professional job. Timothy has good friends and is an active member of his church community, an avid sports fan and weekend athlete, and a news junkie.

Over much time, my experience with such children has only grown, deepened, and richened. Time and time again, I've seen these children engage and play and talk in ways never thought possible. I've listened to them describe thinking, feeling, and imagining that has been said to be beyond the powers of their brains. I've watched these boys and girls smash through glass ceilings and keep growing toward the sky, surpassing by miles the low expectations that professionals once predicted. Thank goodness these children and their parents hadn't taken those prophesies of gloom to heart and downgraded their hopes and aspirations. Admittedly, as I'll detail, these wondrous possibilities didn't come fast, and the work challenged me as much as it did the children and their families.

For decades, children with Asperger's were pronounced to be incapable of certain kinds of experiences. Therapy that involved play and talk was equated with psychoanalysis and judged to be not just unhelpful but destructive. Therapy that talked of inner experience and relationship building was dismissed as quackery tantamount to treating autism with chelation or a testosterone-suppressing drug. And yet, every child I have seen with Asperger's or High-Functioning Autism has taught me that more than anything, they need that connection to others—and more so, to themselves—and that they have all they need to teach us, their therapists, the best ways to reach, engage, and sustain them.

We have come light-years from when autism was said to be an acquired disorder of otherwise normal children caused by cold and unresponsive mothering (Bettelheim, 1967). By 1981, the year I entered graduate school, it was well-established scientific fact that Asperger's and High-Functioning Autism are neurological syndromes involving brain-based deficits in the processing of language, emotion, and social experience. Unfortunately, this enlightenment brought along blind spots and biases of its own. The pendulum was necessarily pushed from its errant and malignant position to its opposite, neurologically accurate side. There, it got stuck.

Consider the authoritative *Journal of Autism and Developmental Disorders*. I felt disappointed when, about 20 years ago, it rejected my article on doing play psychotherapy with a child with Asperger's. As of June 2009, in its 39 years and 2,262 articles published, that journal —"devoted to all aspects of autism spectrum disorders [including] clinical care, education, and treatment for all individuals"—had not published one single article on psychotherapy or counseling for children with Asperger's. A handful of articles made cursory mention that supportive counseling might help but gave no details as to what that counseling would be. There has been a bias in which it seems the whole child got misplaced.

My intent is not to point the finger. Both the therapeutic approach I propose in this book and the children I treat have benefited from my reading that journal and others like it. On the contrary, we all—people with autism, their families, and clinicians alike—owe a great debt to those who righted Bettelheim's misconception, arguably one of the most destructive blunders of modern psychology and psychiatry. The heroic deeds of these autism researchers reversed an entire field, and any bias against approaches like mine came out of a need to guard against echoes of a dark past that should never be repeated. Their vigilance, neither error nor misstep, was understandable as steadfast protection of what research had shown them and to prevent even one more mother from being blamed and one more child from being diverted from the most efficacious education and treatments.

Times have been changing, and so has the world of autism and Asperger's. Knowledgeable and wise clinicians such as Asperger's greatest friend and ally, Tony Attwood, are leading and helping us to grasp the realities and experiences of the whole child so that we can best understand and help. Clinical interventions, such as Levine and Chedd's *replays* (2007) and Greenspan and Wieder's *floortime* (2006), address and employ the relevance of affect, empathy, and connection, enabling clinicians to respond to the child in deeper and more complete ways. Basic research, too, as you will read all about, is finding out new things that suggest there is more to and in children with Asperger's than has been believed.

It is an exciting and opportune time to be working with children who have Asperger's or another spectrum disorder. The research of brain science, neurology, psychiatry, and developmental psychology are propelling our understanding and the futures of children beyond what we imagined. Diagnosis is sharpening and awareness is rising such that parents, educators, and clinical professionals are identifying these children earlier, permitting the early interventions that are key. Educators are designing programs that better address these children, and school systems are seeing the value of building those methods into their special education curricula. Psychiatry is leading the way in discerning the basics of Asperger's Syndrome, teasing out its complex relationship to comorbid disorders and learning which drugs target children's symptoms more sensitively and with fewer side effects. Rather than being rebuked and rejected as the problem, loving mothers and fathers are being given the support they need and deserve so as to learn all they can to effectively parent and advocate for their children. At the end of the day, greater awareness, more sensitive detection, and an actual rise in incidence will guarantee that more clinicians will see growing numbers of children with Asperger's (Hertz-Picciotto & Delwiche, 2009).

Though what these children have taught me seems to be hugely relevant and important, please be clear that my approach and vision in no way makes obsolete or replaces all or any of what we've learned about Asperger's and High-Functioning Autism as neurodevelopmental disorders. The approach to therapy that I'll lay out in detail does not supplant behavior therapies, language therapies, or social pragmatics, to name a few. It is a relationship-based therapy that informs, augments, and enriches all of the other therapies (just as those strategies inform, augment, and enrich what I do). I think of my approach as an atmosphere and view that hovers above and stands alongside other interventions. When facing a challenge such as Asperger's or High-Functioning Autism, children and their families need all there is to offer—the best of all worlds. And the sort of therapy I propose, so my patients have shown me, has a place in that universe of possibility. Whether clinicians embrace my vision or simply add pieces of it to their therapeutic armamentaria, repertoires, or toolboxes is up to them.

A discussion of what Asperger's means, not just diagnostically but to the child, starts off the book. What is the child's subjective experience? The second and third chapters explore the beginning hours of therapy for parents and children, respectively. For the remainder of the book, chapters focus on prominent aspects of the Asperger experience, including: hypersensitivity, anxiety, communication, intellect and creativity, feelings and depression, social difficulties, and theory of mind and other so-called impediments to therapy. Through vivid case material that illumines these experiences in the words and play of the children themselves, each chapter shows what these issues can mean, what has been discovered about them, and how they can be addressed through therapy.

I have come to my view of Asperger's and therapy slowly, steadily, and honestly—case by case, child by child. In nearly 30 years, children and adolescents have taught me better than any books or professors what is real and what works. Although I cannot possibly share those countless hours with clinician readers, I have striven to capture the essentials of all that transpired so that it's not mine but the children's experiences, actions, and words that do the showing and the telling. I will also refer to what's in the literature in order to give my views context, at times by contrast and at other times with surprising and refreshing compatibility. And last, the discussion will sometimes get personal. How can it not when involving such intimate material and mattering? By the book's end, you may not agree with my thinking and methods. But you will, I hope, fully understand how I got to this place and view.

Acknowledgments

Gratitude goes to Naomi Chedd whose thoughtful reaction to my initial proposal inspired and informed the writing of this book. An enormous thank you to Tony Attwood whose constant devotion and insights into children with Asperger's has led all of our ways out of the darkness. More than any, Tony has placed our understanding of Asperger neurology and behavior into the rich context of a real and whole child. A heartfelt thank you to Patricia Rossi, my editor at Wiley, who believed in the need for this book and who carefully guided it to fruition. And hardly last, thanks to Kim Nir, my production editor at Wiley, who with unusual responsiveness and communication led the manuscript to a finished book.

Important Notes

The therapeutic approach described in this book applies to children with Asperger's Syndrome and High-Functioning Autism. This view of therapy rests fundamentally upon the clinician's meeting the child where she is and so, as you'll read, it adapts to each and every child, whichever the diagnosis. Though experts will continue to study the two diagnoses (see Ghaziuddin & Mountain-Kimchi, 2004, for neuropsychological comparison), for the purposes of this book, I've adopted the view that these disorders share more than not and can be discussed in the same clinical context (Witwer & Lecavelier, 2008).

With this diagnostic assumption in mind, and to make for a book that reads more smoothly, I try to use the simpler "Asperger's" instead of the formal "Asperger Syndrome," the clumsy "Asperger's Syndrome and High-Functioning Autism," or the abbreviated "AS/HFA." Also, as Naomi Chedd wisely advised me, we know too much and have come too far to refer to the "Asperger child." Our reasons are less for political correctness and more to convey our deeper and imperative appreciation for the whole child and her humanity (personal communication, March 12, 2009). So, instead, as my book title heralds, I refer to the "child *with* Asperger Syndrome." This phrasing, while reading more awkwardly, stays truer to reality.

The bulk of the therapeutic principles and strategies that I write of apply to children and adolescents, whatever their ages. To speak about children of any age, I refer to "child" or "children "and omit the awkward "children and adolescents" or "children and teenagers." I provide greater distinction as needed.

Finally, for general discussions, I try to use the plural form, such as "children" or "clinicians." When that makes for confusion and I need to refer to a child or clinician in the singular, I randomly alternate gender to avoid the tedious "he or she," "her or him."

1

What Asperger's Means for the Child

As you'll soon read is the heart of this book and approach, what matters most is what children with Asperger's think, feel, say, do, and experience. Their experiences and engagement power their therapies and growth. To grasp and appreciate these subjective and personal aspects of Asperger's, we need to agree on the more objective—what we all can see in and about these children. By necessity, this chapter reads somewhat more abstract and theoretical than the more clinical chapters to come.

We begin by revisiting two early, familiar, and well-articulated descriptions of Asperger's made more than half a century ago by the American child psychiatrist Leo Kanner (1943) and the Austrian pediatrician Hans Asperger (1944/1991). It is indeed a "strange coincidence" that Kanner and Asperger never met, yet they both came from Austria, spoke German, described the same type of children with similar words, and wrote their papers in 1943 (Lyons & Fitzgerald, 2007, pp. 2022–2023). As Hans Asperger's original paper was in German, I, as did many others, first learned of his work from Lorna Wing's 1981 clinical account of Asperger's syndrome. Only later, to my and the field's great satisfaction, did Uta Frith translate the original into English (1991).

Both Asperger and Kanner believed they saw and described a particular type of child whose traits were recognizable and that defined a disorder.

Both researchers spotlighted a "poverty of social interaction and the failure of communication; stereotypic behavior, isolated special interests, outstanding skills and resistance to change" (Frith, 1991, p. 10). Kanner agreed totally with Asperger that the "autistic personality is highly distinctive despite wide individual differences" (1943, p. 67). In other words, while the children's traits varied dramatically, both men felt confident that they could readily identify such a child. Though neither used the term, they implicitly agreed that these children shared a collection of symptoms, odd and ranging, that added up to a *syndrome* exhibiting consistency and constancy.

Both men noticed extraordinarily atypical language. Some of Kanner's children were mute, speaking little or no language. He wrote of children who echoed and parroted phrases as if words were without meaning and who referred to themselves in the second or third person. Asperger's children used words in clever if idiosyncratic ways, coining new words (neologisms) and reshaping words into uncommon forms. These children, he wrote, talked more like adults and stuck out nonverbally, lacking typical eye contact, facial expressions, humor, and, in general, a spontaneity of body and voice.

While the chronicles of both men are exemplary even by today's standards, there are deeper aspects of Asperger's paper that justify mention. While to their credit, both men saw Asperger's as biologically determined, Kanner felt compelled to write in the next-to-last paragraph of his lengthy article that in his sample, "there [were] very few really warmhearted fathers and mothers" (1943, p. 250)—a seemingly innocent aside that tragically didn't go forgotten by Bruno Bettelheim some 25 years later (1967).

Not only did Asperger make explicit his belief that parents don't cause autism, but he further saw that some parents shared Asperger-like qualities with their children. Many of the parents in Asperger's group were obsessive, highly intelligent, eccentric, and accomplished men and women in advanced fields. From his sample of children and families, Asperger inferred that the disorder is genetic, more heavily carried by the male chromosome, and more frequently seen in boys than girls. To Asperger, the fact that the children he met tended to come from one-child families said more about the parents genetically (their being people satisfied with one child). He did not want others to misinterpret this preponderance of one-child families as suggesting that living in a one-child, adult-centered home causes Asperger's in a child who with siblings would have developed free of autism.

Asperger's view toward the parents was modern, enlightened, and sympathetic. In his case studies, he told of one mother who "knew her son through and through and understood his difficulties very well" (p. 41), a second who "fought desperately against [her son's] transfer into a special school for retarded children" (p. 60), and a third who found her mercilessly bullied son a protected situation where he could be educated more safely. Asperger tactfully described how exhausting, frustrating, and ineffective parenting such a child can feel, even for loving parents who understand what's happening. Without blaming, he described how the nature of the condition precludes the child's offering the kinds of closeness, affection, feelings, and empathy to the parents "that normally make life with a small child so richly rewarding" (pp. 80–81). Elsewhere, Asperger underscored the toll that the child's constitutional contrariness—disliking flattery, not wishing to please, oppositional, and neither wanting nor needing human attention—can take on parents and a family, however involved and caring.

In his efforts to know these children, Asperger had their intelligence tested, revealing consistently erratic performances involving average to strong intellects, extreme unevenness in skills, and difficulty concentrating and organizing. The children tended to do well on tasks measuring puzzle solving and factual knowledge but poorly on tasks that involved social understanding and sequential narrative. In reporting the varying IQs of his children, Asperger "anticipated a spectrum" of autism (Wing, 2000). That Asperger so richly and aptly laid out the intellectual profile of the children testifies to a study informed by a modern-day synthesis of clinical assessment, parent reports, teacher observations, and (for its time) sophisticated psychoeducational evaluation that hints at the field of neuropsychological testing to come.

Historically, any sort of autistic disorder was originally diagnosable in the *DSM-I* as *Schizophrenic reaction, childhood type* (APA, 1952) and in the *DSM-II* as *Schizophrenia, childhood type* (APA, 1968). The diagnosis of *Infantile Autism* was added to the *DSM-III* (APA, 1980), with much expanded and detailed criteria in the *DSM-III-R* (APA, 1987). *Asperger's Disorder,* as its own diagnostic entity, wasn't established until the *DSM-IV* (APA, 1994).

Consider the criteria for 299.80 *Asperger's Disorder* according to the revised *DSM-IV-TR* (APA, 2000), which we'll then compare to Gillberg's diagnostic criteria as revised in 1991. I, like Attwood (2007) and others, much prefer Gillberg's criteria. I recognize and fear that diagnostic lists, no less two in a row, can cause clinicians' and readers' eyes to glaze over. I think you'll find our closer attention worthwhile.

DSM-IV-TR Criteria

(A) Qualitative impairment in social interaction, as manifested by at least two of the following:

    (1) Impaired nonverbal behavior, such as eye-to-eye gaze, facial expression, body postures, and gestures to regulate social interaction

    (2) Failure to develop peer relationships appropriate to developmental level

    (3) A lack of spontaneous seeking to share enjoyment, interests, or achievements with other people

    (4) Lack of social or emotional reciprocity

(B) Restricted, repetitive, and stereotyped patterns of behavior, interests, and activities, as manifested by at least two of the following:

    (1) Encompassing preoccupation with one or more stereotyped and restricted patterns of interest that is abnormal in either intensity or focus

    (2) Apparently inflexible adherence to specific, nonfunctional routines or rituals

    (3) Stereotyped and repetitive motor mannerisms (e.g., hand or finger flapping or twisting, complex whole-body movements)

    (4) Persistent preoccupation with parts of objects

(C) The disturbance causes clinically significant impairment in social, occupational, or other important areas of functioning.

(D) There is no clinically significant general delay in language (e.g., single words used by age 2 years, communicative phrases by 3 years).

(E) There is no clinically significant delay in cognitive development or in the development of age-appropriate self-help skills, adaptive behavior (other than in social interaction), and curiosity about the environment in childhood.

Gillberg's 1991 Criteria

(A) Severe impairment in reciprocal social interaction (at least two of the following):

    (1) Inability to interact with peers

    (2) Lack of desire to interact with peers

    (3) Lack of appreciation of social cues

    (4) Socially and emotionally inappropriate behavior

(B) All-absorbing narrow interest (at least one of the following):
   (1) Exclusion of other activities
   (2) Repetitive adherence
   (3) More rote than meaning
(C) Imposition of routines and interests (at least one of the following):
   (1) On self, in aspects of life
   (2) On others
(D) Speech and language problems (at least three of the following):
   (1) Delayed development
   (2) Superficially perfect expressive language
   (3) Formal, pedantic language
   (4) Odd prosody, peculiar voice characteristics
   (5) Impairment of comprehension including misinterpretations of literal/implied meanings
(E) Nonverbal communication problems (at least one of the following):
   (1) Limited use of gestures
   (2) Clumsy/gauche body language
   (3) Limited facial expression
   (4) Inappropriate expression
   (5) Peculiar, stiff gaze
(F) Motor Clumsiness
   (1) Poor performance on neurodevelopmental examination

There is much about Gillberg's system (1991) that adds to its appeal and usefulness. Contrasted with the stilted precision of the *DSM-IV-TR* (APA, 2000), Gillberg's list uses plain language that we understand and relate to. But the attraction goes farther. Gillberg's criteria, as he states them, add meaningful and necessary context to what without such grounding can appear to be a sterile listing of symptoms. Consider some of the differences.

The *DSM-IV-TR* defines "impaired nonverbal behavior," whereas Gillberg defines "nonverbal communication problems," describing such behaviors in clear language that we can't mistake. By couching nonverbal behaviors within a "communication problem," Gillberg suggests why it matters and what it implies for the child's functioning and personal experience. Similarly, the *DSM-IV-TR* states a "failure to develop peer relationships"; Gillerg instead qualifies the child's social impairments as "difficulties interacting with peers," offering a more humane and realistic view that is less absolute, allows for degrees of relating, and again speaks to the child's perspective of having a hard time with social relations. Gillberg's addition of "indifference to peer contacts" further hints to the child's experience. Rather than an "encompassing preoccupation" that is "restricted" and "abnormal" (*DSM-IV-TR*), Gillberg writes of a "narrow interest" involving the "exclusion of other activities." Gillberg also categorizes the "speech and language peculiarities" that Asperger and Kanner both noticed, a characteristic that the *DSM-IV-TR* doesn't mention at all.

Though a chapter could be spent parsing out the differences, we can readily see that Gillberg's criteria are more comprehensive, descriptive, child-centered, and plainly stated. I for one could read and read the *DSM-IV-TR* diagnosis and still not recall what I'd read. Reading Gillberg's criteria, which is basically just a list, begins to leave me with a sense of who these children are, an image that I can recall and from which I can start to think about the real children that I've met. Lastly—and perhaps I see too much in this—Gillberg's list leaves me less discouraged.

ASPERGER'S FROM THE CHILD'S EXPERIENCE

You know that feeling of the sun in your eyes or when someone beside you on a plane hasn't showered? Multiply it by a thousand and run it 24 hours a day. You now are beginning to appreciate what sensory sensitivities are like for children with Asperger's. These children seem not to have the sensory equilibrium and censoring that protect and maintain the rest of us. The world literally pounds on their doors and ears, in their eyes, on their skin, and through their noses. Nails on blackboards and jackhammers next door— that's what ordinary sensations can be like to children with Asperger's. Then, to complicate it more, atop those supersensitivities, these children can be less perceptive of pain or perhaps know sensory synesthesias by which they smell sounds or hear numbers. Besides the obvious sensory onus of having to sense these noxious stimuli, the child's sensory susceptibilities get in the way of life. How, for example, does it affect bonding if the child, through no ill or free will, dislikes the smell of his parents?

Because they have a wish for connection with other people, though it may not look as apparent, vigorous, or invited as with a nonautistic child, children with Asperger's can be alone a lot and experience various levels of loneliness and exclusion, even as it might look utterly self-imposed. These young children are not good at playing with others, and so, by definition, they tend to play less with others. Lacking some of what it takes to read and respond to social cues and data, their best efforts for companionship and affiliation can go unrewarded, to put it gently, leaving them to walk away, give up, and continue to go it alone. While some of the child's being alone is comfortable and desired, it also represents an adaptation, or a solution, to a life problem that's gradually shaped over a childhood. How much social rejection and discouragement could you or I take? How long would we try and try to no avail?

Many times, the child is unaware of or cannot articulate this social estrangement and disconnect, the distress of which surfaces in aggressive or angry behaviors. As their awareness in therapy heightened, several older children and teenagers told me that they were quite lonely when younger but that they felt shame and hid it. They also revealed long-standing feelings of jealousy and envy for the other children who, so it looked, enjoyed and easily interacted with each other. One teen recalled going after and "seeing the enemy in" any child who dealt with life better than he did. And as we'll see, adolescence in itself, with or without treatment, can bring awareness of being different, along with self-consciousness, anger, and despair.

The child's difficulties with reading and expressing emotions create a comparable dilemma. What must it be like to feel all that happens to you in a vague, amorphous, overexciting and overstimulating way that threatens to overwhelm your body and mind? I am not exaggerating. Think of when you have had such moments of feelings that you thought it would drive you mad or cause you to jump out of yourself. Even good feelings can overcome the child's capacity to stay regulated and intact. Add the frustration of not being able to speak what you feel. As one teen looking back on his earlier years put it, "Hitting and biting and screaming were my only options." Unable to process their feelings and social experiences adequately, these children are hindered in their understanding, resolving, and putting it away, all which compromise the development of more coherent and cohesive senses of self.

Then, there is the extreme worry and apprehension, social anxiety and phobias, generalized anxiety and irritability, depression and maybe even suicidal thinking, attention deficits, moodiness, obsessive thinking, and compulsions that often distress if not plague the child. These symptoms, which can be caused by, consequent to, or wholly independent of the Asperger's, are all much worse since the child has fewer internal resources to cope with and master them. That their social support network is probably neither supportive nor a network hardly helps.

Back in 1989 (Bromfield, p. 448), I wrote that "autism represents a syndrome or collection of symptoms originating primarily from a basic [...] neurological deficit [...] in information processing and emotional communication, secondly, from 'psychological defenses against states experienced as a result of those deficits, and (thirdly from a) lack of crucial socializing experiences'" (Bemporad, Ratey, & O'Driscoll, 1987, p. 477). But that's a lot of big words and jargon. What does that really mean for children with Asperger's?

It means that they get hit with a triple whammy. First, they are born less equipped to understand and connect with others, themselves, their feelings, and so on. It's kind of like being dropped in a foreign country with a bag full of U.S. dollars that no one will accept or exchange. After all, what are words, body language, and social cues if not the currency that the interpersonal economy of people and relationships deals in?

Second, inherent deficits shrink and shrink their social worlds. The ways that these children have to protect themselves to survive isolate them further. Because they're biologically less equipped for connection, children with Asperger's rely heavily on more comfortable ways of being to handle the angst and frustration that their social mishaps and predicament create.

Third, these children's self-protective and eccentric ways tend to push people away, leaving them more alone and deprived of opportunities to use and grow their social skills. It resembles a job applicant who is never hired because he lacks work experience or a 90-pound weakling who is judged too puny for the gym. This catch-22 leads the children to get less practice time with others, even though they—the children with Asperger's—are the ones who need social exposure and experience even more than their peers do.

I add to the list of three whammies a fourth and often neglected consequence of Asperger's. Because they can be so hard to understand, children with Asperger's get less understanding, empathy, admiring, and confirming— enormously less. Because they are less adept at the human things that tend to engage others and because what they say and do can be hard to relate to, these children are at great risk of being misunderstood, not just by peers but even by those who love them, whose job it is to parent and teach them. And this is serious, for empathy and understanding are the basics that nourish and sustain human existence and connection, even for the child with Asperger's.

In his award-winning picture book *The Arrival*, Shaun Tan (2007) tells the moving story of a man who says goodbye to his wife and daughter and goes to a new land to find a better life for his family. Tan's illustrations vividly capture this new world that to the immigrant appears strange, different, frightening, and completely alien. Through Tan's subtle story and near overwhelmingly mysterious artwork, readers are halfway through the book before the meaning hits them: This is what one feels as a stranger in a strange land.

I'm not equating Asperger's to the immigrant experience, though I believe the comparison stands. Being misunderstood is part and parcel of a life with Asperger's, and that life includes a childhood. How can having their appeals and occasional efforts to share go unheard not discourage the child? We all know that the child with Asperger's is often an expert at exotic knowledge, but do we realize that the child is even more an expert on living in a constant state of not being understood?

This chapter offers just a glimpse of what it is like for a child to have Asperger's. In the next many chapters, the children themselves show us what it's like, how it feels, and what we can do to help.

2

Meet the Parents

As eager as we are to meet the children, we first need to meet the parents. They are the ones who will find and contact us, make the referral, and arrange for treatment. Without the parents, there are no therapies to speak of and consider.

In a perfect world, parents would come to us as if coasting down a slope of prior good fortune and experience with clinicians, schools, and caretakers. They'd have dealt with a limited number of professionals who quickly and ably responded to their child's needs. If asked, they'd rate their satisfaction with the system high and without complaint. Having known only sound and helpful relationships with caregivers, these parents would come to us with trust, realistic expectations, open hearts and minds. When we met, they would impress us with their good cheer, optimistic outlook, and energetic demeanor.

"Right," I can hear readers chuckle to themselves, thinking of what the rest of parents are like, including ourselves. The reality is that a vast majority of parents who have children with Asperger's come to us having endured a trek of hardship, pain, loss, disappointment, and frustration. They likely have encountered a handful if not a slew of professionals and faced countless and extended detours on the path to assessment and intervention. By the time parents reach us, they may still seek a diagnosis. They may disbelieve or not realize that help is available for their child. While awareness and the potential for early and accurate identification are growing, we still hear from parents who feel lost and confused, as did Mrs. L.

Mrs. L. called me concerning her 6-year-old daughter, Chloe. She and her husband, educated people, for years had sensed that something was amiss. Raising their daughter had felt different to them than it had with their two sons. Mrs. L. described having long known that Chloe was extremely shy. Chloe would throw frequent and wild tantrums when anticipating situations that were new or required that she enter groups of children. Mrs. L. said that she and her husband called Chloe their "mad reader," for she was ever buried in a book, even when walking or eating. It seemed, Mrs. L. went on, that Chloe preferred the company of books to being with other people, especially children her own age or younger. That she would read the same book over and over especially worried them, as did her obsessive interests in textiles (e.g., a need to know and study the makeup of material, especially synthetic fabrics). For example, she would wonder and speculate on the clothing she would see on other children, on television, and even in the stories she read. Being social people and having sons with many friends, their daughter's penchant for alone time interfered with their busy household, and, more so, concerned them about their daughter's mental health.

These issues led the way in my first contact with Mrs. L. My relatively open-ended willingness to hear her story evoked an intelligent, thoughtful, and organized description of her and her husband's concerns. I also heard that after years of being told by various doctors and clinics that their daughter was just anxious, just learning disabled, and so forth, Chloe had been referred for an evaluation through her public school. Mr. and Mrs. L. had met with the examiner for feedback the week before and were told that their daughter was autistic, a diagnosis that they were told was a good thing, for it would help her to qualify for and receive necessary services within the school.

Mrs. L., whom I spoke to on the phone, reported that the diagnosis felt totally out of the blue and fell on her and her husband "like a ton of bricks." She went on to say that she had once seen a movie about an autistic child who lived in an institution and that now she was "scared to death" for her daughter's future. Mrs. L. admitted that in the days since hearing the word *autism,* her daughter had been looking "sicker and more disturbed." "Her eyes," the mother reported, "are looking more vacant." She even wondered if her daughter's hugs weren't feeling cooler or somehow less affectionate. "Maybe I've just been kidding myself," she said.

It was true, as the examiner had said, that the autism label would get their daughter services and was required for that purpose. But the rest had not been explained to Mr. and Mrs. L. When they heard that Chloe had autism, they knew only the form that we clinicians would call Infantile Autism, the classic and severe disorder (Kanner, 1943). The power of that diagnosis overwhelmed this intelligent and capable set of parents. Hearing an authority speak the word *autism* about their daughter was enough to throw their otherwise highly competent thinking into disarray, making them wonder whether they had distorted her entire development and causing them to feel her presence more as an extremely autistic child than as the young girl with Asperger's that she was.

In my first meeting with Mr. and Mrs. L. and Chloe, I was able to put their mind at ease. While it would have been ill-advised and cruel for me to paint a rosier picture than was called for, I felt a need to correct the trauma and misperception they had experienced over the diagnosis. I agreed that their daughter had Asperger's, a condition which I explained to them. I could see right away that her case was on the milder end of the spectrum and felt sure enough to state it clearly, even at that early juncture of the treatment. Though the therapy proper was yet to start, our critical discussion of what Mr. and Mrs. L. had been through helped to set a cleaner and sturdier platform on which to build. In my experience with many other parents, the trials and tribulations of their Asperger "journeys" (euphemistic for *ordeals*) are most always substantial, significant, and worth knowing about and processing. Being more complicated and involving a larger cast of characters, they usually are not unraveled so neatly and in one sitting. Of course, even if Chloe had been more seriously autistic, my sympathetic and curious ear would have been justified to help her parents digest and accept the jarring news the tester had delivered. (See Sanders' book on talking to parents about autism, 2008.)

Beginning aspects of therapy resonate with issues that run through an entire course of treatment, and that is true for the issue of diagnosis. Knowing parents' relationship to their child's diagnosis—how they got to it and now that they have it, *what does it mean?*—is ever a front to keep on the radar. Reckoning with a diagnosis on the autism spectrum can be hard for many parents, but such reckoning is a necessity for healthier acceptance and adaptation. It may require grieving or self-forgiveness. Even when we don't blame parents for their children's illnesses, they can blame themselves—feeling guilty, for instance, for the genetic legacy (i.e., for just having birthed a child with Asperger's). The hope that our treatment can genuinely offer these children and their families can sometimes go great distances in helping parents to see more optimistic and self-sufficient futures.

If treatment goes well, parents will not simply get over their child's diagnosis. They will evolve with it. Rather than deny and forget the diagnosis, they will see it as holding limited value. They will realize that who their child is goes far beyond any label or *DSM* entity. Parents know their child best of all, and they will grow more confident in their capacities to see their children and their needs, maturing into better and more relaxed advocates who can patiently view their child's disorder realistically over a larger and longer time frame. Inviting parental perceptions in the beginning hours sets a tone that tells parents we will always welcome their views of their child as relevant, informative, and valid. Our interest in what parents think shows them that we need their insights and input as much as they need ours.

No two parents are the same; nor do they bring equal attitudes, understanding, resources, and so forth to what is a significant diagnosis. This discrepancy can be more severe between some parents, married or divorced, who cannot come anywhere close to agreeing on the diagnosis, how to intervene, or whose advice and help to seek.

In his first voice message, Mr. S. explained simply that his toddler-aged son had been diagnosed with Asperger's and that he had been recommended to me as a therapist. In a second message, his wife, Mrs. S., told me how a therapist had said her son is perfectly normal and that any attempt to label him was inaccurate and stigmatizing. She wondered if I would be willing to assess her son and declare him not to have Asperger's. In a third message, Mr. S. spoke of his wife's inability to handle their son's diagnosis. He asked me to intercede. "Can you assess our son and mandate treatment?" he asked. There were several more messages, each more plaintive and contentious.

When I returned Mr. S.'s call, I was surprised to hear Mrs. S. pick up. I'd assumed they were divorced. They were married, I learned, and lived together. There was plenty of conflict, Mrs. S. made clear, and it surrounded their 5-year-old son, Kevin. Mrs. S. explained that her husband was an "inveterate worrier" who "had to see problems where they didn't exist." She described how for more than a year, he had "dragged Kevin to a million doctors to shop" for the most serious diagnosis he could find. And, Mrs. S. added, he'd finally found it in Asperger's, a diagnosis that for all of her skepticism, she had a better than average understanding of. She grasped that it was on the autistic spectrum's higher end, and having read a lot about the disorder, recognized that her son had a milder case and that the prognosis was good. She continued to say that she had nothing against me and had heard some good things but saw no need for therapy that mostly risked making her son feel defective, a sense that Mrs. S. believed could hurt Kevin's esteem.

A few minutes later, Mr. S. called and gave his side of the story. For a couple of years, teachers and clinicians had been telling Mr. and Mrs. S. that something was amiss with Kevin. His wife, he said, had an aversion to the mental health profession. "It's not about Asperger's," he said. "She thinks staying far from therapists is the safest place to be." Mr. S. expressed frustration with his wife, for he had also read a lot and talked to many professionals about Asperger's. He knew that the sooner the intervention, the better. "Can't you just treat Kevin in the late mornings, and we won't even tell my wife that we're coming?"

This was a first in my life as a therapist who works with Asperger's. Both parents were well informed and yet held such differing opinions on what to do. I would not treat Kevin without his mother's consent. To proceed on a path that two parents so disputed would guarantee treatment failure. How could Kevin engage in a relationship and therapy that his loving mother disapproved of and, I guessed, feared?

Both parents loved Kevin and wanted the best for him. Mr. S. wanted therapy for his son's Asperger's; Mrs. S. wanted to dilute the focus on Asperger's and just let their son grow up. It took several long phone calls with each parent to schedule a face-to-face meeting. I confirmed Mr. S.'s concern and noted the diligent and capable manner in which he had gotten his son a clear and apt diagnosis. I confirmed Mrs. S.'s loving concern, showing an appreciation for the ways that she felt our profession can harm people. I stated that our mission was not to dismiss or dissuade the other; nor was there an urgency to settle the matter. I stressed that Kevin was young and that treatment, should it be pursued, would be long term. We were in no rush to get Kevin's therapy going on shaky ground. We'd proceed when we'd arrived at agreement and not until. My explicit statement seemed to relieve both parents and made room for mutual validation of each other's love and insights.

Mrs. S. questioned me about my credentials and my views of children, therapy, and Asperger's. I tried my best to answer her questions candidly and without being defensive. I reminded myself that she was asserting herself in her child's best interest. Isn't that above all the most I could want from any parent? Each of my answers quelled Mrs. S. and lead to more open acknowledgment that Kevin might have some need for professional help. To my surprise, Mr. S. showed movement to compare. Our slow and inviting discussions led to his admitting that he felt he could be something of an alarmist. While maintaining his conviction in Kevin's diagnosis, he grew less driven about treatment, seeing Kevin's future and needs from a more reflective vantage point. Each learned from the other. Mrs. S. credited her husband with having identified something very important in Kevin's life (i.e., the Asperger's and the difficulties it created for him), and Mr. S. discovered that his wife's slower approach helped him to put it into a more comfortable perspective. Kevin's therapy soon started, and it went well.

Would Kevin have attained as much in his therapy if I'd begun treatment immediately and without his mother's approval? If, as Mr. S. had requested, we had just gotten on with it, would Mrs. S. have come to join the cause? Who can say? I have no idea. Time after time, my experience suggests that a patient and steady effort to understand, hear, and work with parents' concerns, when it succeeds, leads to strong and fertile relationships that nourish rather than undermine the child's therapy.

That parents need our support probably seems obvious. They will look to us for parenting guidance over the long haul and in specific moments of doubt or crisis. They may look to us as advisors who can advocate for their child at school or other places, or who will work hard to support their doing such advocacy on their own. Parents need the therapist's more balanced and resilient perspective to buoy them through periods that are dark, stressful, and discouraging. The therapist's insights can help parents to grasp the bigger meanings of their child's behaviors so as not to take them so hard and personally or as conveying negativity that the child doesn't feel. The child with Asperger's benefits from a team that includes psychotherapists, speech and language therapists, applied behavior analysts, educators, and so on. Who of this team, though, can best hold the parents in terms of understanding their child, coping with her needs, and venting her frustrations? The therapist may be the best person to perform this critical function. I am pleased when parents credit me with being "a good friend" who helps them negotiate the day-to-day territory of parenting a child with Asperger's.

In turn, the ways that we the therapists need the parents' support may be less obvious. We need the parents to like us and feel good enough about us and our work to continue bringing their child for treatment. We need their assessment of what is going on with their child. For all of their human subjectivity, parents still offer an objective eye that can tell us about home and school life in ways the child cannot. We need parents' endorsement of our work to help show their children that what we do is worthy and to be trusted. And above all, we need parents to be on board with us. However skilled or talented we are as therapists, our efforts will go much farther when parents support our work at home. Child therapists seldom if ever conduct their therapy in a vacuum. This is truer when it comes to children with Asperger's. A sound therapy that is unsupported or undermined by the parents can be as useless as paddling against a fast current heading the other way.

We all know that mutual alliances do not grow overnight. Relationships and trust are earned over time, slowly and steadily. That relating begins at the first exchange between therapist and parent. Words like respect, acceptance, and good listening are easy to type and throw about. Though first prescribed by the client-centered therapists (Rogers, 1949), these ingredients are the essentials to most any treatment that aspires to connect with and move a child to change. If I don't take parents' questions to heart and fail to respond with care, why should they ask me anything else? Parents have plenty to manage without enduring a clinician who's too busy, preoccupied, or uninterested. Spending the time to win over parents to the therapeutic cause is a wise goal to pursue. As Chedd tells us, therapists must not lose sight that however rough their journey, parents "remain highly invested in their child's happiness and success" (personal communication, March 12, 2009). Secondarily and not trivially, a fraction of parents may experience their own Asperger-like anxieties, fears, and limitations that need our caring attention as much as their children do.

But more than any other reason, therapists foster the relationship with parents so that they will allow us to enter their child's personal world, the one that they and their child have shared. It is easy for clinicians to forget the privilege and honor that families bestow on us. It is through those special relationships with parents that we can let our own deeply held beliefs shine through. By seeing, feeling, and sharing our belief in our work and basking in our hopeful outlooks, we can lend parents a renewed hope and vision for their child and family. Every therapeutic today paves the way for a therapeutic and happier tomorrow—especially for loving parents.

3

Beginning Therapy

Children with Asperger's need therapists who not only understand their exceptional needs but who also understand their more ordinary
human needs. Children with Asperger's need therapists who are first and
foremost good enough therapists in the everyday garden-variety sense of
the word—*only more so,* as I'll explain. That need especially applies to the
beginnings of their therapies. This third chapter addresses the beginning
of therapy in its minutiae and glory. Inevitably, the discussion of concrete
strategies requires that therapists heed the psychotherapeutic meanings and
implications that lay underneath. In other words, though we are beginning, the book and therapies quickly throw therapists into the children's
needs, Asperger-related and otherwise. On center stage will be the children
and their experiences as they enter the office to meet the therapist, and, it's
hoped, as they return again and again.

In a field that has a fair share of disagreement, child therapists of all per-
suasions agree that for their brand of therapy to work, children must feel a
sense of safety (Allen, 1964; Axline, 1969; Bromfield, 2007). Without that
safety, there can be no trust. *Merriam-Webster's Collegiate Dictionary* (1998)
defines *safety* as "the condition of being safe from undergoing or causing
hurt, injury, or loss." That definition suffices our psychological purposes and

warrants a closer look when asking what safety means within the therapy office, particularly in the first meetings.

The first half of the definition defines the child's being free from or protected from harm when in our office and presence. That includes the obvious need that the child be free from danger of physical injury or abuse when with us. What else this connotes goes further, deeper, and subtler for the child with Asperger's, and, as I cautioned, will touch upon much bigger issues that underlie all of a therapy and which we'll examine more fully later. Discussion of them, however, cannot be avoided or delayed, even at this initial stage.

When beginning with these children, I attend to their interpersonal safety by heeding how they appear to be doing with me. A therapist beginning with a child with Asperger's probably *can never go too slowly.* I take for granted that the new child client is extraordinarily anxious to be meeting with me. When I encounter a child who seems more at ease, I can adapt and ratchet up my presence. More times than not, I find my wariness well founded and appreciated. How can I tell when a child with Asperger's is growing anxious? There are several signs.

Eleven-year-old Martin was as terrified as his mother had warned me he would be. For the first several meetings, he sat stiffly in his chair, moving only to clear his throat with great exaggeration. He squeezed his eyes shut tightly, and he twisted his fingers and arms into what appeared to be impossibly entwined positions.

During these hours, he spoke at length and without pause about a world of mythical creatures he had long created. The complex, somewhat Latin-sounding names came at a pace that I could not keep up with, and their traits, as interwoven as his limbs, overwhelmed my capacities to listen and remember. If he'd asked me to repeat any of what he had told me, I would have performed miserably. It was not so much boring as unrelentingly intricate. But I kept trying.

As Martin told me more about his extensive imaginary otherworld, his body relaxed a little. His arms unraveled, his eyes opened, and his throat clearing slowed. At one point during Martin's monologue, my mind drifted.

"Are you listening?" Martin asked with clear irritation. He startled me.

"Totally," I replied.

Martin's newfound and relative ease disappeared in a flash. He twisted his arms and legs more intensely. He squeezed his eyes in a pulsing rhythm and cleared his throat louder. His body shivered.

"Never mind," he declared, meaning that he was done telling me about the creatures and the lands that he'd constructively imagined and that he'd worked so hard to share with me.

"Totally," I'd said, caught off guard and thinking that my glib and hollow words would save the day. That feeble attempt to not hurt his feelings made it worse. I rethought my strategy and decided to go straightforward, often the right way in matters of life and therapy.

"You're right, Martin," I began. "I wasn't getting it totally." Martin's body eased up. "In fact, your world is so rich and complicated that I can't always take it all in, like if I was in a lecture on a foreign language or a subject too hard for me. I should ha—"

"Apology accepted," Martin said with an anxious smile. He cleared his throat once more and resumed telling me about his favorite subject.

A majority of children with Asperger's will not say to me in words that I'm making them feel anxious or uncomfortable. They will tell me through their behaviors. Whatever Asperger behaviors an individual child shows may be the same behaviors that serve as reliable "anxiet-o-meters" for therapists to monitor. In Martin's case, it was throat clearing, limb twisting, and eye squinting. For other children, it might be echoing, asking questions, stating facts, looking away, picking their noses, sniffing, curling up, throwing things, withdrawing, and so on. Whenever one or more of these behaviors escalate in therapy, it is a good bet that something is stressing the child. Often, I find it is a stress that I am causing and that I can alleviate to the benefit of the child and therapy.

To avoid harm in the early hours, I do not push the child with my questions, voice, or presence. I don't get too close, and I don't confront. Nor do I expect or force verbal or nonverbal responses such as eye contact. I don't interpret behaviors, correct grammar, ask her impatiently to get on with her story, rebuke habits or tics, or dish tough love.

Researchers of childhood trauma say that above all, therapy needs to show the child that she is safe from future trauma. Most children with

Asperger's have not been abused. (Though, of course, children with Asperger's are no more immune from abuse than other children are.) I assume that even those who come from the most loving and caring homes and schools have experienced trauma of a different kind. I speak of the trauma that their neurological differences bring about; the misunderstanding, overstimulation, neglect, social isolation, teasing, and so on that can pervade the days and life of a child with Asperger's. *Not only will I not do any of these things to you,* I wish to convey to the child in the opening phase of therapy, *but I will also try to undo them, or at least provide some of what has been wrong or missing.* And so to that dear purpose, I try my best to grasp the child's stories, appreciate her humor, share her interests, and accept who she is as she attempts to cope with me, her new therapist. A therapist who provides this kind of safety makes a good impression.

The second half of the dictionary's definition of safety also holds a place in my beginning work with these children: "being safe . . . from *causing* hurt, injury, or loss." Though they may not show or describe it, many children with Asperger's know too well what it feels like to have other people find them boring, irritable, difficult, rigid, or worse. They may not be able to articulate this sense, but they are experts at being on the receiving end of negative interpersonal reaction. It is almost a way of life for the child with Asperger's. How can the therapist protect the new young client from causing harm to others? By understanding more and reacting differently. At least with her therapist, the child does not have to feel that she's bad or inadequate, whatever that means to that specific child.

Later in therapy, some children with Asperger's say it aloud: "You actually like my stories"; "You don't seem bored to death with me"; "You find me interesting"; "You respect my intelligence"; "You don't think I hate you"; "You don't take everything personally. You know it's just my Asperger's, not you!" We are sometimes so sure that children with Asperger's don't feel for others that we utterly neglect the burden they can feel over their condition, especially in relation to those they love and depend on. It can be absolutely tiring and stressing to seem so disagreeable to others. We cannot overestimate the value of a therapist who over time comes to genuinely like the child. Though therapists would routinely consider much of these matters to fall into a general discussion of *rapport,* that term seems far too flippant and casual when considering what the therapist's good, sensitive, and respectful posture can mean to a child who lives with Asperger's. Such a therapeutic attitude is itself consoling and reparative.

I've found that children with Asperger's seem to enjoy the company of therapists with not just an honest but a solid, down-to-earth presence. These children are not ones for psychobabble or tentative hypothesizing. While lovers of concrete imagery and the metaphor, they respond best to direct and clear language, even if representative, that acutely captures experience. It is as if they are so fraught with their own anxiety and discomfort that they are relieved to be in the presence of another person who feels some measure of personal comfort and who appears not to be freaked or stressed by the child's being. These children do not routinely experience comfortable moments with other people.

I try to be as authentic and sincere as I can be with these children. More than 65 years ago, Asperger noted that these children "know who means well with them and who does not, even when he feigns differently" (1944/1991, p. 73). They can read right through our insincerity and have no need for it. My experience thoroughly agrees with Asperger's that these children are excellent judges of other people's characters, and that especially includes their teachers and therapists. More than mere critics, however, these children seem to me to be great admirers of the best humanity can offer, having great affection for those who possess good character. To these children, good character requires honesty in communication and relationships with them.

Nowhere is that honesty desired more than in the realm of thinking. Many children with Asperger's have keen intellects—even those children who have learning weaknesses alongside their assets. These children enjoy our approaching their intellects, for those areas of interest and talent are less emotionally bound and are interpersonally safer. As much as the child will recoil from being asked how they feel, that is how much pleasure he may feel in our asking, "I am not sure how the water monkey's fins differ from arms. Will you explain it to me?" When children offer me detailed information about their interests, I am more than delighted to oblige with my best listening, interest, and queries: "Would you be willing to show me how *your* way of multiplying works? I only know the old-fashioned way"; "Wow, how do you keep so many names and manufacturers of trucks straight in your head?"; "You know so much about military weapons, and I know so little. Would you mind being my teacher in this area?" I have yet to meet one child with Asperger's who isn't touched and pleased to hear me ask such questions.

How do we as therapists keep track of this? How do we know moment by moment where we stand with these children and recognize when we are overwhelming them? As I mentioned before, oft times we can see their behaviors grow more frequent or intense or likewise see them relax or grow engaged. Other times, children's reactions will not be so outwardly visible. As with the rest of us, their inner responses to what we say or do might be hidden from view, despite being felt deeply within themselves. To answer this question summons a concept that will be central to my approach and to every child case discussed in this book: *empathy.*

It is the therapist's empathy to the child's experiences that will lead the way on most every front of the therapy. Our openness to what the child thinks or feels will often represent the leading edge of experience and understanding. Therapists often can sense what is going on in the child before the child may know it. By watching the children closely—meaning with care, respect, and in close contact to what is going on—therapists will accumulate data that will inevitably and dependably inform them as to what's going on in the child. That database builds from the first hello and will continue to accumulate in our ever-refining assessment until the therapy ends. (I say hello instead of shaking hands, for it is apparent that many children with Asperger's have no wish to touch our hands in greeting or have us pat their backs goodbye.)

In another of the many paradoxes that is human nature, psychology, and Asperger's, it was noted that these children were exceptionally clear observers of the other children on the wards (Asperger, 1944/1991). The Asperger clinic children, while hardly claiming their own difficulties, could state clearly what troubled their peers—and they often did, loudly and to their peers' displeasure. These children can be equally adept at seeing their therapist in all of his humanity, even if they do not share their findings. This might seem to suggest that a therapist who works with Asperger's must perform to a higher-than-human standard.

Working with children with Asperger's has taught me just the opposite. I can make honest mistakes, and I often do. My child clients with Asperger's are indeed more observant than they sometimes let on. But I nearly always find them ready to forgive and move on, granted that I own up to the situation.

Natsuki was a 9-year-old girl referred for increasing conflicts with peers, learning difficulties, homework refusal, and compulsive behaviors that according to her parents were "consuming her waking existence." Natsuki entered my office with what on the surface appeared to be conceited arrogance. She avoided my occasional questions, mostly by belittling and dismissing them as "stupid." "What's that got to do with anything?" was her constant refrain for that first meeting.

At one point, I queried about her brother, calling him by a name that though close was not exactly right.

"Can't you remember anything?" she accused me. "My God! You're supposed to be a therapist."

I had many possibilities. I could have defended myself by pointing out that I had heard his name only once and that she spoke rather fast. I could have confronted Natsuki with my clear impression that she didn't think much of her brother, so I didn't get why was she making such a big stink about my mis-speaking his name. I could have interpreted her disapproval and ridicule of me. And I could have apologized. I had learned from previous clients that none of these were my best options. "You told me his name and I couldn't even remember. Some therapist I am," I said. "Join the club," Natsuki said in a much less critical voice. "I don't always remember everything people tell me, either."

My honest acceptance of my shortcoming almost miraculously led to Natsuki's doing the same and to cutting me some slack. My acknowledgment was not dramatic and did not take the therapy to the moon. It was an important small step in our first hour that told Natsuki I was human and knew it. Natsuki had deservedly challenged me, and my response told her that she hadn't done anything bad or regrettable. Over repeated instances, Natsuki would learn that she could confront me about all sorts of things, including my mistakes.

Bringing up Natsuki's attitude reminds us of one other big truth when it comes to beginning our work with Asperger's: Children with Asperger's come not just in all sizes and colors but in all forms. While some present as fragile and fleeting butterflies, others show up as bulls in china shops, pint-sized bulldozers, out-of-control puppies, and computer-driven robots. These children need their therapists to grasp these widely varying outsides while not losing sight of the tender vulnerability that lies well beneath each of these seemingly contradictory personas.

That these children can present so differently compels their therapists to welcome them in correspondingly assorted ways. Verbal and self-assured children will answer direct questions about their lives, functioning, symptoms, and perspectives. Many more will not. So, I ask my questions slowly, infrequently, or in ways that do not corner the child. If the children busy themselves with handheld video games or books that they've brought, I do not take away their distractions or call attention to their avoiding me. I allow them their covers to keep at a distance from me, forging small inroads by showing my shared interest in doses the child can tolerate. For some children, especially younger ones, I allow them to play out of my view, sometimes with their backs to me or hiding behind their parent's legs for hours until they feel ready to venture into the open.

For of all its earnestness, this chapter fails to do service to the complexity, purpose, and potential of beginning sessions. To say that the beginning phase of therapy for the child with Asperger's lasts for a good while—that it goes well beyond the first handful of sessions—is neither semantics nor metaphor. It's true. What we as therapists do in and with these beginnings contains the essential elements for the therapy as a whole. As applies to most every other aspect of treatment, therapy begins the second we meet a child. Equally true, assessment and treatment run hand in hand from day one up to the end. It is obvious that we evaluate early on; but in fact, we never stop evaluating. And while it's obvious that therapy proceeds until goodbye, it starts to take hold from the first instant of clinical contact.

Child therapists know that relationships begin in the first moments. But it's more than that. If therapy is a house that has many different walls (issues), each wall has its own need for a foundation that is deep and sturdy. Each of these foundations and walls, while having some independence, depends on one another. As one brick or a trowel of mortar is to a house, every beginning step and act of therapy—and they are countless—amount to a whole that is much bigger and stronger than their sum. The remaining chapters will spell these beginnings out in greater detail within the context of complete therapies.

In their most ambitious moments, the beginnings of therapy serve the profound function of demonstrating to the child what therapy is and will be like: who we are, how we'll treat them, how we talk and question and answer, how we handle missteps, whether we are sincere, and on and on. Though we'll have plenty of opportunities to show ourselves to these children, we have already begun to do so in vivid Technicolor and high-definition. Just as we will show the child's parents what we are like with their child, we will offer a sampling of therapy and ourselves. Loving parents, many who have probably witnessed one or more professionals treat their child in less than desirable ways, will observe us. They'll take seriously whether we seem to like and respect their child. Just as will happen with parents, our caring, interested, and responsive first moments will tell the children that we, the experts, believe we have the powers to help and that we recognize that child as holding the resources, abilities, and value deserving of that knowledge and assistance. *Together,* our early behaviors pronounce to the child with Asperger's, *we can do this.*

4

Hypersensitivity

Virtually every one of the children with Asperger's that I have known has been troubled by sensory disturbances. I say disturbances, for these sensitivities have shown every variation—from overarousal to underarousal, from aversion to attraction—along with unique patterns that traverse the five senses. In his chapter entitled "Sensory Sensitivity," Attwood (2007) writes that some adults with Asperger's feel it impairs their lives even more than do their difficulties with friends, feelings, and employment. What I've witnessed in my clinical work concurs. I've found sensorial issues to be not only universal but also prominent in the psyches and complaint boxes of these children. It will not surprise any therapist who works with this population that researchers have detected sensory sensitivity in babies who would eventually be diagnosed with autism (Dawson, Osterling, Melzoff, & Kuhl, 2000) and that it can accompany Asperger's right through adulthood (Baranek, Foster, & Berkson, 1997).

SENSORY OVERLOAD

In those early hours when I first meet the child, if I watch closely, I may see visible signs that a child is bothered by the sensory conditions or atmosphere of the office. Such was the case with Hugh, a 9-year-old boy with Asperger's.

> For the first minutes of our meeting, Hugh chose to sit in the big, blue armchair opposite my own. For several minutes, he said nothing while he squinted and rubbed his eyes. He pulled his sweatshirt up over his face.
>
> "It's too bright," his muffled voice said.
>
> I went to my desk and grabbed several sheets of black construction paper, a pair of scissors, and scotch tape. I measured the window pane and cut out a square of paper to match. I covered the top pane that was letting the most light in. "Does that help?" I asked.
>
> From inside his sweatshirt, Hugh gave me the thumbs up. I continued to paper over more window panes, and Hugh each time gave me the okay, until, the job finished, he gave me the ultimate thumbs up by popping his head back out into the open.

Hugh never said thank you, but his engagement around the project and his talking with me said enough. His ending the hour by suggesting we take the squares down until his return so that other kids could have the "sunlight they need to grow" suggested a concern for others that I otherwise would not have seen for some time. It also showed that he was aware his sensitivity was not typical for all children.

The definition of safety includes protection from sensory assault and discomfort. I take care to make my office neutral to the senses. The colors of my walls and carpet are natural and muted. My pictures are calm. I don't use potpourri, air fresheners, scented tissues, or other products with aromas. I strive for fresh air and no smell at all, whenever possible. I don't wear cologne, and should a parent or older patient leave a strong lingering scent of perfume or such, I try to clear it out. My vote for what smells good has nothing to do with what the child senses. I keep the office space reasonably clean. In the summer, I run a dehumidifier whenever I'm not using the office. I find that people with Asperger's—and many without—are sensitive to mold. I've installed dimmers on my overhead light and floor lamps so I can adjust the lighting to the individual's preference. I keep the office relatively quiet by the white noise of an air purifier and the background music from a radio in the waiting room. And as best I can, I try to keep the room temperature near where the child likes it by opening windows or turning up the heat. Not one of us likes to have our senses overwhelmed. Even the most sensorially easygoing of us react negatively when it is too loud, bright, smelly, or in your face. The child with Asperger's is no different, with the proviso that her senses are sharper.

You might think my efforts to insulate the child's senses are indulgent and fear they'll deter the child's growing more sensorially tolerant. After all, she has to learn how to live in a world that's not going to engineer the environment to her sensory liking and needs. But the beginning of therapy is hardly the time to pursue or even think of that. It will be hard to reach a child and do anything constructive when she feels she can't breathe or open her eyes in my office. Even if she likes or thinks well of me and our initial meetings, the child will be reluctant to return to a place that feels oppressive or uninviting.

I am not suggesting that therapists redesign their offices or remove every trace of color or other aesthetic preferences. I realize that many clinicians are limited to offices not their own or for which they have limited control or resources. The considerations I describe are meant to sensitize clinicians, whatever their circumstances, when they make choices as to what their therapeutic spaces will be like or how they'll be kept.

The therapist's best and reasonable attempts to keep the office amenable to the child's senses convey sincere caring in a form that the child can recognize and appreciate. Though her sensory and perceptual vulnerability will prove to hold profound, deep, and far-reaching implications for most every aspect of living, its more obvious and tangible nature makes it a suitable early topic of discussion and interaction.

Questions such as "Is it warm in here?" or "Does the room seem a little musty to you?" run a good chance of being accepted and may be welcomed by the child. I couch the plaint in terms that are general and a bit distanced, stated by myself and asking for no ownership by the child. Hugh had some ability to speak his discomfort; a majority of children will not. I've learned that when I've tried to query these children too fast and too personally about their hypersensitivities, my questions seemed to push them away. However much I've intended my questions to inquire about only what the children have sensed, more than once, they took my questions as unwanted probing into what they're feeling.

So, until the child shows me that she can tolerate otherwise, I say, "Wow, I wonder what that crashing noise outside was?" instead of the more direct "Did that noise startle you?" and the more accusatory "I can see that crash really shook you up." I refrain from going yet a step further. To the uninitiated, a therapist's asking "Are you okay?" sounds rather innocuous and kindly. But the child with Asperger's may hear something unwanted, presumptuous, and intrusive—something that sounds to be a therapist's sneaky ploy to use her sensory reactions to probe inner psychological states. (The child likely won't articulate that belief in such articulated terms, but she can sense and fear it nonetheless.) Children with Asperger's are exceedingly open to candid and genuine attempts to therapeutically join with them. If they, however, come for good reason to believe that the therapist has his own ulterior agendas or comes at them through devious if well-intentioned angles, they are adept at shutting us down and out.

Our responsiveness to the child's sensory discomforts is important not only in the beginning hours but throughout the treatment. I cannot rely on my own senses to tell me what the child wants or finds bothersome. I can only use my own sensations as signals to wonder how the same stimuli are felt by the child. The child has many channels by which to give me that information. She may at some time be able to answer direct questions, but until then, her behaviors will do her complaining.

Behaviors may say exactly what they look like they say. A child who zips and cinches the neck of her down parka may be saying that she's cold. A child pinching his nostrils is likely smelling something he doesn't like. Squinting and covering the eyes, as Hugh did, can reveal a photophobia, and covering the ears with hands or pillows might indicate that something being heard doesn't feel good. I seldom go through a session with a child with Asperger's when I don't have at least one inkling that something sensorially is going on. Oft times, it is just a wonder that goes nowhere; rarer times, it leads me to take an action, like turning on the air conditioner.

As I've gained experience with such children, my sensitivity to their sensitivities has evolved and refined. At first, it took conscious thought and effort; then it became second nature and more natural. For those of us who are fairly robust when it comes to the senses, we go through our days relatively unperturbed and undemanding. In order to grasp what it's like for the child with Asperger's, I needed to recalibrate my own, heartier thermo-, humidi-, and every other kind of "-stat" to detect finer and smaller changes in the environment. The child with Asperger's has endured a life in which she ever guards against what, in no ways a dramatization, can be called a pervasively and perpetually distressing onslaught of environmental stimuli. As her therapist, I do well by growing better at sharing that perception and helping her to micromanage her comfort.

Even as I attend to the child's immediate comfort, my goals are bigger. I wish to help the child better manage her sensitivities on her own. So, here and there I try making little suggestions that I expect to go nowhere. I never cease to be amazed when making what seems to me a ridiculously obvious comment like "Have you considered sunglasses?" and the child reacts as if I've revealed something novel and remarkable. I would think that a child who has squinted in the sunlight for years would have a drawer full of sunglasses. Take nothing for granted. (In all fairness to parents, the child may have a drawer full of sunglasses, and they've likely long lobbied in vain that the child wear them. Many children with Asperger's have unwittingly raised oppositional behavior to an art form.)

Sometimes, I've convinced a child to take long-rejected proaction by appealing to his intellect. One boy for whom sunlight caused headaches grabbed onto my showing him a science article that discussed the various kinds of radiation occurring in sunlight and the physics behind modern sunglasses. Admittedly, he went overboard and became an overbearing zealot for cutting-edge sunglasses, not an inexpensive hobby. But he did put an end to his avoidable headaches. A purely informational tactic likewise moved a girl to take better care of herself in terms of her nutrition and health.

Olivia was a 12-year-old girl with Asperger's. An exceptional athlete with great energy, she often neglected to eat, and when she did, she lived by a very short list of foods she found edible. She would get so lost in video games, soccer, and skateboarding that she would go from breakfast to dinner, forgetting about lunch or snacks. As a result of her high activity and low intake, Olivia would feel lightheaded and tired, symptoms of self-induced hypoglycemia.

With my assistance, Olivia's parents tried various strategies to get her to eat. They instituted behavioral incentives and customized shopping. They tried hard-sell and hands-off. They tried reminding and serving Olivia at her convenience. They tried stocking the kitchen, then her room, with favorite foods and snacks. Nothing worked.

Finally, having listened to a non-Asperger's adult talk to me about the science behind her diet gave me a thought. I photocopied some articles from women's magazines on the health aspects of dieting and gave them to Olivia. She minimized the articles and my efforts as "parental-like" attempts to get her to eat. Recalling the boy with the sunglasses, a few weeks later I tried showing Olivia actual scientific articles that spoke about nutrition. Though it was apparent that much of what she read— about mitochondria, adenosine triphosphate and oxidation—went over her head, the gist of the articles convinced Olivia that bodies need food to run. Armed with objective knowledge that she was willing to take in and digest (puns intended), Olivia began eating. On her own, she made up weekly menus and accompanied her parents to the market where she did her own shopping. Eventually, she even invited her parents into her food experiences, sharing her concoctions and serving as a most passionate consultant to the family table. Coming to recognize, manage, own, and verbalize what she felt—developmental achievements in themselves—proved to be necessary skill-building steps for Olivia's learning to do the same for other internal states and emotions. Also worth mentioning, Olivia made explicit her belief that she had come to her new views and life change to eat well *on her own.* Over and over, I find that children with Asperger's highly value their independence and self-determination.

I ever find that hypersensitivity is one of the first complaints to surface in therapy. The child's perception of sensory stimulation seems to warrant the early spotlight, as it reflects the very place where the child's insides (and mind and experience) intersect with the outside (world), where their bodies and sense organs (skin, eyes, ears, tongues, noses) meet the environment. Being such a readily identifiable problem, sensory issues can represent a doorway through which the child may be more willing to enter an otherwise avoided houseful of Asperger's experience.

THE IMPLICATIONS OF SENSORY SENSITIVITIES

As one works with more and more cases involving Asperger's, it is impossible not to grasp the distress, ranging from annoyance to torment, that sensory sensitivities can cause a child. Consider Clare Sainsbury's self-description (quoted in Attwood, 2007, p. 272).

The corridors and halls of almost any mainstream school are a constant tumult of noises echoing, fluorescent lights (a particular source of visual and auditory stress for people on the autistic spectrum), bells ringing, people bumping into each other, the smells of cleaning products and so on. For anyone with the sensory hyper-sensitivities and processing problems typical of an autistic spectrum condition, the result is that we often spend most of our day *perilously close to sensory overload* [italics mine].

(Sainsbury, 2000, p. 101)

As if not enough of an ordeal, this hard reality holds implications that extend beyond the child's sensory unrest. Perceiving too much too intensely can raise the human life that the rest of us take for granted toward undue levels of stress and difficulty. Sensory sensitivity can wreak havoc at home, in school, and even in the privacy of the child's own bathroom.

Martin's kind and gentle father had told me many times of his concerns over his teenage son's hygiene. "He says he wants a girlfriend, but he does nothing to take care of his appearance. He goes days without showering. When I finally nag him so much that he showers, I can't get him out. He'll spend hours in there," Mr. K. chuckled, "and when I go in there afterwards, the soap is still dry, and I swear the shampoo hasn't been touched. For the life of me, I don't know what he does in there." Mr. K. smiled. "And I don't think I want to know."

Mr. K.'s parental concern and Martin's being hygienically challenged are, I've found, commonplace with Asperger's. I recall Hardy, one of the campers in our cabin at Wediko, who could take 15 minutes to mostly not wash his hands. He would gingerly slip his fingers onto the sides of the faucet so as not to get them wet and then press the sides of that faucet hard with his finger tips. He would close his eyes and just stand there, transfixed. When we counselors, in our youth and not knowing better, physically forced his hands under the running water, Hardy shrieked and would spend the next hour or two angry and shaken. What kind of sensing, perception, and neurology, we try to imagine, can account for such complicated experiences? How can a child like Martin stand under a pouring shower for a solid hour but somehow be unable to actually wash with soap and shampoo? More so, how do I help a child like that take better care of himself?

Consider what it took in Martin's case: a long and detailed discussion about the science of sweat, body odor, and germs. Of course, such illumination does not go smoothly or straight upward. Martin discovered his own scientific writings that said too much bathing is a contemporary fetish that along with soap can overly dry skin and kill the good bacteria that keep the skin in a healthy balance. After attempting what he described as a "good mature shower," he protested for several weeks that his skin itched to the point of driving him crazy, a symptom that he proudly attributed to his having taken my "stupid advice."

Sometimes feeling a burst of self-confidence and autonomy, Martin improved his showering and toothbrushing on his own. Other times, he responded to his parents' bribes or their taking away his iPod until he got on with his self-care. With his showering and many other aspects of his daily life, Martin responded to my suggestion that he edge his way into an experience, heeding closely his discomfort but doing his best to push on. He related totally to this analogy. He gladly came to his next session, chronicling his second-by-second anguish as he soaped his foot and could feel the tingling of the soap's toxic ingredients "eradicating" the good bacteria that kept his skin intact. While listening, I kept my smiles to myself. It was clear this was no laughing matter to Martin.

Martin's struggle with hygiene did not settle overnight. It was a prolonged exercise that paralleled all of his therapy. When he began to show an interest in girls, it struck his parents and me that his wish to be clean and to not smell was not motivating better hygiene. For all of his hypersensitivity, like most of us, Martin was okay with his own smells. It wasn't until he overheard some girls ridiculing another boy's body odor that the switch flicked in Martin's head. This sudden change was hardly an epiphany. It was the culmination of months of labored work—Martin's, his parents', and mine. Eventually, Martin showed insight into the process as he opened up about the ways that his sensory sensitivity and deeper fears that ran beneath led him to avoid many of the life tasks that even his "little cousin can do pretty easily." As we'll address fully and nearer the book's end, children with Asperger's can do amazing work as they come to own and work through their being different, work that wonderfully clears the way to their also growing more certain that for all of these differences, they are even more the same as other people.

My experience has shown the efficacy of a combination of intellectual appeal, behavioral exposure, incremental experimentation, self-determination, reward and punishment, and insight. When confronting such deep-seated and deep-rooted problems (meaning biologically based), therapists, parents, and children need every therapeutic weapon and tool available. Just as it did with Martin, a mixture of these interventions worked wonders in helping Will get over the car sickness that handcuffed his and his family's life. Initially, Will became addicted to medications that helped but did not eliminate his nausea. Relaxation strategies didn't seem to help, nor did the distraction of video games or reading, both which made him feel worse.

Will's caring parents had understandably grown weary of listening to their son's relentless complaining in the car. Will would dramatically make himself gag as if about to vomit. But a paradoxical intervention seemed to help. Rather than replicate the usual and chronic dynamic of Will's moaning and their shushing, they told Will that every 10 minutes he would have 2 minutes to update them on his motion sickness. Will's obligation was to use a little notebook to record every breath of his discomfort, a chronicle that he would have to share at regular intervals; his parents' job was to listen without comment. Will soon gave up his reports. He told me that his nausea just went away. Whatever the reasons, including the obvious demand and bother of keeping a nausea journal, these recurring experiences with Asperger's tell me that many factors contribute to hypersensitivity and that I never need worry that I take these symptoms too seriously or that I am exerting too much thought and creativity on their resolution. It is worth it.

More verbally fluent teens with Asperger's often tell me about the ways that their sensory sensitivities hamper their social lives. Can you remember your first slow dance? "I know I'm supposed to like the smell of girls," Martin confessed. With self-conscious detail worthy of Proust, he spontaneously listed the many sensations that unnerved him: the friction, the fabrics, the breath, the heat, the sweat, all accentuated by the din of the crowd and music. "How am I ever going to get a girlfriend if all those things bother me?" Martin asked with all of his heart and worry. "It's going to be a challenge," I replied.

Martin smiled knowingly, not out of happiness but out of my sharing and confirming the painful reality he lived and knew was real. Diminishing his experience by suggesting it would soon go away or providing false reassurance by telling him that all teens felt that way would have left him alone with his hurt. He didn't have the girlfriend and romantic relationship he desired. At least he had another human being (a.k.a. his therapist) who cared and understood.

"Given all the discomfort you felt," I went on, "I'm impressed that you were able to do two whole dances."

"You have no idea how much I wanted to quit after one," Martin said.

"If you were listening to some other teen tell you this story, what would you think of him?" I asked, wishing to get to the fullness of Martin's disappointment in himself.

"I'd think him very brave," he said.

The child with Asperger's must ever be on guard for toxic and bothersome sensations. How can such a child be socially flexible? He turns every corner wondering what smell, feel or sight will jump out to accost him and his finicky senses. It might be a pulsing strobe or a piercing siren; maybe a wet golden retriever or that green shaker of parmesan cheese. Is it any wonder these children might prefer the constant, familiar, and self-run environments of their homes and rooms? Is it any wonder that they might prefer quarantining themselves with a book in the small, vacation cottage attic than joining the family fun that's happening just outside on the messy, sandy beach that smells like low tide?

The ways that hypersensitivity can throw eternal wrenches into the life of a family are just a diluted reflection of the disarray and inhibition that the child contends with. Whether we're talking about the discomfort of collared shirts, the tightness of socks in shoes, or any of the infinitely unlimited sensations that can dog the child's days, I try to keep my bearing steady and interested and the process as lively as its patient. My goal is not to get the child to brush his teeth right now, no matter what. My goal is to show the child over and over that he can come to own and master these sensory hurdles, making them look more like mere inconveniences to outmaneuver than mile-high mountains to move.

STILL SENSES RUN DEEP

That bathrooms could be loaded when it comes to the child with Asperger's was old news to me. Bathrooms involve water and washing and much else that can be troubling to a child for whom bodily processes can loom odd, mysterious, and disconnected. I had worked with one boy who would hold his bowels and urine for a day rather than use a toilet that had a scary flushing sound. I had heard many parents talk of children who would lock themselves in the bathroom for very long times, even if supposedly just urinating or cleaning up. I had met a child who for each wipe used exactly three double pieces of toilet paper folded perfectly and another one who routinely pulled his bowel movements in and out a certain number of times before letting loose. I assumed that what went on in bathrooms corresponded to some pretty idiosyncratic thinking.

I'd been working with Barclay for several months when in a session he many times excused himself to go to the bathroom. Each time he'd return to the office, he looked more anxious, his eyes averting me more intensely and more jerkily. My queries as to whether he was okay fueled his unsettledness. "I have a sick stomach!" Barclay finally blurted, as if confessing the most heinous crime.

I thought that Barclay might be upset about messing the bathroom, but I couldn't have been more wrong. With much support, Barclay shared his panicked worry that his upset stomach meant he was dying. With deep shame, he spoke of worrying that his intestines were disintegrating and would fall out along with everything else. Every time he went to the bathroom, Barclay felt all alone and scared with his body and its illness and his out-of-control fears as to what was happening. My steady ear, validation of his awful worry, and calm explanation as to what an upset stomach is and how it means nothing bad readily calmed Barclay.

Many children with Asperger's have uncertain relationships with their senses *and their bodies.* I've found somatic symptoms and severely hypochondriacal preoccupations common in these children. They often describe an almost phobic sense of their body processes: "Why is my head hot?" "My teeth feel hollow." "I think I can feel germs in my throat." Despite their sensitivity to bodily symptoms, they can be the worst reporters when at the doctor's office. Describing exactly where and how their stomach hurts can be a task beyond the child. These children can talk about pain or a bowel movement as if it is alien—something that is happening to their body, not an essential and humanly vital part of an integrated and intact body.

Unfortunately, much of this bodily sensing is hidden and secret and goes unspoken by the child who cannot find the words to express herself.

Overwhelmed, apprehensive, and often ashamed by the imagined badness of what she thinks, the child keeps her anguished imaginings to herself lest they be punished or judged as wrong. But what private musings they can be. Barclay's talking to me about his digestive anxieties showed him that he could profitably open up about his fears and that doing so might bring him comfort and reduce his shame. That experience began to teach him a new way of coping and a hint toward future problem solving.

Speaking of the body, therapists also know that oversensitivity is not the only sensory aberration for children with Asperger's. Some children are *hypo-sensitive*, for example—less aware of and reactive to pain signals, a situation that can make a child susceptible to avoidable injuries. Olivia, the girl who wouldn't eat, once spun in my office chair for an entire hour, then abruptly walked a straight line to prove her unbelievable claim that she'd never in her life felt dizzy or disoriented. You've probably seen children who overly enjoy the sensation of spinning, chiming doorbells, the smell of their sneakers, or the inner light show produced by pressing their closed eyelids. Some sensory perceptions can come and go, hyperaroused this hour and underaroused the next, fluctuating with the child's internal state (Bogdashina, 2003). Though research once suggested the rarity of synesthesias—meaning sensorily mixed sensations—it is now known that they are more common. Children with Asperger's have more than their fair share of funny sensing, smelling numbers, hearing colors, or somehow distortedly experiencing these stimuli or not knowing where they come from. All we can do as therapists is help these children by all possible means to recognize, tolerate, and do what they can to make their immediate worlds less noxious and sensorily obstructive.

Many children with Asperger's seem to lack that wellspring of inner calm and self-soothing. They often find the sensations that other children relish—massaging, hair brushing, foot tickling—intolerably irritating and disorganizing. In addition to the strategies I've described, therapists can support parents and others in implementing behavioral methods outside the therapy office. Sensory-Motor Integration (Ayres, 2005) can help the child come to tolerate, integrate, and even enjoy sensations that earlier would have discomforted her. I, for example, often teach the child with Asperger's ways to relax their muscles and stretch at bedtime. Though they usually put up tremendous resistance, I've seen several children come to rely on it, leading to earlier bedtimes and a liking of yoga. Likewise, the children I've treated who pursue martial arts seem to develop an enhanced sense of their own bodies, growing more confident, coordinated, and trusting of their body's integrity. As children grow more connected in therapy, they often grow more willing to face their sensory sensitivities, frequently showing the capacity to expose and desensitize themselves so that the stimuli perturb them less. Children's burgeoning wishes to do more, such as go to parties or date, can motivate their forcing themselves to get used to loud music, the smell of perfume, and so on. These small successes loom large in the child's psyche and can lead to pride and enthusiasm to keep moving on and past their sensory sensitivities.

For all the attention we've now given to the child's sensory sensitivity, we have only pricked the surface, for senses and the data they receive do much more than keep us apprised of the weather. Our sensory perceptions affect the most essential aspects of the human condition—most notably, love and attachment. What effect does it have on the young child's attachment to his parent if the smells, sounds, or feelings of closeness are felt as aversive? Can those of us who love a hug truly grasp what it would mean to our relationships if those same hugs hurt or physically repulsed us? What if that beaming smile that lightens your life instead hurt your eyes as if a laser-guided dart? You probably feel confident that you could never get close to a skunk, but what if the one you loved smelled that way to you? Could you maintain your love? Could you even feel and know it in the first place? Human attachment is a miracle. It is even a greater miracle when it comes to children with Asperger's. And beyond the ways their unusual sensitivities can impair their connecting to other people, doesn't it make sense that the child with Asperger's can be disconnected from herself as much as she can be from others and that her body can feel apart from her mind? While it takes more than some sensory adjustment to make for attachment, helping these children grow more comfortable can make way for interactions and connections that might be averted or confounded because of sensory overload or repulsion.

Children with Asperger's endure and suffer the sensations and consequences of their sensory eccentricities. Like one with a god-awful headache caused by the jackhammer down the street, these children would like nothing more than freedom from their sensory oppressions. They try to overcontrol their environments—not in an attempt to be pests or get attention or because they are princesses sleeping on a single pea. These children's sensory burdens are real and substantial; their actions and protests serve to make their living in this world more bearable. Sensing and perceiving involves physiological stimulation in association with brain perception and cognition *and* the attribution of psychological meaning, too. More times than not, we find together that these sensorial difficulties hold profound and complex implications for their social lives and most other aspects of their daily lives. By going patiently, steadily, and creatively, therapists can help these children know and own their vulnerabilities, the acceptance of which can allow for problem solving and adaptive behaviors that bring relief and freedom.

5

Anxiety

Even after its neurological and developmental realities were established, anxiety was not always seen as a primary aspect of the Asperger experience; nor, according to current psychiatric criteria (APA, 2000), is it requisite to diagnosis. However, as any clinician who works with this population soon learns, children with Asperger's often suffer symptoms of anxiety. Regardless of whether it rises to the level of a comorbid diagnosis, anxiety can cause extreme distress, hinder functioning, and exacerbate the traits and vulnerabilities of Asperger's. This chapter examines the many faces of anxiety in Asperger's, how it's experienced, and what can be done to alleviate the angst and interference it brings to an already difficult existence.

ASPERGER'S AND ANXIETY

Sometime in the late-1980s I was fortunate to hear a woman speak about her firsthand experience with autism. She first spoke at Grand Rounds, where she gave an enlightening talk on what having autism felt like. She had already earned a doctorate in animal science, and given her unusual sensitivities to animals and remarkable visual skills, Dr. Temple Grandin was on her way to a notable career in the designing of livestock facilities. Dr. Grandin described how she could walk through a blueprint of a not yet built facility and see it as a cow or horse might. Unlike anything I had read in the literature on autism, Dr. Grandin described in vivid detail how uncomfortable hugs felt to her as a child. From her childhood, she recollected how much she detested the scratching of starched petticoats against her skin and how much she loved sneaking into the "squeezing machine," used to hold animals tight for farm procedures, where she'd self-administer a different kind of hug. To say that Dr. Grandin held the audience spellbound is understated. Her presentation was articulate, powerful, and confident in its truth.

A few lucky ones of us were invited back to a more intimate lunch where we could ask Dr. Grandin questions. Whereas that morning, she had spoken from behind a podium in the distant front of a large auditorium, Dr. Grandin sat just across the corner of the table from where I sat. She continued to dazzle us with her candid, genuine, and beautifully expressed experiences, all of which were entirely novel and unheard of by any of us, from trainee to the most senior faculty. But something else, something different, was noticeable in this more personal setting. Dr. Grandin appeared visibly less comfortable and more nervous than she had at Rounds. When I asked how she had come to such comfort as a public speaker, she openly described the horrendous anxiety and panic attacks that had come in her twenties (and which, she reported, medication alleviated). She compared them to a case of stage fright that never went away. Dr. Grandin explained her view that anxiety was part of Asperger's. She saw the anxiety, in turn, as making the hardships of Asperger's only that much worse (e.g., compromising and obstructing social experience). She conceptualized anxiety and Asperger's as mutually contributing to a vicious cycle that was hard to derail. Though so much of what Dr. Grandin told us enlightened me, it was her emphasis on the need to see anxiety that most stuck and stayed with me. Her revelations and ideas confirmed what I had been seeing in the children with Asperger's that I'd thus far treated. Almost without exception, the many children with Asperger's who I've known have all struggled with anxiety, sometimes to paralyzing proportions.

But for all of what my clients were showing me and for all that Dr. Grandin revealed in her talks and a then newly published book (1986), the field was hardly noticing. Despite significant advances in the understanding of its biological and developmental nature, the syndrome itself was relatively misunderstood, particularly in the United States. As a result, a majority of children with Asperger's went undiagnosed, and in terms of epidemiology and incidence rates, the number of cases went grossly underreported (Fombonne, 2003). Clinicians and researchers were apparently having enough difficulty seeing and agreeing on what Asperger's was without refining associated or comorbid symptoms and diagnoses.

This is not to say that the relationship of anxiety and Asperger's was totally missing. In her 1981 clinical report on Asperger's, a classic that coined the term *Asperger's* and that nearly single-handedly brought the disorder to the light of day, Lorna Wing warned that Asperger's Syndrome can resemble "[s]uperimposed psychiatric illnesses[, including c]linically diagnosable anxiety." Since that time, research has shown that anxiety symptoms and disorders can be found in well over half to as many as 80 percent of children with Asperger's (de Bruin, Ferdinand, Meesters, de Nijs, & Verheij, 2007; Ghaziuddin, Weidmer-Mikhail, & Ghaziuddin, 1998; Leyfer et al., 2006). Yet, for all our current knowledge and methods, the diagnostic refinement of Asperger's and associated disorders remains relatively immature and in need of study. While clearer criteria have increased the identification rate of Asperger's more than tenfold (Fombonne, 2003), as of 2004, a substantial number of cases still were not diagnosed (Fombonne et al., 2004). Anxiety is not just something that children with Asperger's are stuck with. It warrants high priority as a treatment goal of Asperger's (Volkmar & Klin, 2000).

HIDDEN FROM SIGHT

In her initial call to me, Derrick's mother sounded both urgent and ambivalent. She asked for a quick appointment before adding that she wasn't sure she was looking for therapy and that maybe she and her husband just needed "a little guidance" around their 6-year-old and only child who could be "a little trying." She spoke of Derrick's having obsessions that scared her while almost at once dismissing them as typical boy stuff. She also intimated that he could get out of control but diverted my gentle attempt to find out more. At the end of the call, Mrs. P. thanked me, adding that I had given her lots to think about. We agreed to let it go for now and that she would call if in the future she felt stronger about her son's need for professional help.

Later that day, I received a message from a dean at a local private elementary school. She said that she'd given my name to Mr. and Mrs. P. and that she hoped I could see their son that week or as soon as possible. The dean described a history of peer problems, odd communication, stereotypical behaviors, and distractibility. She described how the school had recommended therapy in the past, and how Mr. and Mrs. P. had not followed through. She said that the school was now pushing it harder, as Derrick had grown more provocative and aggressive.

The following week, I received another message from the dean. She said that Derrick had hit a boy in the face with a trumpet and that he'd made some disturbing threats to other children in the classroom. The dean said she'd discovered that the family had again chosen not to take action, so she'd set an ultimatum. She reported that she'd suspended Derrick as of that day, adding that he wouldn't be allowed back in school until he'd begun working with a therapist.

That afternoon Mrs. P. called me again. She said that she'd been thinking and thought that it might be a good time to try a little therapy. "Nothing big," she said—just maybe giving Derrick a strategy or two to help him behave better. We scheduled a meeting for the following day.

When they arrived, Mr. and Mrs. P. couldn't get Derrick into the office. He threw a major tantrum in their car and then threw a second one in my waiting room. The 6-year-old cursed and threw things at his parents. At one point, he bit his mother's hand. He's just a little upset because we told him he might have to shut off his Gameboy while you meet with him," his mother said. Derrick stopped his flailing and intently watched for my reaction. "If he can go get his game quickly," I said calmly, "he can keep playing while we talk."

In a flash, Derrick ran to get his Gameboy and rejoined me in the office. Derrick played his game and paid no attention to me or my questions. On the few occasions when I pushed, he squished his face and played his game more intensely. I did little more than stay out of his way in that first hour. The parents made it clear that they had little desire for help. But they wanted Derrick to stay at his school. They asked that I try a few sessions with him. Naively, I signed up, believing that my efforts would be so helpful Derrick's parents would sign on for the lengthier treatment their son needed.

We met three times and were beginning to ease into a more comfortable rhythm. Derrick came to therapy with less of a fuss and on a few occasions had shared with me his exasperation while playing his video game. At the end of the third hour, Mr. and Mrs. P. announced to me that this was my last time to meet with their son. "You've helped us a lot," Mrs. P. said. "We think we can do it on our own now with all you've taught us." Mr. P. nodded that he felt the same, though I had no idea what possible lessons I might have imparted.

I tried to persuade them to stay. I spoke of the continued threat of Derrick's aggression, and, referring to the first day's tantrum, how he posed a danger to peers and his family. I spoke of his unspoken anger. Blah, blah, blah. "Thanks again for everything," his parents said as they left my office, never to return.

I don't know what happened to that Derrick. But I do know what happened when I met my next Derrick. Several months later, I was referred a similar case of a slightly older boy who also had grown frighteningly aggressive. This time, I did not forget what both the school and parents had told me. Anthony was bright in an odd way; he knew more than most adults about stuff that most kids and adults don't care about. He liked to spin and rub things. He had a terribly hard time with other children. He often accused them of breaking school rules and saw himself as an unofficial deputy to the principal. He gave speeding tickets to children who walked the halls too fast and attempted citizen's arrests of children who he judged to be unruly on the playground. Anthony felt justified manhandling peers who he deemed needed his disciplining. The referral came on the heels of several incidents within a few days, each of which involved his hurting another child. Anthony's anger, lack of self-control, and need to be right seemed to school staff to be escalating for reasons unknown.

Anthony grabbed my dog puppet by the ears. He pulled and wrenched them cruelly.

"Ouch! You're killing me!" my puppet yelled. "Those are my ears you're ripping off!"

"Serves you right," Anthony said in a serious and somber tone. He was not kidding. "Schools have rules, and you broke them."

"What did I do?" my dog cried.

"*What did you do?*" Anthony exclaimed, looking at the ceiling and laughing to himself. "What didn't you do?" Anthony tied my puppet's ears tight with a pipe cleaner. "That should keep you quiet for now."

For many weeks, Anthony played a sadistic cop to my rule-breaking animal puppets. Each week, he grew tougher and meaner. Over the course of this play, the immediate precipitants to Anthony's angry and willful aggression grew a bit clearer. He accused my puppets of running wild in school, bullying other kids, and asking stupid questions. He accused them of all the things that could threaten a child, especially one with Asperger's. "You mean kids care?" I made my dog puppet ask. "Yeah, I keep kids safe from guys like you!" Anthony shot back, meaning it.

Anthony's play displaced his aggression and his underlying fears in a format and at a distance that he could tolerate and find solace in. As time went on, Anthony's play showed me that indeed, much of his aggression was a reaction to the great anxiety and vulnerability he felt being a child in a school community that scared and overwhelmed him in most every way. Acting as cop to the other kids was his attempt to cope with those fears and demands. Though Anthony and I had yet to speak more directly about his aggression or fears, his teacher happily reported that his hostile behaviors were diminishing. Anthony came to her on his own and explained that he no longer had the time to help out policing the other children. His teacher possessed the caring and wisdom to take his apology seriously. She told me that she'd thanked him for his previous service to the school while agreeing with his judgment that his time was best spent being a student himself. Though I hadn't made one remark or asked one question that suggested to Anthony that I knew about his fears, his play—me as a dog puppet and he as himself, the school sheriff—did the trick.

As preoccupied as I was with Derrick's aggression, I'd been wholly taken in by his behavior with me, which felt arrogant, controlling, and on the edge of an explosion. As a young therapist—and sometimes as an older one—it's hard not to feel responsibility for a child's dangerousness. I was so focused on Derrick's aggression and the possibly of his losing a spot at his school that I lost sight of his Asperger's.

Not only did I keep in mind that anxiety and fear might be propelling Anthony's aggressive and controlling behaviors; I also bothered to explain that clearly and carefully to his parents, saying that the remedy could take some time. No longer was I willing to gamble on my hooking a child and family into a course of therapy that they didn't want. In all likelihood, Derrick's parents' denial and withdrawal from therapy had involved their own fears and anxieties, neither of which I'd addressed in any way with them. Maybe they had rightly sought a therapist who would see and address such concerns?

Over time, Anthony's play incorporated discussion of the ways that other children could mistreat him, as well as ways that he always felt one down when playing with others. Through this play and talk, on his own he came to the sterling insight that he had become "enforcer of the rules" because deep inside, he had never felt as if he knew the unwritten rules that guided life with kids in school and beyond, rules that all kids just got naturally, even much younger ones.

These cases harken back to our wondering why the anxiety of Asperger's can go unseen. The reason is that anxiety in these children can look like a different species of problem. As we'll soon discuss, it's easy to identify shaky knees, a quivering voice, sweaty palms, and a fear of snakes. When anxiety shows up in disguise, however—as aggression, arrogance, irritability, impulsivity, anger, or a need to control—it can distract and delay the clinician, particularly one who feels pressure to quickly resolve disruptive or other troublesome behaviors. Clinicians who use methods that focus exclusively on those behaviors may make progress, but they run the risk of getting therapeutically waylaid and handcuffed as the anxiety that at least partly feeds the child's difficult behaviors continues to percolate. How do we assess for anxiety in a child whose demeanor and behavior may not look anxious? Before we talk actual strategies, we must talk mindset and therapeutic attitude.

One, therapists can play the percentages. Studies and clinical reports suggest that anxiety symptoms or full-blown diagnosable anxiety-related disorders can be found in a vast majority of children with Asperger's. This doesn't mean that we see and diagnose anxiety blindly even in children where it doesn't exist. False positives are not the goal and don't help the child. However, the certain and strong connections between Asperger's and anxiety should sensitize us to watch and listen for anxiety. That is, we should entertain the possibility that anxiety lurks behind or aside behaviors and symptoms that at first glance can appear unrelated.

Two, we train ourselves to watch more carefully, meaning on a smaller and slower scale. In therapies that can move so slowly and with a child who may not be the clearest or most willing reporter and responder, how do therapists tell if their hunches concerning anxiety are grounded and worth pursuing? When assessing a child with Asperger's, we recalibrate our scales to match. Moments that might last seconds with a nonautistic child can represent minutes or hours when doing therapy with a child with Asperger's. Alternatively, it can be the minute reactions of the child with Asperger's that tell us she is growing more anxious with our questioning. She might like to pick at her knees *all the time;* it still means something when her picking accelerates or goes deeper. A somewhat dependable gauge of what's going on with the child (in terms of stress and anxiety) is to notice what's going on with stereotypically autistic behaviors and habits. Tics and odd body movements (or withdrawal) that intensify can warn us of stress, which then can guide us to back off or to take some action to help relieve the child's tensions.

Three, we experiment, as I did with Gerard. Gerard was a first grader referred for a panoply of behaviors and symptoms that included aggression, repetitive and eccentric body movements, odd language, compulsive interests, and pronounced social immaturity. One of the symptoms that most troubled his parents and school staff was his sudden discharges of energy that seemed to them to come out of the blue, that disrupted the classroom, and that could escalate to dangerous levels in a flash.

I'd seen milder variations of his tantrums several times in my office; they seldom seemed to rise out of nowhere. They appeared to erupt out of some clinical circumstance in which, so it appeared, Gerard felt stressed or frustrated. And they seemed to follow an observable prodrome, even if small and short-lived.

Gerard sequestered himself in the corner behind my rocking chair. He had done this only a few times before, each time just seconds before going into one of his hyperkinetic free falls. I grabbed a stuffed skunk from the toy bin. "Leave me alone!" I yelled for the skunk. "And don't try to stop me." Gerard studied my strange behavior. "And don't tell me I'm being bad or wild. I am sick of hearing that. I'm just scared," I said for the skunk. Gerard watched, utterly rapt. "What are you scared of?" I asked the skunk. "I don't know!" I the skunk replied. "People, school—maybe I'm afraid of everything."

Solidly regrouped, Gerard walked over to the skunk and gently put his hand around its shoulders as if to comfort it. "It's okay. You're safe. Don't be afraid," Gerard said. The skunk said that no one knew what it felt like, and Gerard answered that *he himself did*.

Believe me, this was no miracle. Gerard didn't return the next hour eager to talk of his anxiety; nor did his teachers or parents report new behaviors after he left my office. But it was something worth noting. My effort to grab his attention and divert his going inwardly nuclear worked, making him open to hear me and to put his anxiety into words and gesture. I no longer had to speculate whether his explosions and aggression involved fear and anxiety. He had proven to me that they did. That certainty gave me further confidence and motive to keep at it.

This puppet play resembles the *replays* of Levine and Chedd, a technique that uses play to "help children who have behavioral difficulties due to intense responding" (2007, p. 13)—a method, incidentally, that seems to work with all children, Asperger's or not. By this method, the clinician creates a play scenario that replicates a real-life event in which the child, overwhelmed by emotions, reacted with maladaptive behavior, such as melting down, erupting, or withdrawing. This psychologically safe and fun intervention offers the child an opportunity to reenact the event or circumstance while reexperiencing it and the associated feelings in small and bearable doses, enabling increased mastery of the feelings and self-regulation of the behaviors. The intervention aptly combines elements of virtually all worthwhile schools of child therapy, including the behavioral, cognitive-behavioral, client centered, and psychodynamic. The method can help to reduce and eliminate problematic behaviors by strengthening the child's ability to cope with transitions, haircuts, doctor visits, frustration at school or in play, and other trials of daily life. But the method's beauty goes well beyond improving immediate behaviors—though is itself a valuable goal. Every ounce of growth that the method yields is like a small seed that grows into bigger and enduring gains such that the child experiences less anxiety, an ability to withstand greater stress, enhanced problem solving and self-control, and so on.

As Levine and Chedd might have predicted, Gerard embraced my puppet's *replaying*. Over many sessions Gerard's play evolved and clarified under his direction. In each hour he encouraged me to repeat this play. He instructed me to escalate my puppet's tantrums. Gerard absolutely delighted in the playful and exaggerated discombobulation that my puppet displayed. "Louder!" he ordered. "Wilder!" Gerard, in return, took over the role of a kindly and understanding grown-up, trying in vain to calm my puppet and learn what it was that upset it. Of course, in doing so, Gerard's guesses about my puppet's problems sounded a lot like what was triggering his own meltdowns. "You and me are a lot alike," he eventually told my puppet while consoling it. "Maybe next time," Gerard said, gently patting the puppet's head, "you can tell your teacher when you're feeling scared," a piece of self-advice that Gerard actually took with him back to the classroom.

The anxiety in the child with Asperger's is not always subtle or surreptitious. Many children show up to our offices visibly tense and withdrawn, fraught with bodily symptoms that speak of nervousness—talking incessantly or remaining near mute. Children with Asperger's may be referred for extraordinary separation anxiety, fear and avoidance of social situations, and so forth. We'll meet children who will ably answer questions or complete checklists about their anxiety symptoms. They or their parents may report fears and phobias, nightmares, or generalized anxiety. They may speak of being a worrier with a capital "W." Of course, the age and developmental stage of the child will have much to do with their individual anxieties and the ways that therapists can help.

ADDRESSING ANXIETY

There are many avenues to approach the child's anxiety and its sequelae. As with many children, each therapeutic strategy can assist, doing its part and fair share in helping the child with Asperger's come to grow beyond fears and anxieties that can range from mild to paralyzing to, so it can feel, annihilating.

The therapist's gentle and accepting attitude toward the child's anxiety helps to hold the child who much else of the time must bear that discomfort alone, oft times under the hostile conditions of everyday existence. "Your anxiety and worry are welcome here," my therapeutic stance says to the child. "You and I can together bear and manage that anxiety, however colossal and frightening it may feel."

The therapist's ability to help to share and contain the child's anxiety itself serves several functions. Foremost, it provides the child with an important (human) other who can share the burden. Second, the therapist's capacity to witness and bear that anxiety validates the child's experience and helps her to know more clearly what she feels, a necessary precursor to owning and integrating affect. Third, the safety of the office provides the child a respite from the unrelenting onslaught of such anxiety, allowing her to take a breath and rejuvenate before heading back into the anxiety-stimulating world outside the therapy room. Fourth, having her anxiety reduced for a time being can free up the child's intellect and coping. That is, her not having to spend so much energy guarding against anxiety (while in therapy) lends her greater awareness and cognition to examine and process therapeutic talk and play. Fifth, and arguably the biggest, experiencing that respite shows her that life can be easier (i.e., less anxiety ridden), which in turn gives her new hope and inspires her to further work (in and out of therapy) to grow less anxious when possible, and when it's not, to grow stronger in the face of anxiety that can be neither reduced nor avoided. In other words, the very therapeutic acts that help prepare, invite, and sustain a child in therapy from the start integrally facilitate the child's coming to better terms with her anxiety.

In the case of Gerard and the meltdowns that so hampered his life at home and in school, we worked slowly but diligently to help him recognize when he grew anxious. Commonly with Asperger's, anxiety mounts until it discharges physically, aggressively, or verbally. Jack Wall, a director at the TEACCH center in Charlotte, North Carolina, conceptualized this process as an important one in the education of the child with Asperger's (Faherty, 2000). Teaching the child to "mind the gap"—a phrase that Wall adapted from the London Tube's warning to riders to watch their step between the train and platform—increases self-awareness of the space between "anxiety-building" events or experiences and the behavioral reactions that follow (p. 262). The ultimate goal is to help the child read the signals in her anxiety and expand her "decision zone," where she can learn to exercise more restraint in the face of stress and come to feel some willful choice in how she responds to a stressor.

All clinicians, from the most dynamic to the behavioral, concur that the anxieties of the individual child must be fleshed and teased out clearly in order to target them more sharply. In doing so, clinicians often find that the child with Asperger's holds many fears. These children are worriers. Nearly half of these children's worries attain the level of a diagnosable phobia (Leyfer et al., 2006), with prominent fears of crowds, noise, groups, needles, and according to a recent study, routine medical visits (Gillis, Natof, Lockshin, & Romanczyk, 2009).

When working with these children and fears, I regularly employ a range of methods that each add up to a treatment more effective than the sum of their parts. Sometimes, as happened with Rory, I find that by appealing to the child's intellectual and logical prowess, information can loosen the fixedness of those fears.

Rory was ever fearful. He saw personal and lethal threats everywhere. When his parents tried to watch the news, he would cover his eyes and squeal to drown out the audio. He lived in perpetual terror of accidents, illness, and being kidnapped. Before our meeting one day, his mother told me that they'd seen a dead squirrel in the road.

> Rory shivered in his chair, unable to talk or cry. "Are you afraid that could happen to you, Rory?" I asked. Rory nodded. "But you aren't anything like a small squirrel," I said. Rory listened as I described the ways that a 10-year-old boy differs from a small squirrel. I explained that squirrels are small animals with limited intelligence and awareness, especially about the modern environment. "They don't understand about crossing streets safely."
>
> "I always look both ways," Rory said softly. "And I know all about cars."
>
> "You're nothing like a small rodent," I said.
>
> Rory smiled. "But it is still sad," he added.
>
> "It is," I agreed.

Just a small dose of facts—in this case, the distinction between a rodent and a high-functioning human—lessened Rory's fears that he would get run over like a small animal. It left him with a sadness for an accident of nature. That was less of a problem to be repaired and more a perception and feeling to be understood and shared. This sort of intervening resembles that used in the Middle East, for example, when showing children the infinitesimal odds of their being harmed by terrorism or that used when showing adults who are afraid of flying similar statistics proving the safety of air travel.

Behavioral therapies based on exposure and desensitizing extinction have a major place, too, even in a relationship-based therapy such as I conduct and propose. Extending a behavioral approach built upon a discrete hierarchy of stepped exposures, I employ a method that follows Attwood's astute conceptualization that a child with Asperger's copes with anxiety over an entire childhood, day by day and minute by minute. In that "incremental development," the child develops "compensatory mechanisms to avoid anxiety-provoking situations" (2007, p. 17). I believe that the concept of *incremental* is key to our understanding and intervening. The growing child does not cope with major events that happen every fortnight or two. The child with Asperger's copes with anxieties that come all the time, or at least often and regularly, and that can feel like a blazing and endless assault by Cylon Raiders. So, the child develops (much unconsciously) ways to sidestep and avoid daily experiences that threaten and overwhelm him. The defensive persona and maneuvers that he creates and refines are tough, interrelated, and in every crack and crevice of his life. How does a therapist help a child to undo such a complicated defense system that's accrued bit by bit and that has in many ways been adaptive and protective?

Such children profit from what I call an individualized plan of *microexposure*. I help the child learn to recognize and master every little situation that unnerves them. Consider this example of a teenager with pronounced social anxiety whose self-consciousness made being at school a nightmare. The child described having to walk down the school corridors on a path defined by the fourth row of oak strips out from the lockers on the right. As you might guess, this created its own set of problems, for the boy's rigid route often bumped into people and called attention to his odd behavior. I suggested to the boy that he try meandering in and out of the fourth row, as might a driver who weaves between lanes. He tried and survived, edging out until able to walk down the middle of the corridor. It didn't matter how far out from his *comfort zone* the boy dared to venture. Even a few inches brought him deep feelings of success, confidence, and hopefulness for the next step outward. We likewise worked on his being able to sit anywhere in a classroom and so forth, until he felt much greater belonging and freedom at school. "I can walk and sit anywhere now!" he announced with pride after months of such self-led exposure.

Inch by inch of anxiety, the motivated child with Asperger's—which many are—can desensitize herself to the nearly imperceptible anxiety-stimulating events that rule her daily life, essentially reversing the incremental compensation that Attwood conceptualizes. Focusing on microelements of a child's fear or phobia nearly insures that the child will be able to succeed and move to the next step. These steps add up. Soon, the child describes feeling freer, braver, and psyched to face and overcome bigger anxieties. In spite of what the conventional views of autism have suggested, I've found that many children with Asperger's welcome the self-directed and spontaneous nature of this strategy of microexposure. They grow to become observers of their anxieties and able self-guides to their desensitization. They enjoy being captains of their destiny, for their growth is limited only by how much and how fast they wish to push themselves. I've now witnessed many children and teenagers employ this method to overcome anxiety associated with eating and ordering at restaurants, talking to teachers, and interacting with peers. I also often find that children with Asperger's have the intellectual rigor to attack and analyze their anxieties. The process can feel very empowering to the child. After all, the child is leading the way out of his own anxiety toward a more confident existence.

Cognitive-behavioral methods, such as correcting faulty beliefs and using self-talk, have their proven place in the treatment of anxiety for all children, including those with Asperger's (Attwood, 2004b; Beebe & Risi, 2003; Reaven, 2009; Sofronoff, Attwood, & Hinton, 2005; Sze & Wood, 2007). Such therapeutic correction and education can help reduce the apprehension, negativity, and critical self-talk that can absolutely plague a child with Asperger's. For reasons no one has yet explained, the child with Asperger's is prone to having his most negative thoughts and fears "obsessified," thereby guaranteeing a continual cascade of unhelpful inner talk and expectations that can amount to utter self-torment. Similar to the way that children have taken charge of their microdesensitization, as just described, Sofronoff, Attwood, and Hinton (2005) presented their cognitive-behavioral intervention to children by using a metaphor of "the child as scientist or astronaut exploring a new planet" (p. 1155). This, it should be stressed, is neither gimmick nor trick. That metaphor captures for the child exactly how they feel, trying to navigate a world that can seem to move way too fast and in ways that appear alien and unnatural. Such education often finds a place in helping to promote my client's growth, even within the relationship. Besides reframing and substituting positive self-talk, I find that some teenagers with Asperger's grow capable of discussing the larger process itself, examining why, for instance, they harangue themselves with fearful, discouraging thoughts rather than more encouraging ones.

Conventional clinical thought would suggest that a more time-limited cognitive-behavioral approach to anxiety should come first, and then, if the child and family is wanting and able, a more in-depth and broader therapy involving relationships, self-awareness, identity, and such should follow. While this holds true for many children, in my work with Asperger's, I have paradoxically encountered the opposite situation. I've seen a handful of my long-term clients graduate from their work with me and go on to pursue more circumscribed cognitive-behavioral treatments with high motivation and success. Their therapists have told these former clients, now teenagers, how impressively articulate and aware of their problems they are. Contrary to what we might otherwise expect, these adolescents begin those cognitive-behavioral treatments with a strong wish and commitment to tackle specific distresses and problems associated with their having Asperger's and can make use of them in a way that they could not have early on, given their fears, social inhibitions, and lack of communication.

The methods of cognitive and behavioral treatment can be varied and modified to fit the developmental needs of the child or teen. Attwood's *Exploring Feelings* workbook for anxiety (2000b) leads the child through an accessible and relevant series of multiple choice questions, fill in the blanks, and other strategies that access and raise the child's awareness concerning his feelings. Concepts such as one's "emotional tool box," *social stories,* and the "antidote to poisonous thoughts" keenly respond to children and their anxieties. While exercises in themselves provide relief and self-knowledge, they evoke productive revelations and discussions that go beyond what we imagine the child is capable of. With both younger children and even teens, I often find that drawing their situations and feelings—I am not any sort of artist, but that doesn't matter—can capture the child's interest and understanding and often leads to their responding in kind. Our illustrating becomes another communication skill in our joint repertoire, as it also becomes another tool in the child's "tool box" for emotional expression. Simple stick figures and hand-drawn emoticons can perform small and similar wonders.

When it comes to the child with Asperger's and anxiety, our therapeutic repertoire cannot be too large or varied, and it should include strategies for stress management (Attwood, 2003a). Because these children can carry great tension and anxiety in their bodies, behavioral methods for relaxation are justified. I have taught children to meditate and visualize. I've found that showing children how to stretch their arms and legs at bedtime can help them to fall and stay asleep. I've suggested, with success, that they go to the gym or an aquatics center or that they take a yoga class. Several children, both boys and girls, have found martial arts training to help with their social anxiety and confidence. These alternative methods tend not to cost much, are readily available, are convenient, and can occasionally be self-directed.

Many of the children I've seen have benefited in both the short and long term from medications—particularly selective serotonin reuptake inhibitors

(SSRIs), as well as other drugs. Prudently applied medications have especially helped the large number of children who suffer obsessive symptoms. Some children with great shame describe horrible and compulsive thoughts that they cannot shake, however hard they try. While the talk and play of therapy can help over time, there's no virtue in a child's suffering needlessly. These behavioral and medicinal approaches to anxiety can also reduce tics and Tourette's-like symptoms associated with anxiety and stress.

The concept of inner psychic conflict has its place with these children, too. The children I have met with Asperger's frequently have highly developed moral ideals that invoke guilt and self-doubt about not just their behaviors but what they think. And why wouldn't they? They typically have good minds and good homes, with parents who give love, are caring, and set inspiring models for good character. This was the case for Martin, whom you've already met.

Martin often looked away while he talked. But in one session, he'd swung his chair 180 degrees so that his back faced me. "I don't even know what I'm saying. I mean, I don't get it. I don't get what they are doing. It seems so wrong," Martin had said. For most of that hour, Martin struggled to explain why the bathroom and sex jokes his peers made bothered him so much. "I don't laugh and can't join in," he said. "I just walk away and look like a stupid prude."

For many months, Martin talked of wanting a girlfriend. Whenever he stated that wish, he made clear that his desire had nothing to do with sex or physical attraction. He'd mention a girl's name, then launch into a rant, near monologue, as to how other guys only want sex from girls and see them as objects. One day, Martin had been going on about how a guy friend had spoken rudely to a girl.

"I couldn't believe what he said," Martin exclaimed, throwing his hands up in offense. "I was so offended for her!" Martin's face blushed.

"What did she do?" I asked.

Martin awkwardly slammed his hands to the table in anger. "Nothing," he said. His hands and arms shook, nearly vibrating. "I mean, she laughed, and they hugged."

"They hugged?" I asked.

Martin's eyes teared.

"You like her, too?"

Martin nodded sadly.

Martin and I spent many hours talking of his frustration. He wanted a girlfriend mostly for the love and acceptance. But he noticed their bodies, too, and was feeling things in his own body. "How come other guys know how to look at girls?" he once asked in all sincerity. "When I look at them, it's like I'm a dirty old man ogling them."

Martin and I worked hard to understand what he was trying to convey. He tried so hard not to show that he was looking at girls, that he'd sneak stares in a way that he said made girls feel "creeped out." Martin eventually learned that his guilt over his sexual attraction ironically led him to not be able to look at girls more openly and affectionately. It also blocked his forgiving himself for having human reactions when it came to such matters.

Although seeing how his inner conflict confounded his Asperger's-compromised social skills and made the problem more complex, Martin felt buoyed and hopeful by the humanness of what he was discovering within himself. He lacked some of what other teens had to pursue girls. Then again, he knew some of the same wishes, fantasies, and even shame that all good kids knew, and that made him feel more okay and hopeful. Had we not opened therapy to his inner conflicts and had limited our discussion to Martin having social deficits, we would have missed the boat and left the job at least half undone. The best therapeutic route considers anxiety from both sides—that which is Asperger-related and that which is not—especially as they weave together into a dialectical experience that was, in Martin's case, his life. As I would have done with any teenager, I explored with Martin why he felt so guilt-ridden about his wish for a girlfriend. Not as with any teenager, we also discussed and problem solved in concrete details how Martin could glance at girls in class, look at them during conversations, and even ogle them across a room without making them uncomfortable and without making himself feel like a pervert.

Even as I support a child's stretching to new and enhanced ways of functioning, behaving, and living, I ever honor and respect who she is, which includes how she has to this point dealt with life and her anxiety. It is no coincidence that children with Asperger's adore, live for, and protect with ferocity hang time that is free of scheduling and outside demands—*time that is all their own.* Our goal is not to get rid of hang time. It's necessary and as therapeutic to the child as anything else can be. The child's learning to recognize her own anxiety and stress levels and guarding herself against them is healthy and self-protective. Being on her own is the time where she can catch her breath, stay put for a while, then replenish and recharge to face a new day with its challenges and opportunities for growth. Ireland's Kenneth Hall's words say it best:

> I like quiet places best, such as my room, and I like to spend a lot of time playing or reading on my own. I like to spend a lot of time at home in my house. Sometimes I don't like to go out much. I like my room a lot. This is because it makes me feel brilliant, cosy and happy. The best thing about my room is that it is *homely*—*roomly* [italics mine] if you want to be very accurate.
>
> (2001, p. 31)

The therapeutic strategy toward anxiety is as multipronged and complex as is the anxiety itself. We as therapists employ any and all strategies that can mollify the distress of anxiety and reduce its impairing and inhibiting other aspects of functioning, such as the child's social life. Our goal is not to push the child to places or activities that we judge as right as much as it is to help the child herself (be free enough) to get to places, people, and experiences that she wants for herself and that will both enrich and advance her life in directions that she endorses and values. Even young children with Asperger's have strong convictions about what matters to them. Though we therapists, like parents and teachers, may know a lot, we will do well to keep those matters in our sights, whichever ways or by whatever methods the therapy goes.

6

Communication

Consider the commonplace meaning of the noun *communication*: "a process by which information is exchanged between individuals through a common system of symbols, signs, or behavior," and the verb *to communicate*: "to transmit information, thought, or feeling so that it is satisfactorily received or understood" (*Merriam-Webster's Collegiate Dictionary*, 1998). Together, these definitions encompass the basic nature of communication and suggest the places where children with Asperger's find themselves challenged. This sixth chapter reviews what we know about the communication of these children and its implications for their development, functioning, experiences, and of course, the therapy.

> *My therapeutic approach has much to offer the child in terms of communication. It is not a substitute for other strategies and interventions. Speech and language therapists lead the way when it comes to the communication and social issues that confront these children. Their education, training, skills, experience, and focus make these professionals the experts on language and communication. Referring the child with Asperger's for a formal speech and language evaluation is wise. Language therapy helps the child in ways that go beyond talking. The sooner and younger language therapy begins,*

the better. A speech and language therapist is an essential member of the Asperger's team and should be looked to as the primary consultant on issues of communication at home, on the playground, and in the classroom.

In Vienna in the early 1940s, Hans Asperger noticed the language patterns of the children he called "autistically psychopathic" (1944/1991). He described their difficulty with casual conversation, the odd melody and flow of their speech, and the discrepancy between their immature language abilities and their inclination to big or rarefied words and complicated sentences. In much the same way that students' errors captured Jean Piaget (1928), the children's "intelligence, neologisms, unique expressions, and points of view, and . . . 'surprising maturity' in their ability to see things from a new perspective" intrigued Asperger (Klauber, 2004, p. 56). He believed the children capable of being "rich in original language productions" and gave the following examples: "I can't do this orally, only headily." "My today sleep was long but thin." "To an art-eye, these pictures might be nice, but I don't like them." "I wouldn't say that I'm unreligious, but I just don't have any proof of God." Look past the awkward phrasings and one hears the innovative, accomplished attempts to convey deep thought and thinking that's original and genuine.

Kanner observed the children's tendencies for echolalia, difficulty generalizing word meanings, and pronoun reversal (1943). Gillberg (1991) expanded the picture of language in the child with Asperger's to include "superficially perfect expressive language"—"formal and pedantic" with a "flat delivery"—and "non-verbal communication problems, with limited or clumsy gestures and little or inappropriate facial expression" (p. 123). (Readers wanting more on the history and assessment of language in Asperger's should read Attwood's chapter, 2007.) The diagnostic criteria of the *DSM-IV-TR* (2000) reflect the assumption that the language of the child with Asperger's, atypical and eccentric, is not generally and significantly delayed (as with other disorders on the autistic spectrum). That is, the child has been speaking in single words by age 2 and in sentences by age 3.

HELLO

Where to begin therapeutic work on the child's language? We begin by saying hello and something like "How are you?" Though we don't expect or demand a reply, we do the cordial thing anyway. It sets a tone and example.

If the child replies or invites more, we're happy to talk on. We refrain from acting overly happy or chummy or enthusiastic. A hearty and hail good fellow, "Hey champ, how's it going?" may not go well and a welcoming slap on the back will go worse. Friendly and civil reserve is the order of the day. While the child may choose not to talk much, they are usually okay with our talking some. Some children appreciate silence, many more find it threatening, especially if the therapist grows frustrated, lost, or uninterested.

We strive to use language that's clear and direct, devoid of psychobabble and psychic inference. Depending on our delivery, "How are you?" can come across as an innocent query or an intrusive probe. The child will give us immediate clues to his communication style and how he wants ours to be. The child's easy and straightforward reply gives us the green light. We can imagine less comfortable verbal and nonverbal reactions that cue us to adapt and proceed otherwise. To use a football analogy, we can come out of the huddle with a planned play. When we see how the defense reacts we may decide to call an audible and ad-lib a new tactic.

There is no one way to approach the child. The constant goal is to communicate *responsively.* One child may want down to earth, while a second prefers intellectualized questions. Little is left up to our guesswork or imaginations. It is continuous experimentation. The child with Asperger's will withdraw from attack or dishonesty. She rewards the therapist for earnest learning, regrouping, and trying again.

What is good communication with a child with Asperger's? We assume that the child wants to communicate, and we strive to create the conditions that make it safe to do so. We listen well. When the child lectures me or speaks monologue, I try my best to hear it. Surrendering to a monologue often brings out in me an unexpected and open curiosity. I may not enter with a burning interest in commercial aircraft, but now that you mention it. I remind myself the child is not trying to put me off. He wants nothing more than my joining his fascination with his favorite subject. *The child is sharing.*

Therapists' boredom endangers their connection with the child. At some time in the future, it may work to discuss the effect their monologues have on listeners. For now we allow ourselves to find and fall sway to the monologue's charms. Keeping in mind how much the child wants to connect with me heightens my wish to grasp what they say: "I know you've said it once, but can we hold on until I've really gotten clear on how those five species differ?" Holding the child accountable to help me get it tells him that I care and facilitates my getting involved. If I get lost in the first 5 minutes and don't catch up, I risk growing permanently bored and disengaged, as if I'd missed the first few classes of a difficult course.

When the child dares to express himself, I am candid if I don't get it: "I'm a bit slow, can you say that again?" "I want to make sure I understand just what you mean. Would you explain more?" Attwood has found children with Asperger's to be "remarkably patient in explaining particular topics" (2007, p. 205). I have likewise found such children willing to repeat themselves. They seem flattered and respected to have me take interest in what they say. That children with Asperger's care so much about their precise language—about putting it just right—suggests that they would not like and might resent their therapist nonchalantly moving on, even though he hadn't a clue of what was being told to him. None of us feel good talking to people when they are happy to dismiss our miscommunications with a flippant *whatever*. Children notice when their therapist goes out of the way to find out what they said. The child gets plenty of people tuning him out in his life; he needs his therapist doing that like he needs another hole in his head.

Communication is a two-way street. I don't proceed until I am sure my communications have been received by the child. Sometimes it's natural to say "Never mind, don't worry about it" when people don't get what we say. The child with Asperger's needs help communicating; it is all about the process. When I speak, I watch and listen and maybe query to make sure what I've said makes sense to the child. "I know I'm not explaining this very well," I might say. "Would you mind if I tried again?" Said with a smile and sincerity, it's a rare child who declines my offer. My patient response to the child's verbal and nonverbal messages make it clear that he's free to communicate with me in any way that works. The child may blame himself for not getting what I say. Until proven otherwise, *it's my bad*. I make clear it is my responsibility to keep expressing myself until I am understood. This behavior models my willingness to work at being understood by others. It also pulls the child into a more active role as a listener who bears responsibility for helping the speaker have his message heard.

SOME WORDS CAN SPEAK A THOUSAND WORDS

We live in a world of communication and words. Talk mediates relationships and social connections. Talk is a major vehicle for the work of therapy. And words are germane to what goes on inside the child. Language is the format and internal translator by which a child's experiences are processed, synthesized, and integrated. Language is a key to the construction of a self. And whatever the therapy and moment, communicating is ever both the goal and the medium.

When Stan and I met, all he could do was grunt and moan when distressed, which was often. "I don't speak bear too well," I'd say, appealing to his preoccupation with wildlife. I encouraged him to devise sounds that I could recognize as anger, frustration, sadness and so forth. Stan initially laughed my comment off. Nonetheless, over months, he grew a bear vocabulary to express feelings. Eventually, Stan replaced his growls for words that telegraphed his feelings: "Me angry"; "Me sad"; even "Me pissed off." He ultimately came to use sentences and paragraphs to speak what he felt.

When I meet a young child with Asperger's, he might not be able to express the fear, anger, or jealousy he feels. That doesn't mean he feels it less. It means that he's stuck unexpressed and devoid of my understanding and help. Without my clarifying, he might not know what to do with this unknown black box of feelings. The child can be taught to help us both discover what that is.

Tokens and candy do not motivate a child to communicate; the natural rewards of true communicating are what prompt the child to talk and share. The child with Asperger's can go through her day deprived of the fun, satisfaction, and connection that communication brings to most children. Once experienced, the wonder of reciprocal communication becomes the carrot that the child works, talks, and listens for.

Five-year-old Brady stood in the corner, wringing his hands and looking at his feet.

"Simple Simon met a pie man." Brady repeated that line over and over, maintaining the cadence and simple rhyme with the constancy of a digital recorder.

"I wonder what happens next?" I asked, looking to the window.

"Simple Simon met a pie man," Brady's mantra continued, as if I had never spoken.

Brady was referred for Asperger's diagnosed the previous year. His parents, bright and informed, had enrolled him in intensive language and occupational therapies. They saw Brady as frightened of everything and everybody. They wished to expose him to social opportunities yet feared overwhelming him. "How much is too much" they asked, "and how much is too little?" They realized that Brady would require substantial services for a long while. While they had read enough to wonder about the kind of therapy I did, its whole child view appealed to their sensibilities. They asked that I initiate a trial of therapy.

For the first handful of sessions, Brady wouldn't come in without his mother. He'd sit on her lap and hold her leg with his back turned toward me. More than a year into his language therapy, Brady had yet to meet without his mother in tow. "Don't you want to play with the nice doctor?" his mother would invite cheerily in my waiting room. Brady responded to his mother's gentle suggestions by tightening his grip on her.

That Brady was standing in the corner, gripping a pinwheel, looking at his feet, and repeating "Simple Simon" was a giant step for us. He had walked into the office on his own, the first time he hadn't dragged his mother along. He had looked around the office and picked up the pinwheel, the first thing he had seen, though he hadn't tried to make it spin. He immediately began reciting the first line of the nursery rhyme.

Brady had taken steps to come in alone in two previous hours. His mother's exclaiming "You want to go in without Mommy!" startled his senses and sent him running to her. His third try did the trick; Brady's wish to come in himself was robust. There, for 30 minutes or more, Brady had stood, unable to even blow on his pinwheel as he repeated, "Met a pie man. Simple Simon met a pie man." Over and over.

What was I to do? Brady had insisted that his mother stay for the first hours. He'd let me know with his body and gestures—holding on, blocking her way, starting to cry, wailing. I'd tried to talk with him. On a few occasions, he'd shown interest—at least, he'd looked up at me. He hadn't yet spoken a single word. But his mother's report was upbeat. "He comes more easily every week," she'd said. "He likes it here." When I asked how she could tell, she explained with confidence that his formidable opposition was waning. Her wisdom, keen observing, and smile reminded me of what extraordinarily competent and plodding troopers these parents could be.

"We only have about a minute left," I warned. Brady didn't move or show any reaction; nor did he react when I announced time was up. I opened the door, steering clear so as not to block Brady's running to his mother. He stood there and recited "Simple Simon." His mother peeked into the doorway, amazed. "Would you like a little extra time to stand there and sing 'Simple Simon?'" I asked.

"Yes, I would," Brady replied in a monotone.

"I'd like that too, if it's okay with your mom," I said.

Brady's mother gave us the okay, and so, with door closed, Brady kept on keeping on as he had, until we had to stop.

"Goodbye, Brady," I said. Without a word, Brady quickly stepped out to join his mother.

When Brady returned the next week, he walked quickly into the office by himself. He went to the corner and looked around.

"Are you looking for the pinwheel?" I asked.

"I am," Brady answered.

"It's in that pile," I told him, and he looked to where I pointed.

"Do you wish me to find it, or would you like to get it yourself?"

Brady thought, then walked over to the toys where he rummaged to easily find the pinwheel. He picked it up and took his former position in the corner. It looked to me that he was standing perfectly in his last week's footsteps. "Simple Simon," he said.

"Met a pie man," I interjected. Brady smiled and waited.

"Simple Simon," I said.

"Met a pie man." Brady got the game.

Our communication was on the surface as small and simplistic as it was interpersonally huge. Brady and I went back and forth like that for not just the rest of this hour but for successive hours. We'd even go freestyle, alternating words then syllables. Brady was very good at this, never once making a mistake on his turn. Most of all, he enjoyed it.

"I don't know what you're doing in there," his mother told me at a parent meeting. "But whatever it is, it's working wonders." She described how Brady would run to the car and then to my office. "He loves coming and every day asks if it's Wednesday. And best of all," she went on, tears in her eyes, "when he leaves your office, he's a little chatterbox. He can't stop talking about school and his friends and everything. I'm not sure what all he's saying, but it's the first time he's seemed interested in sharing his world with us."

I write this not to say how wonderful the therapy or I was for Brady. It's to counter the skepticism that most of us can so reflexively feel when facing such uncommunicative children and cases. Relatively speaking, Brady had become supercommunicative with me. He went from frozen statute to my chorus. And what did I make of his becoming a chatterbox on the way home from his hours? The good feeling and confidence of having dared to grow communicatively closer with me, his therapist, energized and excited Brady for more verbal sharing, especially with the parents he adored. Neither Brady nor I told his mother what we did in therapy. Nor had Brady and I done explicit work or discussion on his need to verbally communicate more with either me or his parents.

> "Brady has a surprise for you," his mother announced prior to his next meeting. Brady pushed the closing door against his mother, letting her know that he wished to get on with his session.
>
> "Simple," Brady said.
>
> "Simon," I replied quickly. And so it continued, until Brady, having just said "pie man," took a second turn.
>
> "Going!" he exclaimed with glee. He flapped his arms and squealed in delight. "Going! Going!" he said again.
>
> "To?" I replied.
>
> "Yes!" Brady said. "The."
>
> "Fair," I said.
>
> "Hurray!" Brady ran around the room, shaking the pinwheel.

At the hour's end, Brady's mother told me he'd asked her to read him the original rhyme, though she had no idea why. Brady started to explain, talking so fast that neither his mother nor I were sure what he said. Finally, she got it. "You wanted to know it for Dr. Bromfield?" she asked.

"Yes, I did!" Brady replied. He jumped on his mother's lap and gave her a giant squeeze.

Innocent bystanders might hear this and shake their heads. *This is therapy?* There's no way I can frame this in terms compatible with utilization review, HMOs or short-term treatment. It is what it is. Sometimes, and often with Asperger's, slow is the fastest route. No therapy that forced or bribed Brady's talking could have gotten him to speak more. At the end of the (therapeutic) day, *it is the non-Asperger's and utterly human wish to communicate with other humans that most motivates and propels the child with Asperger's.* The inherent wonders of reciprocal communication became the key motivator in Brady's communication.

What any of us think, feel and experience are *precious goods*—as precious as it gets. Children like Brady spend days upon days frustrated by their inherent difficulties with putting what they feel into words that can be shared with others and that can lead to the responses they want and crave. But days upon days, children like Brady have trouble getting their messages heard, so they endlessly are at the receiving end of unsatisfying, hurtful, rejecting, cruel, [fill in the blank] responses. How many times would I try to explain my predicament or upset to a person who usually misheard or mistreated me as a result? Not too many. Brady took a great risk in doing his rhymes with me. With each sing-along, he saw I listened, that I got it, and that I accepted him where he was. And he saw my pleasure, too, at his joining with me.

LITTLE PROFESSORS

Hans Asperger noted that children can sound like little professors (1944/1991)—children like Leonard. Leonard was a large 12-year-old who walked and talked slowly. His speech was deliberate and dramatic, full of grownup vocabulary and a condescension. Leonard had no friends and his arrogance turned off teachers, too. He gave off an air that he knew more than everyone. He did know a lot, yet with his disorganization and learning delays, he got poor grades and his academic skills lagged. Leonard spend many of his sessions playing a judge.

Leonard wore my sports jacket over his shoulders as a judge's robe. He lamented that he didn't also have a white wig he could wear. When presiding over our pretend courtroom, Leonard exaggerated his typically highfalutin voice (and sounded like the British actor Charles Laughton). That day's case involved a man, played by myself, who'd robbed a bank. As usual, Leonard asked the accused to explain what happened. Judge Leonard didn't listen to my answers. He pounded his "gavel" and loudly declared, "I've heard enough of your nonsense, young man. The court has no interest in your sob stories and your alibis. Take him away!" The cases always ended with Judge Leonard delivering a harsh sentence involving hard labor and oft times execution. Leonard enjoyed the play. One day, when I as sentenced defendant was about to walk to my jail cell, I decided to speak my thoughts.

"It's true," I said, employing Leonard's theatrics. "I am guilty as charged. I stole another man's money. But," I continued, "I wonder what has happened to make this judge so bitter?"

Leonard took off his robe and soberly put away his props.

"I don't try to talk this way," he explained. "It's just how it comes out of me."

I asked Leonard if he would like some help with this. He said he did. We decided that we'd work on ways to talk more like a kid. Leonard would say something and I would write it down. I would then read it aloud and Leonard would try to translate what he'd said into the way regular kids spoke. At first, it was impossible for him and I'd have to provide most of the translation. Slowly and steadily, Leonard got better at speculating how his peers would say it. In examining and dissecting the adult way he spoke, he came to think about the impact he had on other children. He also came to see that he dealt with his sense of exclusion and estrangement by acting superior to everyone. He made a successful effort at stopping habits that kids found obnoxious such as his answering the teacher's every question, correcting kids when they were wrong, and walking around the room critiquing classmates' work.

The therapist can apply similar strategies around a child's tendency toward monologues, as I did with Buck. Buck was referred for severe peer difficulties, loneliness, and constantly disrupting his class with long-winded answers and off-topic lectures. Peers teased him and teachers lost their patience and kindness. In response, Buck argued back. He accused both peers and teachers of discriminating against him.

Buck came to therapy presenting himself pretty much the same way. He consumed every hour with a monologue about a new video game and his progress playing it. I mostly listened, cultivating my interest and nudging him to be clearer and more tolerant of my own confusions about what he told me. Buck tried to answer my questions, but he would grow brusque and unable to conceal his annoyance. "I already told you that last week." "My memory is human, you know. It forgets things," I replied. "That's okay," Buck replied with irritation.

I'd gradually try to shape the monologue and discussion. For example, I'd point out that if Buck spent the whole hour telling me about one level of one game, he'd have no time to tell me his impressions of the game itself. Buck would gather himself and start again with a broader focus. Likewise, I'd stretch him by saying if he spent his hour talking of video games, he'd have no chance to tell me about the other things on his mind. Luckily, there were generally other things on his mind that he did want to bring up. Buck grew to appreciate my gentle pushes and reminders and would congratulate himself for raising new topics.

Interruptions proved to be another obstacle. Buck forever spoke over my few and brief comments. On the other hand, my interruptions of him, however tactful and brief, visibly shook him. When I was done with whatever I'd said, Buck with exasperation would pick up exactly where he'd left off. I suppose that a more behaviorally-oriented therapist might have taught and rewarded his learning to be interrupted. I went at it differently. "I'm sorry, Buck. I wanted to make sure I'd let you know. But I didn't mean to throw you off like that."

Buck took my apologies in stride. They evoked his greater forgiveness. Over time, we addressed how much people's interruptions frustrated him. He described how even while he knew that he "kind of held people hostage" with his stories, he resented having to stop talking and felt a need to get right back to where he left off. That, he described, was just the way he felt when his mother told him to turn off his video games. Each small discussion helped Buck to process his feelings. He steadily grew more "interruptable." One day, he didn't even want to go back to his story, a change that he crowed to his mother about and one that foreshadowed his growing more reciprocal at school.

These advances led to my asking Buck what he imagined it was like for someone such as me to listen to him talk. This labored and painful work led to Buck noting how he feels when others talk, which was bored, uninterested, and angry that he couldn't do all the talking. He grew to realize how unfair and imbalanced his expectations were. "You listen to me for hours and I roll my eyes to put up with two minutes of your talk," he said. Our work was not all in our heads. We practiced taking turns at interrupting each other rudely, not so rudely, and nicely. "Shut up and listen just to me!"

I screamed, to which Buck laughed and said, "You can't say that to someone, even if it's what you want to say."

SMALL TALK

The trouble that children with Asperger's have socially is enormous and complex. We know the language difficulties that come along can obstruct interactions and relationships with peers and others. The casual conversation central to play and friendships and that comes secondhand to many people baffles and eludes the child with Asperger's. Akin to a game of four square, the give-and-take of banter on the corner, in the cafeteria, and at the kindergarten climbing gym follows an organized system of rules and equations that a majority of kids pick up incidentally. To those children, conversation is no more challenging than are breathing and kicking a ball. To the child with Asperger's, such conversation looms large, discouraging, and a constant source of failure and bad feeling.

Teenaged Martin wanted friends more than anything in the world. But being with them in any situation involving conversation unsettled him. He described standing next to kids at the bus stop and sweating bullets as he tried to figure out how to enter their conversations. He knew plenty of ways to not fit in. He butted in loudly and frenetically. He asked questions about what they'd been discussing before he got there. He pretended to laugh at jokes he didn't like and that offended him, and he tried telling his own. "How do I break in?" he would ask with great upset, as if seeking the code to some ancient mystery.

One strategy that helped Martin was to state the problem, and then together, he and I would imagine possible scenarios and solutions. We would do our best to anticipate how his proposed action might make other kids feel. When we thought we'd found something that held potential, he would practice it on me and then go try it out with the kids. More times than not, it went poorly. Martin always learned something that led to some sort of solution and improvement. For example, Martin would sit at a cafeteria table and feel tensions in the "valence of his relationships" with the students who sat near him. These tensions pressured him. "How can I ask Tamara how it went with her boyfriend when I don't know if Robbie and Chris even know she has a boyfriend?" he asked. "Who do I talk to first? Who do I look at when in a group?"

While Martin problem solved and experimented, we paid close attention to what he felt. He found much solace and validation in my witnessing how hard it was, how brave he was, and how worthwhile it was to plug away. We problem solved ways to recognize and deal with sarcasm and other forms of verbal aggression. Martin worked hard to learn to be random, something that he said regular kids had a knack for. "How come their random stuff makes more sense than the logical stuff I say?" he asked. We even worked on ways that he could flatter a girl without offending or embarrassing her. While Martin's work on this bears resemblance to social pragmatics and scripting, it differed in that it occurred within our relationship, meaning that even as we worked on skills, we focused equally on the feelings and issues of esteem that dogged every inch of behavioral change.

Martin also learned to give himself space and understanding, like allowing himself to hang out with kids without having to speak or become a major participant in the discussion. Learning to be an active and engaged listener was a new experience for him and one that transformed Martin's ability to enter, follow, sustain, and even end (and be able to leave) conversations. "I used to think that I just had to stay there and keep talking until the other people were done," he said. By engaging in real-world conversations and coming back to analyze and refigure them, Martin grew to see conversation as fluid, robust, and organic. By seeing that he could always return and do better, he came to recognize, as Attwood so aptly puts it, that conversations can be repaired (2007), a lovely corollary to the bigger truth that relationships can, too.

When we work to facilitate the child's growing more communicative, we take care not to trample on who she is. We are torn. We wish to help her find new and improved ways to express herself—ways that make her life easier, connected, and fulfilled. We meanwhile don't want her to think that she has to become a new creature, nothing like who she is. If we push too hard when teaching a child English as a second language, we can damage her inner sense of who she is, dismissing her heritage, her culture, and her identity. We never want a child to feel that her authentic self, language and all, is bad, undesirable, or in need of replacing. The child needs our sincere respect and liking of who she is and how she communicates, even as she reaches out for enhanced competencies and skills.

As I said when introducing this chapter, speech and language therapists are the true experts. Even while our psychotherapies devote themselves to language, our clients benefit from language therapies and interventions such as semantic- or social-pragmatics groups, where they focus specifically on learning to converse and interact with peers. In such therapy, speech and language therapists actually break down the unspoken rules of social communication and teach it to the children in a manner that's immediate, experiential, and relevant. When a child is struggling to catch up on so much, one doesn't have to worry about providing them too much good help.

YOU GOING TO EAT THAT PICKLE?

When my grown son was small, he and I watched an episode of *Bewitched* in which Samantha was expecting. For some reason, Samantha's husband, Darrin, kept asking people, "Are you going to eat that pickle?" I cannot recall why it was so funny, but for some time afterward, my son and I would ask that of each other, even when there were no pickles around. Sometimes, it was when we were eyeing each other's food or sometimes in situations that were utterly unrelated. It made us laugh, and we both knew what we referred to. There was a context that held meaning for us, and that phrase became special to us for no other reason than *it was ours*.

One of the most profound ways that therapy wields its power for children with Asperger's is by the creation of a world that shares language, concepts, and understanding. This mutual language includes idiosyncratic phrases, coined words and neologisms, words that we mispronounce or misuse—virtually any aspect of language that holds some joint and exclusive appreciation. For example, whatever the discussion and however serious, one teen client with Asperger's and I adopted god-awful imitations of a cast of characters, real and cartoon—Yankee Doodle, Dr. Evil, and our favorite for some reason, Sean Connery—that I suspect will forever be loosely associated only in our minds.

For example, I recently noted how this adolescent had avoided going to an after-school club where he'd anticipated expanding his social life. "There wasn't enough sex," he replied with a heavy Scottish lisp, a la Sean Connery. "And this troubleth you?" I asked back. "Your Shakespeareth doth bothereth me," he shot back. And so it went on for some minutes, keeping the matter at hand at just a distanced-enough place so that he could deal with it. "Yes, yes, I admit it," he then cried out. "I'm afraid of girls." The rich and oft times funny context that we share has enabled us to approach all sorts of hard problems.

Often, a long period of such camaraderie lays the ground for a short minute or two of important problem solving, as in the preceding case, where this adolescent thought about ways that he could start to overcome his shyness.

I always chuckled when Timothy, a boy you met in the introduction and who will return later in much more detail, would take the hand crank out of my window, hold it up and say "I'm feeling a bit cranky today." His maturing capacity to poke fun at his irritability notwithstanding, I laughed not for its wittiness but because of Timothy's wish to tickle me with his pun. Why do our children laugh at their fathers' lame jokes? Because they get funnier and funnier after 20 tellings? No. It is because they are being shared and groaned at by people who hold affection for one another.

Another boy who I treated many years ago spent sessions setting up elaborate Playmobil scenes for which he had little time then to play with. Whatever the scene, Nikolai always found a cameo role for a little brown plastic owl. With great enjoyment and a smile, Nickolai would end every session and scene by finding a perfect place to put Owly, as he named him. Owly was wise and shy and very bright, and deep down inside he wished he could be more comfortable with the attention of friends, which sounded a lot like someone else I knew. Almost 10 years after Nikolai had ended a successful treatment and had moved far away, he wrote to say hello and tell me of his recent accomplishments in school and sports. He ended the letter, "Owly yours, Nikolai."

As so many have observed, the child with Asperger's is prone to use language literally: "Boy, my arms are out of breath." Rather than generalize the meanings of words, they tend to take them at their face value. "Break a leg! Well, isn't that a nice thing to tell someone?" Such concrete thinking can invite the therapist's doing the same. So, when working with these children, we try to speak in images and words that can be grasped. Metaphors and analogies run amok in the therapies I do with these children. I make up my own and sometimes borrow other people's, such as "that's as much fun as a porcupine in a balloon factory." (I think I heard that one on *Andy of Mayberry.* When doing therapy, we don't have to worry about plagiarism.) I strive to put ideas and feelings into words that are palpable and tangible—that can be felt and manhandled. The child's reactions and responses will soon enough tell us whether our hunches and ways are working and relevant.

Speaking of humor, what, I wonder, would children with Asperger's answer if I told them I would like to walk *inside their shoes* for a while? "Okay, but you'll have to shrink your foot to a 6D." "You can't. I only wear sneakers." "And I could swim inside your hat?" "You obviously haven't smelled my shoes." "You aren't going to get much exercise in there."

I don't really know what children would say. I know what the research says about the Asperger's brain and its lack of humor (see Lyons & Fitzgerald, 2004, for a most interesting discussion). The individual children with Asperger's who have crossed my threshold have told me something different. They've said that the number of jokes a child with Asperger's makes doesn't matter, nor does the number of times that he doesn't laugh at himself or the fact that he takes himself too seriously. Want to bring out the humor in somebody, Asperger's or not? Enjoy them and their attempts at humor. The more time I spend with children I've known with Asperger's, the more pleasurable it becomes (and almost always involves much humor, granted a sometimes unusual brand of humor). In fact, I know what one young child with Asperger's would do if I told her I wished to walk in her shoes. She would carefully unfasten her Velcro straps, take off her pink shoes—the only color she deigns to wear—and hand them to me, fully expecting me to try and put them on, smiling and giggling even before I could get my own shoes off, knowing just how silly my feet are about to look. Finally, when the giggles faded, she would call me "you silly goose!" That's what she would say. And that makes me smile.

Whatever a child's gifts and weaknesses, her language is ever going to be primary in every aspect of her functioning and development. It will determine much of her social relations and contribute to who she is in terms of identity and esteem. Language is a process that helps the child to understand and connect; it can also obstruct and detach a child. We know that for many reasons, the child with Asperger's has problems with language that ironically deprive her of ongoing communicative exercises and rewards that other children enjoy. While more formal speech and language therapies can effectively target language—especially its social impact—relationship-based therapies such as the one I propose can help to make a child communicatively happy, effective, interested, and successful.

7

Intellect, Cognitive Style, and Creativity

As it did for communication, everyday English has something to add to the discussion of intelligence as it applies to the child with Asperger's. Once again, turning to the *Merriam-Webster's Collegiate Dictionary* (1998), we find that definitions of both *intelligence*: "the ability to learn or understand or deal with new and trying situations," and *intellect*: the "power of knowing as distinguished from the power to feel or to will" together set the stage for our look at the intellectual abilities and traits of children with Asperger's. This chapter spotlights issues of intelligence and cognition, especially as they affect the whole child. I, too, focus on the ways that intelligence and cognition influence what we do in therapy, and conversely, how therapy can influence them in return.

While there's been little studied and written about psychotherapy and Asperger's, there's a considerable body of research, some experimental, on the cognition of the child. Assessment of Asperger's has been a fixture of study since early on. Much is known and published on the intellectual assessment of Asperger's in a child. My therapeutic approach has much to offer the child in terms of using her intellect, coping with her limitations, and performing academically. It is not, however, a substitute for or improvement upon strategies and interventions that target cognitive and academic functions and skills. Neuropsychologists and educational specialists are the experts on these. Any child suspected of having Asperger's should be assessed by such an expert who, if warranted, can then consult to the team and school, ensuring that the child's educational plan does all it can to meet his or her needs.

More than 70 years ago, Hans Asperger had already made keen observations concerning the intelligence of the children he studied and would soon chronicle (1944/1991). Combining his sensitive observing skills and those, it seems, of an equally able team of professionals and educators, Asperger characterized the intellect and cognition of the children with an acuity and subtlety impressive by current standards. To his credit, Asperger went beyond his own diagnostic and intuitive senses, which were considerable, to include systematic psychoeducational testing. Anticipating contemporary neuropsychology, Asperger's testers were more interested in the qualitative process, the mechanisms by which the children thought and performed, than in the quantitative IQ.

Much of what Asperger and his testers found have formed the core of what we know about these children's cognition (Baron-Cohen, 2008): usually being of average or above average intelligence, splinter skills that can occasionally approach the level of a savant, extreme and obsessive interests, a penchant for self-taught masteries, difficulty with more mundane and simpler academic tasks, disorganization, verbal development and language skills that significantly exceed the nonverbal involving the visual-spatial, tendency toward distractibility, and poor social comprehension.

Current researchers have confirmed Asperger's insights, further delineating the children's intellectual complexity and the dilemmas it poses. In spite of what in many ways are formidable intellects, children with Asperger's are prone to attention deficits, executive dysfunctions, and other learning disabilities (Thede & Coolidge, 2007); weak adaptive life skills (Klin et al., 2007); and most sadly (and avoidably), underachieving lives full of highly distressing and obstructive symptoms (Saulnier & Klin, 2007). From this point on, I refer readers interested in the neuropsychology of Asperger's to scientific journals, where the literature grows. (Also see Ghaziuddin & Mountain-Kimchi, 2004, for neuropsychological differences between Asperger's and High-Functioning Autism.)

I also need to mention nonverbal learning disability (NLD), a diagnosis that is often discussed and debated alongside Asperger's. While both disorders reveal relatively weak nonverbal development, neuropsychological assessment finds that children with NLD fare significantly better on tasks involving language, whereas the children with Asperger's fare better on visuospatial tasks. This suggests that NLD is more of a purely right-brain origin, whereas Asperger's involves both hemispheres (Dumitrescu, 2006). For the purpose of our discussions, I am relying on the guidance that clinically, we not focus too much on the differences (Dinklage, n.d.), at least for what we're doing as clinicians—wisdom based on the fact that NLD and Asperger's appear to be "converging" disorders, with a large majority of Asperger's cases showing the central features of NLD (Klin, Volkmar, Sparrow, Cichetti, & Bourke, 1995). The thinking and strategies of my approach will hold relevance for the majority of children with both Asperger's and NLD. While research that aims to better distinguish between these two diagnoses is important and being pursued, as therapists, we are yet left with our perceptions, experience, and judgments to decide when we need to modify our method or go in an entirely different direction.

Children with Asperger's Syndrome are often of average intelligence or brighter. But for all their smarts, they tend also to be distracted, disorganized, and in other ways learning challenged. And hardly last, they present as unique individuals with intellectual profiles that can show unique and extraordinary variability.

ASPERGER'S AND IQ

The values and limits of IQ are familiar to most of us. That they do not equal destiny and are somewhat fluid is yet truer when it comes to the child with Asperger's. I have repeatedly seen children with Asperger's who—coming to me with records full of explicit and dire prognoses from senior clinicians, hospitals, and learning clinics—went on to pulverize the glass ceilings that were set well beneath their potential. Like Fritz V., the boy whose school had referred him to Asperger's clinic after deciding that he was "'uneducable' by the end of his first day there" (Asperger, 1944/1991, p. 39), many of the children were found to be varying degrees of untestable by their experienced clinicians. And as has been the findings of today's researchers, testers, and myself in my practice, Asperger's team found that for all their intellectual strengths, these children could be uncooperative, unmotivated, distracted, and socially apprehensive in the testing room. As a result, the test findings often failed to adequately portray the child's optimal cognitive abilities. For that reason, and ahead of his time, Asperger wrote, "We adapt the way we test according to the personality of the child, and we try to build up good rapport. Of course, every good tester would do this anyway," adding that the assessment task "demands experience" (p. 53).

For example, one boy I treated came to me with an up-to-date assessment from a comprehensive learning center clinic where a neuropsychologist had found him to be in the borderline range of intellectual functioning. Though she described him to the parents as the most challenging child she had ever tested, she did not hesitate to hold his results as valid and to predict to his parents that he would soon need a self-contained residential school, that he would never be able to engage in much learning, and that his parents should start makings plans, financial and otherwise, to provide for what would be a lifelong and sheltered dependency. "It felt like they'd torn my insides out with their bare hands," Iggy's kind and devoted mother said as she revisited that memory many years later, after her son, now a man, had graduated with honors from a public high school and college and was gainfully employed in business management and well connected to people at work and home. "It was as if they'd told us that we had no reason to hold out any hope for our son. And what if we'd listened to them?" she asked. "Where would he be now?"

I can't blame the tester for having found Iggy difficult. He had been one of my most challenging therapy cases, too. For weeks, he wouldn't move out from under a chair; he spent other weeks hiding behind his mother's legs from where he would grunt and spit at me. At that time, I couldn't have gotten him to do one small thing for me, much less engage with a lengthy and demanding test battery. That his tester was able to get him to do enough work to score at the borderline level is itself a testimony to her skill and rapport building. My issue with the testing has more to do with what was made of it. Given the multiple ways in which Iggy couldn't and wouldn't comply and produce in the testing, how could the results not be qualified as something less than valid? I fully grasp that his performance reflected his then current level of functioning. Indeed, that was what he was like in school. But that in no way showed his true intellect, capabilities, and what he could eventually learn and attain. And to make such predictions? The powers of self-fulfilling prophecy are to be respected. What horrors can come from experts authoritatively prophesying gloom and doom to parents of a young child! Why, I had wondered, couldn't they have told his parents something such as, "Given that Iggy was so frightened, fidgety, distracted, uninterested, preoccupied, exhausted, and so forth, the best he could do and the best we could elicit, was . . . " What made them so sure that they knew all that he would never achieve or grow into?

There are children with Asperger's who love the intellectual challenge of a testing, a puzzle for their mettle. But it is not uncommon for many other children with Asperger's to not like it at all—to fear it, hate it, oppose it, defy it, hide from it, and maybe even fight it (and the tester). Such children do not produce much and do not give much of an effort. Of no surprise, their scores are low, often below or well below average in intelligence. But over time, as they grow in so many ways, they become more able to engage with the tester and the testing, perhaps showing motivation to do the best they can. The assessments start to grow valid, and we find the children are found to be of average intellect or brighter. I have seen many children whose IQ scores from young childhood through young adulthood go steadily up. The significance of this is not so much that they get higher scores; it's that as they psychologically grow, with all that can mean, their capacity to summon and apply their intellectual powers can rise and rise—not just in the testing cubby but in the classroom, at work, at home, and in their lives. Please forgive my rant here. I know that much of my protest is now obsolete and that testing today takes these things more into consideration.

COGNITIVE STYLE

While we wish to help the child with Asperger's cope with and extend her intellectual capabilities, applying them more fully, we must first and ever work with the reality that is, at any instant in time, the child's way of thinking and processing. Meeting the child where she is—a basic tenet of psychotherapy—is respectful and more likely to engage the child, whatever the therapeutic matter or aim at hand. It also is the surest route to creating a meaningful moment of life teaching. Consider what can be done with some cognitive traits common to the children with Asperger's.

> "I asked for tuna on toast, not egg salad." Terence's knuckles were bleeding, but he kept picking at them. "Tuna is tuna, and egg salad is not tuna," he said. Though the chair was not a rocker, Terence's rhythmic back-and-forth accelerated. "Tuna. Tuna. Tuna! I said tuna. I did not say egg salad."

Terence had spent the session talking about tuna and egg salad. He had in fact asked for tuna. But the counter waitress had ordered and brought him egg salad. I knew, because his probation officer had filled me in on the whole story. When the waitress brought Terence an egg salad sandwich, he in layman's terms had gone ballistic, screaming at the young woman that he had ordered tuna, not egg salad. Hearing the ruckus, the cook came out. It escalated until the police were called. Knowing Terence well and that he came to the clinic, the police brought him in. The probation officer understood and was very sympathetic to Terence's situation. But she emphasized to me that he couldn't just keep going off like that. "He's going to end up in jail," she warned me, adding that it's the last thing she wanted and the last thing, she knew, that would help Terence.

When the police brought Terence to the clinic, I was tempted to get right down to business. I needed to get through to him that he just couldn't behave so poorly, to make him see that he was his own worst enemy. "Keep it up," I would have liked to say, "and you'll end up in jail. And you know what kind of food you get in jail? They won't be asking whether you want tuna or egg salad." But I knew that kind of confronting wouldn't help Terence at all. Instead, I tried to express the feeling that I suspected lay underneath his upset.

> "What's so hard about tuna? Tu-na. Tu-na. Tu-na," Terence said each syllable loudly, while pounding his things with his palms. "Tu-na. Tu-na. Tu-na."
>
> "You were so disappointed. You wanted tuna."
>
> "Tu-na. Tu-na." Terence spoke louder and faster.

"She frustrated you."

"Tu-na. Tu-na," Terence said once more.

We were down to the last 5 minutes of our hour. The police were waiting to hear how it went with Terence and to get word that he had gotten the significance of what he'd done. I had worked long enough with Terence to know that I couldn't directly ask or force him to say or do anything he didn't want to. Feeling helpless, I reminded myself to listen to what Terence said. And that was the key.

"You are right, Terence. Tuna doesn't even sound like egg salad," I said. Terence's rocking slowed a bit. "Listen to me, Terence, and you tell me." Terence sat up straighter. He stopped slapping his hands and cupped his ears toward me. "Ready?" I asked.

"Ready," Terence replied.

"Tu-na," I spoke slowly. "Should I say it again?"

Terence nodded.

"Tu-na," I repeated. "Now, listen to this one. Egg salad. Egg salad."

His forehead wrinkled in concentration. "You tell me. Do they sound alike?"

"Nope," he said. "They don't sound alike."

"This can only mean one thing, and you know what that is?" I asked. Terence waited for the answer. "If you said tuna and she brought egg salad, she must have…"

"Screwed up?" Terence replied.

"Bingo," I exclaimed.

Terence's face beamed.

"You figured it out!" I told him.

Terence's eyes got teary. "She didn't mean to hurt me. It was an honest mistake."

"No, Terence. I think you are right. She heard you wrong, and that was a mistake. But it was only a mistake."

Terence cried openly.

"I'm sorry," he said through his choking sobs.

Having gotten me to understand, on his own Terence decided to tell the police that the waitress had made a mistake, that he took it wrong, and that he would like to apologize to her. The police listened, saw his tears, and let it go. Over time, Terence came to discuss the incident in more detail. He spoke of how people frequently misheard him and how it hurt and enraged him. He eventually learned to grow more adaptively assertive. Months later when a similar situation occurred, he politely asked if his order could be corrected, which, of course, it easily was, bringing Terence joy and pride in his patience and ability.

Though we could conceptualize this incident in terms of feelings and that would be justified, the magic of the moment, I believe, owed its debt to a synchrony between the therapist and client at the level of cognition. Terence's thinking was rigid and perseverative. As long as I stayed on the level of affect, our discussion was stuck. When I finally understood what Terence was telling me, how the incident and feelings were being perceived in his own head—"tuna doesn't sound like egg salad"—the therapy moved onward.

The value in our staying with the child's thinking and cognitive style cannot be overstated. One girl explained her social world to me in terms of numbers. Even-numbered groups of people (e.g., 2, 4, and 6) were problematic, because those numbers are divisible by 2. Odd-numbered groups of people (3, 5, 7) were problematic, because there's always a remainder of 1. My "wordly" attempts to talk of loneliness, partnering, and rejection left this child cold. When I responded in her language of arithmetic, however, I touched this girl deeply. "You're right. It's either all two's or a one left out," I said. "I never realized math could be so unfair." "It is," she replied. "Math can be very unfair."

Eventually, the girl verbalized her sense that numbers could represent people and relationships and she came to expand the hidden meaning of her last comment. Her advanced mastery of mathematics had for years been her forte and her love. But as she passed through adolescence, she could feel lonely doing math. She described wishing that she had more friends and a boyfriend and that she could know how to be with them without needing a complex equation to calm her.

NEED FOR SAMENESS

Anyone who works with children with Asperger's soon observes a need for constancy that can range from an inclination to a singular quest. Younger children with Asperger's can oft times notice when I've moved a marker or mug on my desk. It's as if they possess some sort of radar that picks up every tiny change in the environment. Some children rush to move the mug back to where it was, restoring the scene to its original state. And I let them. Over time, children may come to accept verbal confirmations of what they've seen: "You don't like that space where the tape used to be"; "You want my office to stay the same, always." The children frequently respond with sad, worried nods or subdued yeses.

"There!" Seven-year-old Daria wasn't kidding. She pointed at my big, blue armchair. For all of her colossal timidity, she meant what she said. She directed me with all the determination and authority her little hand could muster. I stood up from my gray desk chair and moved over to where she wanted me. I sat down. "I'm supposed to be here?" I asked. Satisfied, Daria returned to her block building.

Daria was a handful for her parents and her teachers. She combined exquisite delicateness and shyness with a ferocious need to control. With a chuckle and concern, her teachers described how Daria would try to move the other children like furniture. She would walk up and rearrange other children's and the teacher's desks. When she couldn't, she'd cry and throw tantrums. I indulged Daria's demand that I sit in my chair. I gently nudged her when she tried to control how I related to other objects in my office. Each time that I took a sip of water, Daria moved my glass back to the place where she thought it should be *precisely*. I went along until I thought I saw an opening to make it a bit of a game. Each time Daria moved my glass, I slid it back an inch.

"No, no! You can't do that!" Daria yelled in frustration.

"But it's my glass," I said.

"Then it's my glass!" Daria replied, again moving it. She held on to the glass with both hands.

"Now it's your glass and I can't move it?" I asked.

"Hmmmph." With all of her might, Daria held the glass in place.

I suppose I could have done some tough love therapy, provoking her by gluing my glass tight to where I wanted it, sliding it every which way, telling her that it's mine, or maybe by messing her blocks and seeing how she liked it. Any and all of this might have worked. However, I chose to work with her way of cognitive style, which included a need for sameness. That need may have grown into a full-sized oppositionalism. But I couldn't afford to forget where it had gotten started, in her Asperger's-related brain differences. Rather than going head-to-head with her need for sameness, I played with it by showing Daria small and gentle reactions that confirmed, challenged, and stretched her. When she made demands, I approximated her requests, partly giving her what she asked for while leaving her to accept a bit of me, reality and the resulting frustration. Slowly and steadily, Daria's ability to accommodate changes at home and school grew. Time and time again, I've witnessed children with Asperger's use therapy to play out these issues and in doing so grow less needy for sameness and less needing to control parents, teachers, and peers.

One could suggest that the best thing for these children would be sloppy, unreliable, unaccountable therapists who arrive to appointments early and late, take lots of vacations, frequently cancel or reschedule appointments, and convey little constancy. The tone of my question gives away what I think the answer is. To these children, sameness is not a frivolous wish; it's an absolute need. Changes frighten and unnerve them deeply. Changes can arouse unspeakable apprehensions and terrors involving loss, danger, and the hurts of everyday life. For example, one child's distress around inconsistencies in my office and therapy evoked fears that I was dead and gone.

OBSESSIVE INTERESTS

You might be familiar with what Gillberg described as the child's "all-absorbing, circumscribed interest in some area such as meteorology, astronomy or Greek history (or indeed any area)," an interest that "goes to extremes, excludes most other activities, [and] is adhered to in a repetitive way and relies on rote memory rather than meaning and connections" (1989, p. 520). These interests can last for a long, long time, as they did with Luc, a very bright boy who I treated.

Luc was very bright. His standardized test scores put him in the 99th percentile. Yet, he had extreme difficulties at school. Two private schools had expelled him permanently for disruptive and hostile behavior that no one could manage and that was usually aimed at a popular, socially facile child. Luc loudly and publicly ridiculed peers and staff and questioned their intelligence and competence. When called on his behavior, Luc's only reaction was to mock the adult who confronted him.

Throughout his treatment, Luc spent his sessions lecturing me on issues of politics and government. At first, his lengthy rants sounded to be verbatim transcripts from talk radio, full of hateful speech and extreme ideas. Even when his life was falling apart, Luc couldn't be budged to face what was happening. He preferred to voice his complaints and stress through hour-long monologues that debated right versus left, poor versus rich, and so on.

Early on, I mostly listened, checking here and there that I'd heard Luc correctly. I showed respect for his thinking, though it could offend me morally. I would occasionally try to reason with him and show him a more balanced view. But it was always for naught and would lead to either withdrawal or a sudden belief that he no longer needed the help of therapy. Premature attempts to uncover the psychological and interpersonal meanings of his tirades fell flat. Sometimes, he went on as if I hadn't spoken; other times, he would shut me out with conscious determination.

What turned out to work most effectively with Luc was my intellectually going to where he was. "But poor children can't help being poor" flew in one ear and out the other. I would instead make comments such as "You're just stating facts about the world." Luc would smile, say "exactly," and his viewpoint would soften, expand, and evolve. Luc's monologues gradually acquired a bit of mutuality. He would ask me my opinion, though he'd immediately dismiss it. Or he'd invite me to debate him on a point, only to quickly ridicule my argument. Rather than behaviorally reward good (and polite) behavior, I slowly brought awareness to Luc's rudeness. "Why thank you very much," I'd say with a smile. Luc would laugh and rephrase what he'd said to be less negative.

Luc's hours spontaneously morphed from singular and angry monologues to lectures with questions, debates, and vigorous discussions full of humor and reciprocity. The social and personal meanings of his ideas and obsession grew clearer and more undeniable. The people that he once held such broad and degrading prejudice for became, in his intellectually broadened vision, respected competitors for an American dream that Luc feared he would never attain. Luc once believed it was because of his whiteness, goodness, and deservingness. But he came to acknowledge that the more likely reason for his failure to achieve was due to himself and his behavior: his learning disabilities, his social anxiety, and so forth. Paralleling the evolution of his preoccupation with social issues, Luc's grades, athletics, and friendships all blossomed. Luc finally came to therapy and talked about his problems more directly. He still talks about politics and society, and when he does, I am glad to oblige. By running alongside the intellectual fence that Luc exerted such effort to erect, we found the shortest and speediest route to his emotional life and lasting behavioral change.

What Attwood calls the "circumscribed interests" of the child with Asperger's can take many forms. Younger children can grow obsessed with a toy, a game, or a book. In older children, the matter can grow more complex, extensive, arcane, and involve greater effort. In girls, the interest can focus around dolls, animals, and fiction (the same things that can occupy nonautistic girls). As clinicians, we observe such interests and, using our own curiosity strive to understand what they mean for the child. As Attwood illustrates (2003b), such interests can both facilitate and obstruct the child's daily existence. I, for example, have known children who are so busy with their own interests that they have no time for school work. Obsessive interests can get in the way of home life, leaving parents needing our guidance on how to manage them (Bashe & Kirby, 2001). In short, I find it to be an ever moving give-and-take that simultaneously accepts, sidesteps, and extends the child's interests. (See Attwood, 2003b, for other strategies and a more thorough and highly relevant discussion.)

HONESTY

I was talking recently with a psychiatric nurse who worked on an inpatient unit for adolescents. She was telling me about an admission the night before over which there had been some discussion of whether the teenager had Asperger's. She had been going through an interview inventory and had asked the boy whether he had been having sex.

"Oh yeah," the boy replied. "All the time."

My friend, the nurse, waited.

"Well, not all the time. But a lot."

Pause.

"Here and there, actually."

Pause.

"Well, not that often."

Pause.

"Truthfully, never."

Pause.

"But I think about it all the time."

That candor, the nurse said, sealed the diagnosis for her. Though it is far from a hard rule, the fact is that many of the children with Asperger's we'll meet happen to be honest to a fault. As Simon Baron-Cohen explains in his fascinating commentary "I Cannot Tell a Lie" (2007), neuroscience suggests that children with Asperger's are "hardwired" to be that way. This honesty can reveal itself in many ways, both good and bad, so to speak.

Intellectual honesty is a good thing. Many of these children are not just fact-checkers. They are truth seekers, driven to understand what makes a theory hold together or what makes an object function. They live by an integrity of knowledge that may in the best of circumstances carry them to careers—such as scientists, professors, and writers—where their deep and abiding sincerity will be both an admirable trait and asset, where their profoundly sincere way of looking at the world is understood, shared, confirmed, and rewarded with respect and companionship. These children do not want glib and easy answers; they want the truth.

But of course, not everyone can take the truth. As Kenneth Hall, a boy with Asperger's and author of the fascinating *Asperger Syndrome, the Universe and Me,* wrote, "[I]f a 790 lb lady asked if she was fat then you would say yes" (2001, p. 65). These children are the ones to say what everyone else might really be thinking when Great Aunt Ethel asks how the Thanksgiving table is enjoying her raisins suspended in tangerine-flavored gelatin. "Your breath smells." "You farted." "Your haircut makes you look like you're wearing a toupee." *Thank you, thank you very much.* I, for one, do not try to teach these children to be white liars. Such reframing of the truth might be good social grace, but it totally asks the child to be untrue to herself. What do I do instead? I engage them in making euphemisms, playful word shaping that allows them to be sincere and a tad more tactful. I talk to them about qualifying what they say. They learn that asking "Do you really want me to tell you what I think?" isn't such a bad thing to say before stating their opinion. "I'll happily tell you what I think about the pie, but people say I can be a tough critic," is another. And then, for some children, one of the hardest lessons they learn is that not saying anything is an option, too.

I agree totally that honesty in the child with Asperger's is to be respected, admired, and cultivated as much as it would be in any other child, including one built to be a scoundrel. This trait of honesty—which can run contradictory, so it seems, with the child's relatively weak need to share what he feels and experiences—is an unequivocal advantage in doing therapy for both child and therapist. Children with Asperger's quickly grasp my saying that they can refuse my queries or tell me straight on that they would rather not tell me something. Even when feeling little urge to share any experience with me, the child likes knowing that not only can I hear the truth but that I prefer it that way.

SELF-ACCEPTANCE AND COPING WITH LIMITATIONS

There are many paths to self-acceptance. Here, I refer to children's self-acceptance of who they are intellectually and cognitively. Such acceptance is key to the child's fulfilling her destiny, being all she can be, academically and otherwise. While the road to self-acceptance is arduous and rocky, it can begin in any child at most any age.

"Go ahead!" Judy Ann squealed. "Ask me another one."

"What about pizza?" I asked.

Judy Ann thought. "The *BSG*'s favorite food for every sleepover. Yes!" She punched the air in triumph, then laughed. "They call pizza a food group. Ask me again."

"Let's see, how about . . ." I looked around the office to get some ideas, "a juice box?"

Judy Ann smiled broadly. "Avery sipped the last of the juice into her mouth. One more question, please!"

Judy Ann had come in that day asking if I'd remembered the names of the *Beacon Street Girls,* a book series that she adored and that according to her mother had for months been consuming Judy Ann's free time. My recalling three of the names and almost the fourth pleased Judy Ann and led to her asking me to test her on the books. I had started easy and asked if any of the books had music. Judy Ann said at least two. She gave the books' titles and then described a singer at a beach party and a karaoke contest. Handling my questions with ease, she pushed for harder ones.

"How about a hair dryer?" I asked. Judy Ann closed her eyes. "Stumped?" She held up her hand for me to hold on.

"There's a hair curler in *Crush Alert,*" Judy Ann spoke with excitement. "Katani's coming over to give Charlotte a makeover. More, please, more!"

Judy Ann and I were well into our second year of therapy. She had begun in a very painful place (as I'll tell more about in Chapter 9). Although Judy Ann had been making good progress with friends, her obsession with reading concerned her parents. For example, she had read every one of the 20-plus books in the *BSG* series. What troubled her parents most was that she would read each one over and over and over. Some days, her parents described, she would be happy doing nothing else.

"This is too easy."

I took a few minutes to think of harder ones.

"A mosquito?" I asked.

"*Freaked Out.* Maeve asks, 'How do you get West Nile Virus?'"

"Balloons?"

"*Crush Alert,* at the Valentine's Day Dance," she answered.

"A weird color?"

Judy Ann smiled. "This is going to take me a minute or two." She closed her eyes and seemed to talk to herself. "Katani's favorite color is Tuscan Gold!" she exclaimed.

"I can't believe it!" I said.

Judy Ann glowed. "My parents think I read too much. I mean, the *Beacon Street Girls* too much."

I asked Judy Ann how much was too much. She giggled and explained that she had read each book as many as six or more times. She added that there is "so much to see and hear" in the stories that she keeps reading them to get it all. "You don't like missing a thing?" I asked. "I hate missing anything!" she replied.

I then asked Judy Ann how she could remember so much about the books. She said that she didn't exactly remember everything, though she did remember a lot. She said for the harder questions, she read the books in her head. She described flipping the pages in her head and scanning the text for what she was looking for. She said that sometimes, something jogged in her mind, and other times, she actually saw the words and could read the exact sentence from the books in her head. "You are amazing, and *so is your brain*," I said. "Thank you," Judy Ann said, meaning it, her eyes welling up.

It must be tough enough to have a brain and intellect that can work so differently. The same brain and intellect can lead to interests and behaviors that push away the very children and adults whose attention, affections, and friendships are craved for so dearly. *As if it's my fault that I'm built this way?* the child might ask in frustration. We must be wary, for when we try to discourage or extinguish the child's interests, we risk discouraging and extinguishing who they are. Imagine if someone we adored made us feel less worthy or special because of our devotion to gardening, traveling, or the Red Sox?

My unbridled interest in Judy Ann's interest in no way encouraged her to go off and read by herself. It did the opposite, giving her a much needed opportunity to show off her interest. When someone, including a child with Asperger's, spends so much time pursuing an interest, we know it has to mean a lot to them and has to feel special (and vulnerable to the threat posed by others' critiques and apathy). In addition to confirming her wish to share her love for reading with me, my interest *in her interest* opened up a candid and enlightening discussion of Judy Ann's thinking itself—the ways her brain and mind work.

When they're able and the time is right, children with Asperger's can find it very helpful to share their experiences as learners and thinkers. I am ever impressed by the ways that these children can articulate the ineffable processes that go on in their heads and thinking. In trying to understand how Lincoln, in spite of his strong intellect, found school so hard, he said that his brain was like a "file folder full of other file folders, on and on"—like an infinite loop of cats in hats—an image that captured what to Lincoln was his powerful, obsessive, and disorganized brain. He used that image as a springboard from which to elaborate his experience and to problem solve ways that he and teachers might be able to better help him to learn and succeed academically. What makes more sense than applying their own intellects to (understanding and promoting) their own intellects?

While it will be the skilled educators and allied professionals who most directly help these children to learn and perform in the classroom, we as therapists can support their efforts by helping the child come to accept her limitations and need for help. Nothing ignites the growth of a disabled child than her growing to accept her needs and to want and use the wonderful help that's available. How do we help a child with Asperger's get to that place?

We believe in the child, nurturing him or her and finding even the smallest kernels of motivation, caring, or interest. We don't try to deflate or deplete her energy because it tires us; we embrace it and work to find suitable places for its channeling and expression. We take care to notice and marvel at the islands, more like continents, of intellect and skill, ever giving these best parts the spotlight they deserve. We respect the child's self-will and the ways in which she prefers to learn, which often include a liking of self-directed learning. Rather than squash the child's love of certain learning, we try to inspire and expand it to engage more and more, be it new information, other subjects, or life skills. Through patient and plodding missteps and repair, we help the child to learn that she can make mistakes and move on. We try to create the opportunities and conditions for the child to recognize who she is cognitively and intellectually and to know that it is better than okay. We try to help her to see that there are many kinds of intelligences and that they all matter deeply. As Temple Grandin, with her characteristic good sense steeped in a life of first-hand experience, instructs us, don't mistake the label for a whole child; keep in mind that each child with Asperger's has her own style of thinking and learning, and hold high expectations for what the child can learn and attain (2008).

PERFECTION

Learning requires risk and mistakes. But children with Asperger's often show a perfectionistic striving that can grow tyrannical. The child with Asperger's can fear making mistakes so much that he will not fully engage in his learning, a deterrence as unsurprising as it is tenacious.

In her paper on anxiety co-occurring with High-Functioning Autism, Reaven presents a lovely example of how cognitive-behavioral treatment was used with a boy named James to overcome his perfectionism and the worry and self-defeating behavior that it wreaks (2009). Reaven coached James to replace his harsh self-talk with more helpful comments. Instead of "I hate making mistakes; I'll fail math if I make a mistake on this test," James was urged to try saying to himself that "People make mistakes all the time; being perfect is impossible" (p. 197). The hierarchy of exposure that Reaven created asked James to make mistakes on an increasingly larger stage, starting with "1. Read a sentence out loud and intentionally make a mistake reading one of the words in front of a parent or teacher" and running all the way to "9. Intentionally make a mistake on a test, do not correct, and turn in the test" (p. 197). Any therapist, teacher, or parent can only imagine what a huge accomplishment and benefit such a hierarchy would be for any child living under overly high (and self-imposed) standards, with or without Asperger's.

It is common to see these children react fiercely and negatively to self-perceived failures. These children rip up drawings, quit projects, angrily blame their own errors on teachers and other children, and so forth. Some children in therapy will spontaneously reenact scenes of frustration and self-hatred to work through what happened. Other children require my helping hand and initiative in recreating play situations that allow them to replay and reprocess the original experience, with all of its tumultuous self-disappointment and rebuke, by reenacting situations where the child's reaction to self-perceived failure led to behavioral explosions (Levine & Chedd, 2007).

LEARNING DISABILITIES

Executive dysfunction, attention deficits, and learning disabilities often accompany Asperger's. As I stated explicitly at the beginning of this chapter, the Asperger's team should include a neuropsychologist, educational specialists, and teachers with the skills and temperament to engage and appreciate the child. As strong as we may be as clinicians, we do not substitute for such professional and educational intervening. We can, however, play a supportive role in the child's educational life.

Consider these examples. I regularly use therapy to help children deal with their frustration over school and work with child and parent to make homework less of a hardship and battle. I check in with children to ask how they like their classrooms, their classes, their teachers, and query them as to how pleased or unpleased they are with their own progress and effort. I often witness and celebrate their hard work to overcome a learning difficulty. For example, I have invited children to give me a tour of their backpacks and binders, making clear my great interest and shared pride in the new ways in which they're trying to be more organized in school. I offer children my laptop keyboard to show off the typing skills they've acquired to offset their illegible handwriting. I listen to what laments them about their academics—for instance, when Judy Ann confessed sadly that even after reading and rereading 20-plus volumes of the *Beacon Street Girls,* she wasn't sure how to spell two of the heroines' names. I encourage children to exploit and sublimate their special interests into forms that'll be welcome and that can flourish in the classroom environment. And hardly last, I do much work with parents, supporting their support of the child at home and at school, doing what I can to make the parents better advocates, and, when needed, "velvet bulldozers" who can get their children's needs heard and met in ways that build rather than burn relationships (Row, 2005). (Clinicians who consult to schools and educational programs will appreciate Silverman and Weinfeld's thorough and well-informed guide to insuring school success via best educational practices, 2007).

CREATIVITY

Among the several sad and mistaken myths of conventional thinking on autism is one believing that the child with Asperger's lacks creativity. It makes my blood boil just thinking about it! Nothing is further from the truth.

Back up and take note of the world that surrounds us. Our richest mines of innovation, invention, insight, and discovery are full of people with Asperger's. I mean places like the Ivy League, graduate schools and schools of medicine and business and writing, Silicon Valley and the Triangle area, engineering departments and libraries, accounting firms and financial institutions. Asperger's is everywhere. I am hardly dismissing the impact and challenges that Asperger's implies. But then, there is an aspect of the broadness of normalcy, isn't there?

We can mistakenly see creativity as confined to pastel-colored butterflies in a child's drawing or her emotionally accessible poem about her family vacation. To create is to bring something new or different into existence. And that can and does happen all over the place, all the time. Some of this creativity happens in computer science, medicine, psychology, and every other discipline. Some creativity happens at work, where employees come up with neater, faster, or cheaper ways of getting a job done. Creativity can be seen in most every kitchen and woodworking shop; it can be seen in engineers and journalists, in bankers and librarians. And though I cannot tell you who specifically these people are, I can promise you that many of them have Asperger's.

All children I've met with Asperger's are intriguing in their thinking and ways of approaching their world. As Asperger put it, "Autistic children have the ability to see things and events around them from a new point of view, which often shows superior maturity" (1944/1991, p. 71). That lovely phrasing and the observation beneath it made me think of the way literary agents ever seek fresh voices whose words speak the familiar in new and palpable ways. If things go as they should, these children will grow enough to fulfill their intellectual dreams and maybe become creative there. But in the meantime, they are at risk of coming to share some others' view that they, in fact, are not creative. How do we as therapists help? By treasuring what they say, do, show, and produce; by anointing with our undivided attentions and curiosity the tiny pearls of creativity that they display each and every therapy hour. Through our heartfelt presence, we let them know that their different ways of thinking bear merit and wonder.

Using whatever materials are handy, Seth ever builds lovely and oft times humorous things, as appealing as they can be complex. Teenage Lincoln takes lines from movies, cartoons, and books and weaves them into novel combinations to create hysterics, and now teachers are noting that his school writing is taking on his own idiosyncratic perspective that's humorous and evocative. Grown out of his prolific mythological world, Martin now writes intriguing blogs on teenage life and is working on a very good short story. Luc uses magnets and Legos to create machines that test and demonstrate principles of science. Devon experiments with cardboard blocks to build structures that are increasingly simple without losing strength. Iggy ever ponders ways that his work site can be greener, efforts that recently earned him recognition as employee of the month. Young Brady used the sticks from Tinker Toys to hit everything in my room to see what they sounded like, after which he played songs by doing so. Tiny Sheila would use blocks and figures to construct elaborate movie scenes that ultimately featured a theme related to her aggression and the remorse and loneliness that often followed. Judy Ann worked to find faster strategies for assembling puzzles and worked out new dance steps for her jazz dance. And you probably don't recall Carlos, the Wediko camper from the Bronx. He made a fishing pole out of a branch and by trial and error learned to cast so lightly and quickly that he could catch sunfish after sunfish in the same pond that defied all the other kids and staff.

There is no question that the child with Asperger's has plenty to work on. But we must be careful not to forget the other stuff, too—those natural gifts and talents. This "beautiful otherness of the autistic mind" has been relatively overlooked in both brain research and education of children with Asperger's (Happé & Frith, 2009). I would go further and suggest that our professional focus itself has been askew in terms of what can promote the child's growing into all she can and wishes to be. Both the science and lay media have made it easy and likely to conceptualize the talents of the child with Asperger's as *savant* skills that rise like "islands of genius" out of a sea of handicap nowhere (Treffert, 1989, 2009). This limiting purview has been further compromised by the realities of school systems. It's a challenge to meet the needs of a child who all at once can be so bright, capable, and disabled, particularly by teachers already overburdened to meet the collective needs of a classroom. Gifted and talented programs, never the norm, have grown rarer in these harder economic times. Ellen Winner (1996), who studies both giftedness and creativity, reminds us of our duty—parental, educational, and social—to foster exceptional talents. Listen to what Winner wisely cautioned in a 1996 interview:

> "I know it sounds elitist, but I think it's unfair to treat these children like you treat everybody else, because they're not like everybody else. They know and understand too much too soon and they are feared as strange, oddballs or freaks. But they are America's future leaders and are much less likely to become successful, creative adults if they don't have the right kind of education." Not all the children she studied had high IQs, as one might expect, nor were they well-versed in all academic and artistic areas, Winner said. However, each of the children displayed an obsession with a particular skill and, whenever possible, looked for or created opportunities to express their specific talent. One with a fervent interest in painting constantly recruited playmates to be his models, for example; another seemed to turn every situation into a mathematical equation, such as calculating distances every time she passed a road sign while on a car trip.
>
> (Howe, 1996)

When children with Asperger's don't "find a compatible learning environment most such children will fail to realize their potential and suffer from some degree of under-achievement and frustration. For the intellectually gifted child with a learning disability this is doubly the case" (Rowley, 2001, p. 11). Whatever their nature, the children's strengths, intelligences, and interests need constant feeding and challenge. Just because some children cannot do more basic or rote work doesn't preclude them from needing individualized music study, creative writing tutoring, or advanced math instruction. Programs such as the Johns Hopkins's Center for Talented Youth (CTY) and Stanford's Educational Program for Gifted Youth (EPGY), which offer summer and long-distance, self-paced curricula in many subjects, can sometimes fit a child who in other ways does not manage school well. Nothing, by the way, buoys a child's working on deficits than the satisfaction and pride of taking his strengths to new heights.

Nurturing the talents and interests of children with Asperger's may hold extra treasures, too. Children with Asperger's can sense the emotional impact of music (Heaton, Hermelin, & Pring 1999). They often share a love of words and writing. And given their passions for less seemingly romantic endeavors, such as science or math or historical facts, is it possible, or even likely, that many subjects besides music can sing to these children and touch their souls? Perhaps honoring and feeding their talents and preoccupations is itself an effective intervention for developing their emotional and communicative selves.

Not every talented child has Asperger's, and not every child with Asperger's is savant (Happé & Frith, 2009). And of course, a majority of these children's talents do not reach the level of a savant. Maybe, we will do best by following Temple Grandin's advice to not focus too much on the Asperger's diagnosis or label (2008) and instead strive to see the child in his own completeness and reality. Perhaps the child with Asperger's will fare best when we can take his unusual and unique strengths and weaknesses in stride with an even mix of marvel and responsibility, remediating, supporting compensation, and promoting and enriching, all implemented with our admiration and enthusiasm.

8

Feelings and Depression

As clinicians know firsthand, the basic issues I've been addressing do not run on their own, either in real life or real children. We can use a metaphor from the realm of textiles, where threads of all colors weave in and out and around each other in the most intricate of tapestries. But that image is woefully inadequate for what I'm aspiring to portray. Threads are inert, discrete, and independent. The child's issues, or threads, are organic and messy and influence each other in ways too subtle, pervasive, continuous, and profound for easy analysis. A patient weaver with good eyes could tease out the individual threads from a tapestry in ways that a clinician could never do to a child. With this in mind, we move on to feelings, arguably the lifeblood of human experience.

Feelings can bring cheer and its opposite, leading too many teenagers to hurt themselves, need medications—prescribed or recreational—and even take their own lives. Feelings are the energy that glues and sustains relationships. Feelings can bring out the best and the worst in us, with or without the added burden of Asperger's. In this chapter we examine what feelings can mean and not mean to the child with Asperger's? Are their versions of feelings equal or comparable to the feelings the rest of us know, or do they differ in nature (qualitatively) or degree (quantitatively)? What roles do feelings play in the daily functioning and the evolving development of the child with Asperger's? What do feelings have to do with the child's therapy, and what do therapy and the therapist have to do with them?

FEELING ONE'S FEELINGS

I would be the last to know. I'm not sure who first made that remark, though I have two witty Irish friends who both use that phrase when asked how they're feeling. Of course, their poking fun at themselves belies their actual capacities and willingness to both know and express what they feel. (The phrase, however, might not be a bad one to teach some children with Asperger's, even as we try to help them better learn to know, recognize, and state their feelings.) As Attwood succinctly put it, the child with "Asperger's syndrome has a clinically significant difficulty with the understanding, expression and regulation of emotions" (2007, p. 129). Ironically, this hardship is a prime object for therapy, even as it poses major obstacles to that same therapy. As Hans Asperger wrote when trying to imagine what or how these children suffer: "They *are* strangely impenetrable and difficult to fathom. Their emotional life remains a closed book" (1944/1991, p. 88). Jacob was one such boy whose therapy reveals how that book and child can be opened.

Seven-year-old Jacob was referred by school staff who held considerable concern. They ran down a lengthy list of "misbehaviors," many of which involved what they rightly judged to be "worrisomely aggressive." Jacob had hit another boy in his gym class with a plastic hockey stick hard enough for that boy to need stitches. In a game of playground soccer, he'd shoved a boy to the pavement because the boy had beat him to the ball. Other incidents involved knocking a boy off the school stage and tripping a boy on the stairs. School staff saw his aggression as escalating and feared that it was a matter of time before there was a "very, very serious injury." The kindly principal explained to me that while she much cared for Jacob and his education, she had a school and children to keep safe.

Jacob's teachers also described his "detached demeanor," how they often felt unable to reach and communicate with him. They felt particularly helpless when they'd try to discuss these incidents with him. Jacob would shut them out and appear clueless as to what had happened and what he'd done. He, they said, didn't seem to know how to be with other children and tended to play provocatively, for example, getting them to chase him. He hoarded things such as crayons in the classroom and got angry and retaliated when other children touched them. Occasionally, he accused classmates of stealing *his* crayons, though they were in fact crayons that belonged to the class and that he'd taken from them. "Can a child that young be paranoid?" his teacher asked me, apologizing for having what she judged to be such a bad thought about a child. Jacob refused to do school work or pay attention in class. The teacher also noted stereotypical motor behaviors that looked like tics, only stranger and more intense than she'd seen with other children. And he would eat things that weren't food. Lastly the teacher, very experienced and with a reputation as being both kind and firm, made clear her upset that she was not educating and helping Jacob as she wished. "Nothing's working," she said.

When I met Jacob, he looked like the child I'd been told of. He came through my door in a burst of energy and fear, running by me, hopping on my waiting room furniture, seeming all at once to hypervigilantly assess me while ignoring each and all of my attempts to engage him. I asked him questions, and his parents, trying in vain to control his climbing and running about, answered on his behalf. "You can see that we really need help," Jacob's father said while his wife tried to get their son off a table.

Though it would prove to take much therapy to understand and help Jacob, plenty was apparent in our first hour. Jacob never once answered a question; instead, he jumped from chair to chair as if a squirrel navigating roof eaves and high wires on its tricky way to a bird feeder. Jacob talked to himself in a kind of mutter. My gentlest verbal approaches led to his abandoning whatever he was playing and a renewed dashing to nowhere and everywhere. While Jacob didn't aggress at me, his utter and rare disregard for my stuff was striking. He purposely tried to break small cars, and when he couldn't, he tossed them at the wall. He flippantly emptied bins and buckets, mostly to make a ruckus and a mess, so it seemed, as he showed no interest in what was inside once he'd poured the contents onto the floor. I tried asking him to help me clean up, but he had no interest and made clear that he was no helper.

When Jacob talked, he referred to himself in the second person. "You are going to school after this." "Your favorite color is green, isn't it?" His facial expressions appeared mostly flat or frightened—except, when studying to see how his misbehavior affected me, he displayed a sadistic grin that hinted at pleasure. He showed no such smile in the rare moments when genuinely engaged in constructive play. He seldom looked at me, though in his perpetual testing of me and this new environment, he often glanced sideways to watch for my reaction, so it appeared.

I was torn in that initial meeting. On the one hand, I sensed that Jacob was checking me out as much as I was checking him. I wanted to give him good messages that would start to show him what kind of person and place this was. I wanted him to feel acceptance for who he was while wanting also to demonstrate that he, I, and my property were safe from his destructive impulses. And yet, my experience in working with some very aggressive, arguably violent children taught me to tread carefully. Did I really want to set a limit on breaking stupid little cars that cost all of a dollar or less? If I was sure that my limits on his aggression would have generalized to his aggression at school, I would have spoken up in a flash. I wasn't sure.

It was clear that our work was going to be large and time consuming. I wasn't going to undo his aggressive behavior and feelings overnight. I knew I could readily clamp his aggression down with me in the office. I worried that, if I did, he'd leave my office even more vulnerable to acting it out at school. So, when Jacob started to rip the head off a play figure, I tried a more tentative strategy.

"Jacob," I said twice, to get his attention. He didn't look my way, though he did stop wringing the doll's head for a moment. "I don't usually let children ruin my toys." Jacob smiled that smile and went back to his twisting the head. "But I know you're having a hard time not hurting children at school. If hurting my toys can make you feel better or help us figure it out, I'm very okay with that." Jacob flipped the doll backward into the wall, head intact.

Jacob tested me a few times. He picked up toys and worked at breaking them. "It's up to you," I said. He twice put them down. On the third try, he broke a toy. I didn't say or do anything, and that was that, at least for the rest of the hour. When time was up, Jacob moved slowly.

"Jacob, I can help you. Would you like that?"

"Yes!" Jacob screamed as he exploded back into the waiting room to join his parents, his departure turning into another round of parent-child mayhem.

When I met Jacob's parents, I discovered warm, loving, intelligent, and generous parents who minimized the problem. They spoke of Jacob's being a little "rambunctious" and "overenthusiastic" and of his "adventurousness." They described him as suffering most from a bad case of "being a young boy." I heard nothing about strange behaviors, a lack of connection, or unusual language; nor did I hear much about aggression, anger, irritability, or anxiety. At the hour's end, I relayed to them what the school had told me. They neither appeared terribly distressed nor did they disbelieve what the school had reported. "Does any of this happen at home?" I asked them. "Not really," was their joint reply. "He's mostly just a little too mischievous."

Jacob jumped on a chair, then off, and then on another chair, doing a handstand against its back until he flipped over its top and slid down between the wall and the chair back. *Squeak, squeak, squeak.* I looked over to the chair. I could see Jacob's legs kick and fidget beneath the chair.

"I think the chair is talking to me," I told him.

"What's it saying?" Jacob screamed.

"It's saying that it feels excited." The squeaking stopped. Jacob wiggled his way out and zipped over to the blocks where he worked by himself for quite a while, ignoring me for the rest of the hour.

Jacob had tried to communicate with me, and I'd gone for the bait (really a heartfelt appeal), as I should have. I failed miserably. I thought that my attributing feelings to the chair would have provided distance and camouflage. I may have used the guise of the chair, but I'd gone straight to what Jacob felt, mainly his excitement. That to Jacob, was my seeing too much too fast. Fortunately for parents, teachers, and even child therapists, children give us lots of second chances. And so did Jacob in the very next hour.

In almost a carbon copy of the previous session's play, Jacob ran from chair to chair, to headstand, to back flip, to hiding behind the chair. *Squeak. Squeak, squeak.* Jacob's legs kicked under the chair like a competitive freestyle swimmer. I waited for the cue.

"What's the chair saying?" Jacob asked.

"I think it's saying . . . Jacob is kicking me." Jacob's squeaking turned into an exulted squeal.

"What else is it saying?"

"It's saying that Jacob climbs on me."

"What else?"

"It's saying that Jacob jumps on me."

"Does it say anything else?"

"Yes. It says that Jacob can do whatever he wants to me, 'cause I'm just a chair." Jacob could not contain his joy. With a huge smile, he ran out from under the chair, headed straight toward me, and ran into my side before running back under the chair.

Jacob never said "thanks," "eureka," "you got it," or "you understand me." His behaviors said it for him. For all its speed, hard bump, and quick retreat, his fleeting wish for contact with me was a moment of affection and connection.

Jacob was settling in nicely with me and therapy. He liked coming and disliked leaving. He played and he communicated. Meanwhile, school reports were discouraging. He stabbed a boy with a pencil bad enough to require the nurse's attention and for the principal to notify that boy's parents. Jacob's parents and I held an urgent meeting. They feared Jacob would be removed from their beloved neighborhood school and be sent to a special school for troubled children. Under the pressure of their fear and the situation, Jacob's parents talked more candidly with me.

They now reported that what went on in school hadn't been news to them. They'd been seeing and worrying about Jacob's behavior for a long time. They described incidents in which Jacob had aggressed at home with his brothers and sister. These episodes went back years, as when he'd tilted over a crib and when he'd hurt his baby brother's cheek by feeding him with a spoon roughly.

I explained that he needed to know what his parents thought, felt, and expected about his aggression. Along with the school, we devised a plan that tied Jacob's two worlds together. (It was clear the school would have an easier time following through on our plan than would Jacob's parents.) At the meeting's end, with my querying, they also acknowledged that Jacob attacked them when he was angry, deprived, or told to stop something he was doing. That, I said, was a clear indicator that he needed clearer limits, structure, and expectations.

In about a month our renewed collaboration showed traction. Jacob appeared slightly less out of control and less in need of controlling others. His play was a tad more cohesive and coherent. A play sequence might last 2 minutes now instead of 1 minute or seconds. Occasionally, he engaged in construction projects that held his attention for longer. He approached me more frequently, even if his visits were short-lived and awkward. During this phase, I repeatedly reminded Jacob's parents that progress comes slowly and needs to be measured in baby steps, signs of progress, I underscored, that Jacob needed the grownups in his life to notice, admire, and validate. This newfound perspective relieved much of the pressure that Jacob's parents felt and gave them hope to offset their discouragement and fear.

A pebble fell out of Jacob's pocket. Jacob turned red and quickly pushed it back in. "I didn't steal them," he said. He put his hand over his bulging pocket. "I bought them somewhere." The stones had unmistakably come from the walkway to my office.

"Oh, okay," I said. "By the way, if you need any more stones, I have a ton of them outside. You can help yourself."

"You can have mine," Jacob blurted, as he ran outside and dumped his pocket of stones onto my pathway. He ran back in and went right to my container of markers. He crammed as many as he could fit into one pocket, then did the same with the second, and then a back pocket.

There was much I would have liked to say. "Hey, that reminds me of your marker hoarding at school." "Hey, by the way, how come you lie and steal?" "Hey, how come you took my rocks?" "I wonder what you feel when you take other children's markers." I knew that any of these comments would only chase him away and bring me farther from the truth. "Markers. Markers. Markers," I said aloud.

"Yeah," Jacob replied, still stuffing his pockets. "You can't have enough markers."

"I have a few more in the waiting room. Should I get them?" Jacob nodded that I should. He left with all of my markers.

Jacob came to his next session very eager to come into the office. He carried a plastic bag of markers, which he promptly returned neatly to their box. "Thanks so much!" I said. Jacob blushed with pride. It was obvious that Jacob had plenty of feelings. But I wasn't hammering them, nor was I demanding that he expose or work on them. I perpetually reminded myself to go slowly, to not say what I was thinking, to not ask or probe, to not reflect what I thought he was feeling right near the surface.

Whenever I'd slip, Jacob gave me a reprimanding refresher course, as he did one session after he'd gotten in trouble at school for having blurted inappropriate comments. "You don't mean to get in trouble," I said softly. Jacob bolted from my office and ran out the outside door. Hearing the sound of the gate, his mother went to get him. "It's okay," I said. "He needed to get some space."

When Jacob returned, I didn't bring up the previous session or apologize for what I'd said. Nor did I pursue the school issue or his fleeing the office. I didn't want him to feel that he'd been bad or suggest that he wasn't allowed to find space away from me if he felt the need. Conversely, I did not make a big deal of his return. This brings up a critical element of therapy and feelings when it comes to the child with Asperger's. If we as therapists want the child to grow more able and comfortable with his feelings, we must take care not to step over feelings that are being expressed in a vaguer, more primitive, and inarticulate state.

When Jacob, for example, took my markers, my not saying anything showed him my acceptance—not for his stealing but for the feelings that underlay his need to hoard markers. And when he brought them back, my saying nothing showed acceptance for what he felt—a pride, and who knows what else. Likewise, when he fled my office and then returned, my quiet welcome showed acceptance for whatever feelings had threatened to overwhelm him. My point is not that we therapists don't speak; we do and must speak. I'm saying that when a child cannot yet speak what he feels and cannot yet bear my words too, my heartfelt acceptance provides an all-important confirmation early on that I get what he feels and that I am okay with the way that he has to express (or not express) it. If I had made Jacob feel inadequate or defective at this early stage of sharing, what reason would he have for trusting me with his feelings in future meetings?

Jacob's aggression, while abating, could still rear itself under social stress. One day, I got a message from his school that he had thrown his lunch pail at another child's head. The child had bled. The school was most distressed that when confronted, Jacob smiled that smile, appearing not at all sorry or concerned for the boy he'd hurt. As was usual after bad days, Jacob came to his session looking weary and beat up. He said nothing about the incident and spent his session building structures out of a building set of small magnetic bars and steel balls.

"Is something up?" I asked. Jacob put his structure down. He squinted and pulled his sandaled foot into his stomach. "A boy bled in school today," he said.

"Really?" I asked. "What happened?"

"Nothing," he said. He stuck a magnetic bar between his toes. Jacob pointed to the small space between the outer edge of his eye and eyebrow.

"Is that where the boy bled?"

"That would be the place," Jacob replied. He squinted.

"Is he okay?" Jacob didn't respond. I tried asking a few more questions. "Did you see what happened?" Jacob shook his head, no. "Did he get stitches?" Jacob nodded. "Was it upsetting?" Jacob squinted harder but said nothing. I backed off. I wanted to help him get a hold of his aggression. But I reminded myself that overpowering him had never gotten us to anyplace useful. "Do you have any idea how you feel about that boy bleeding?"

Jacob turned his head as if trying to look to be thinking about my question. "I can't say that I do," he said.

"You don't know or would rather not say?"

"I believe I don't know." At this point, my dog woke up from the corner where he had been sleeping. "What's *he* feeling?" Jacob asked about the dog.

"Ivan," I said, as I looked straight into the dog's face. "What are you feeling?" I put my ear to Ivan's mouth. "He says he is wondering if you had some feelings about that boy." Jacob smiled that smile and it troubled me. I wanted Jacob to be worried sick about the boy he'd hurt. Maybe, went my thinking, if he could begin to worry about hurting other children, he would stop doing it.

"Did he *really* say that?" Jacob asked.

"No," I said. "I don't know what Ivan feels. He doesn't tell me. What do you suppose he's feeling?"

"How would I know? I'm not a dog."

"That's true. But you know how a nine-year-old boy would feel?"

"You should know. You were a boy," Jacob said, enjoying his deft deflecting of me.

"And any guess what I might have felt when I was a boy?"

"I bet you felt just like a boy your age would feel." Jacob laughed, more relaxed, apparently realizing he could fend me off forever. He went back to building with the magnets.

When Jacob rejoined his mother in the waiting room, she noticed that his mood was lighter. "You must have done a lot of good talking with Dr. Bromfield," she said. The next day, I spoke with the school. They reported that Jacob had apologized, and though he didn't look nearly as regretful as they would have liked, he did show some discomfort and a tear in his eye, they said. They added that the incident had thrown them for a loop, because Jacob had been doing better. He'd been provoking peers less and sometimes played cooperatively.

Children who cannot express their feelings make me think of Melville's stammering Billy Budd who, unable to speak when falsely accused of mutiny, strikes out in frustration and accidentally kills the master-of-arms Claggert, a maritime crime for which Budd is sentenced to hanging. I seldom lectured Jacob on his hurting other children. I never believed that a boy who could read advanced books and who could explain black holes didn't intellectually know that it wasn't okay to hit, kick, and physically mistreat other children. Of course he knew. My careful approach to Jacob's aggression and irritability focused on what he might be feeling, which was yet inexpressible. For instance, when on a couple of occasions he spit at me, I let my disapproval be known. I added that I felt very sad that he was stuck spitting so that he couldn't even tell me what he wanted me to know. Such interactions left Jacob very sad. I did the same with his aggression, explicitly expressing my dearest hope that one day Jacob could be free enough to speak what he feels, just as do other children his age. As Jacob progressed in his play and talk, he edged his way closer to feelings.

"Pick one," I said. Jacob, who loved for me to make him math and word puzzles, looked curiously at the page I had just scribbled in bold, blue marker. He had just spent several minutes ripping to shreds a paper airplane left on my desk by another child. He read aloud the choices I had given him: *angry, jealous, hungry,* and *sleepy*.

"That's easy!" Jacob exclaimed, as he took the marker and circled both *angry* and *jealous*.

"You knew just what you're feeling," I said.

"That's a piece of cake," Jacob said with a happy smile.

That jealousy and envy played a big role in Jacob's life and world was an old, familiar song. That, however, didn't help us help him manage the feelings that ever threatened to rise up and overwhelm him until, too late, he'd struck out at a sibling or schoolmate. As his therapist, I worked to help Jacob grow able to know, speak, and manage his feelings. It could only happen through real-life experiences that held genuine meaning for him.

While playing a game about feelings can help a child to recognize them, it is when he actually is in a life circumstance in which those feelings are truly felt that the greatest clarity and growth comes. Had I out of the blue greeted Jacob with mimeographed feeling worksheets on jealousy, he would have used them far differently. But when I brought them out in the heated moment of his upset over his younger brother's upcoming birthday party, he was able to convey the upset he felt.

I saw my job as a big one that moved in tiny stages across a huge landscape. At first, my task was to help protect Jacob from feelings that were too much for him in the real world, the kinds that led to his aggression and impulsivity. I then strove to capture each little piece of feeling and translate it into a palatable form that Jacob could digest and integrate. (Cognitive theorists might prefer words such as "process.") I insulated Jacob from overstimulation by raw and indistinguishable blobs of anxiety or excitement that ran loose in his body, the ones he couldn't express. Steadily, at a snail's pace, we came to deal with simple feeling states that with my help, Jacob could own, perhaps through a guessing game or by agreeing with a puppet or confirming my stating it outright: "You seem so sad today."

Eventually, Jacob learned to occasionally use his words to express strong feelings: "I hate you." "You're a jerk." "I hope you die." "Nobody likes you."

This progress created a new problem. Jacob's parents and teachers expected me to promptly put an end to this "bad talk." *But,* I had to say aloud to both his parents and school staff, *he's gone from aggressing his feelings to speaking them.* For a child like Jacob, mean-spirited put-downs were a major breakthrough. After all, using one's words is a sign of socialization, a step beyond impulsive action and a necessary way station on the way to self-regulation. Over time, Jacob grew more able at mastering his frustration so that he could put it into better words, meaning words that didn't get him into as much trouble, words such as, "You make me angry when you won't let me play."

Though, like every child with Asperger's, Jacob presented with a unique mixture of traits, his relationship to his feelings was *alexithymic,* meaning that he lacked the words to express his feelings. He was somewhat disconnected from what he felt and thus couldn't express it, share it, or problem solve around it (Fitzgerald & Molyneux, 2004). Some researchers suggest that the disconnection occurs at a very deep and basic neurological level. Their findings say that children with Asperger's don't, for example, register "embodied pain" signals physiologically (Minio-Paluello, Baron-Cohen, Avenanti, Walsh, & Aglioti, 2009) and don't experience stimuli at the subcortical level of the amygdala (Critchley et al., 2000). Other researchers disagree, finding that children with Asperger's did not differ from nonautistic controls in their physiological reactions to separating from their mothers as measured by skin conductivity and heart rate (Ben Shalom et al., 2006; Willemsen-Swinkels, Bakermans-Kranenburg, van Ijzedorn, Buitelaar, & van Engeland, 2000). Wherever the deficits reside, the emotional lives of these children are fraught with difficulty and challenge.

Fortunately, we do not have to wait for those uncertainties to be biologically unraveled in order to help the child grow more emotionally intelligent and competent; nor must we rely on longer-term therapies such as those I describe in this book. Child-centered programs for emotional education such as Attwood's *Exploring Feelings* (2004a, 2004b) and Faherty's workbook for self-awareness (2000) can help children to grow more emotionally aware, intelligent, and fluent. The interactive play structures of Levine and Chedd's *replays* (2007) and Greenspan and Wieder's *floortime* (2006) offer clinicians eminently concise and doable methods for helping children with Asperger's better read, manage, and express their feelings. Both of these interventions have the additional beauty of being well fitted for parents and educators to incorporate at home and school. (Emotional learning is, after all, a full-time job that can profit by being addressed in all parts of a child's life.) Expressive therapies also can play a wondrous role in helping a child with Asperger's to grow emotionally (Elkis-Abuhoff, 2008; Henley, 2000, 2001; Meyerowitz-Katz, 2008). While art therapists possess the training and skills to optimize the therapeutic value of children's drawing, sculpting, and so on, clinicians will inevitably find that many children with Asperger's use art to express themselves, often in ways that they cannot yet do with words. Our awareness of what art therapists can do is sure to enhance our own efforts when encountering children and their artwork. There is, I suspect, no limit to the ways in which skilled, motivated, and kindly therapists of any persuasion can employ music, drama, movement, storytelling, or any of the arts to engage and promote the affective growth of a child with Asperger's. (See Judith Martinovich's rich and pragmatic book on creative expressive activities and Asperger's, 2005.)

DEPRESSION

As early as 1981, Lorna Wing, in her clinical account of Asperger's Syndrome, wrote that "diagnosable anxiety and varying degrees of depression may be found, especially in late adolescence or early adult life" (p. 118). More recent studies have confirmed that teens with Asperger's, in particular, run a significantly higher risk of depressive symptoms and full-blown depressive disorders (Ghaziuddin, Weidmer-Mikhail, & Ghaziuddin, 1998; Kim, Szatmari, Bryson, Streimer, & Wilson, 2000; Leyfer et. al., 2006) and may be at higher peril for suicide (Wolff, 1995). Conversely, higher frequencies of Asperger's traits were found in clinic adolescent patients being treated for anxiety and depressive disorders (Towbin, Pradella, Gorrindo, Pine, & Liebenluft, 2005). "For teens with Asperger's," writes Attwood, "an additional mood disorder is the rule rather than the exception" (2007, p. 29). My own clinical experience has seconded these observations, as was true with Trudi, a fourth grader whom I'd seen for many months.

Having spent much of her hour silently sitting in the corner, Trudi walked over to the dollhouse, which she cleared of all the figures and furniture. For several minutes, she leaned her chin on her hand and studied the cleared space until, as deliberate and inspired as any artist, she set aside one of the child figures, a girl with brown hair and a red dress. Trudi took the remaining child figures, about a dozen of them, and formed a circle on the top floor of the dollhouse. She then stood that special girl right in the center. How nice, one might have thought, seeing the children playing ring-around-the-rosy. But Trudi was far from done.

She showed no sign of pleasure as she placed tiny hatchets, swords, and spears in the hands of the children surrounding the girl. She turned the figures' heads to stare at her and raised their arms in attack. With each small change, the scene grew more sinister.

"She's scared," Trudi said, sounding scared herself as figure by figure and bit by bit, she closed the circle in on the girl.

"Why is she scared?" I asked.

Trudi hid her eyes with her hands. "Because everyone hates her. I know what I want to do!" Trudi shouted, ending Act 1 with a swipe of her arm that sent the figures flying. She walked to my shelves, took the oversized cardboard construction blocks, and began to build.

Trudi had had a rough time of it. Though pretty, athletic, and smart, nothing went very well for her. Her disorganization and learning troubles frustrated her, and teachers found her trying. She would avoid the work they wanted and ask question after question about tangential topics. She would get in other children's space and ask them personal questions that annoyed and chased them off. She'd even gotten into fist fights at school. Her parents described their pain at watching her wander the playground alone. Even sports were a failure, as her social awkwardness curtailed her participation in sports teams.

I checked the clock. "We only have a few minutes left, Trudi."

"I know," she said. She built a tall tower of bricks. "That's the Empire State Building," she said, accelerating her pace. "And this"—she laid a brick on its side—"is a hot dog stand." She put figures here and there: pedestrians, window washers, and a newspaper hawker.

"We're just about out of—"

"I know, I know," she said. Trudi searched through a large straw basket of puppets and other stuff until she found a rubber dinosaur puppet and put it on her hand. She walked it around the tower. "He just wants to get a hot dog." She made the T-Rex gently approach people in the streets. The people screamed and ran and called for help and the police. The more the people panicked, the harder Godzilla tried to be nice to them. "Kill him!" they cried. "Kill the monster!" Just as Godzilla went to share his hot dog with someone, the police shot him. Godzilla cried out. Trudi gently laid the puppet on its side.

"They killed him," I observed.

"No one liked him," Trudi said soberly. She stood beside the tower that came to her knees, making no move to either clean up or leave. Far below, the people of New York City milled around the dead dinosaur. "He was bad inside," she said. "He deserved to die." Like public workers shoveling up a disaster, Trudi went to putting the toys away.

"Do you want help?" I asked.

Trudi shook her head. "It's my mess," she said. I held out a block, but she waved it away. She wiped her eyes with the side of her hand. "I wish they'd respect me." Trudi spoke quietly, looking away. "I just want them to respect me," she said, this time taking the block. I felt her tears when her hand brushed mine. I handed her a tissue.

In a final miraculous moment that I had witnessed too many times to question, Trudi suddenly came to life. Like a human vacuum, she cleaned everything and marched to the door. "I don't like leaving, you know," she said.

"I know."

She looked at me with a teary smile. "I don't feel like I'm bad when I'm here." I smiled. Trudi took a deep sigh, gave a little wave, and walked out to meet her mother at the car.

The ways that Asperger's affected Trudi's life was getting to her. Fortunately, she had much support, some capacity for emotional expression, and had really taken to therapy. She had people with whom and places where she could share her pain. When children with Asperger's are ensconced in a therapy where they can share their emotions, their risk for debilitating depression goes down. Honestly put, however, therapy does not eliminate all the risk or likelihood of depressive feelings. The awareness that therapy brings can temporarily heighten depression.

As with an Agatha Christie mystery, we suspect there are many culprits contributing to teenagers' vulnerability to depression. Depression can result directly from the Asperger's or follow an associated neurological or physical disability (Tantam, 2000). That depression seems to blossom during adolescence suggests other mechanisms, too. That teenagers with Asperger's have fewer and less satisfying friends is well documented, as is the critical role that friendships play for the adolescent. Teens with Asperger's who describe having less friendships report higher rates of loneliness and depression (Whitehouse, Durkin, Jaquet, & Ziatas, 2009).

It's been found that the more intelligent the teen, the greater the depressive distress (Barnhill, 2001), presumably as brighter teens are more aware of their circumstances, the disorder and its limitations, or as Wing (1981) proposed, the social and other ways that their disability makes them different from peers. We could suppose, too, having attained the ability to think abstractly, brighter teens can grasp that their Asperger's is a lifetime thing, evoking feelings of despair and helplessness. Although Asperger's begins biologically, environment can influence its fate. How the child or adolescent reacts to his Asperger's, as well as the ways that others react toward him, can profoundly affect and exacerbate depressive pain and dysfunction (Tantam, 2000).

While research works to better identify and understand comorbid (psychiatric) illness, our clinical experience tells us that the many, if not a majority of, teenagers with Asperger's suffer depressive symptoms and dysfunctions. Even if it is not to the level of a diagnosable depressive disorder—one study found 46 percent of teens with Asperger's reported depressive distress within the range for all adolescents (Barnhill, 2001)—it concerns us. For when the adolescent with Asperger's faces the "average" depression, she does so with less social support and fewer inner resources than does the average teenager. Our collective experience with all children, with or without Asperger's, suggests that these depressions spread roots in the tween years, if not before. Both Jacob and Trudi, in the mid-elementary grades of school, were well on their way to seeing that they were different and that they were being rejected because of it. Trudi wished that she could be like and liked by her peers—"just respected." Jacob's jealousy and envy for peers and my other child clients grew out of his intense feelings for his younger siblings who could make friends, express feelings, and just be and live so much more easily than he could. Though Jacob could not yet articulate his feelings as having to do with Asperger's, he could tell from early on that his brother and sister gave and took love more freely and successfully than he did. We can easily grasp why that is something to be envious of and grow discouraged over, even depressed.

While children and teens with Asperger's commonly know depression or a disturbance of mood, they do not have to suffer needlessly. Talking to a trustworthy, empathic, sympathetic, knowing other such as a therapist can invaluably alleviate depression and related distress. Therapy can be a setting where the child or teen with Asperger's comes to acknowledge difficulties, climb out from under shame and guilt, problem solve better decisions, and see reality more clearly and optimistically. As I'll discuss in the next chapter, social and therapeutic groups that provide safe and relevant experiences can also profoundly help these children and adolescents better understand and manage their social lives, especially given the relationship disadvantages their Asperger's brings to them. Receiving the support and understanding (and maybe even friendship) of like-minded beings can be a powerful antidote to feelings of isolation and self-hatred.

Cognitive-behavioral therapies can be especially useful for the teenager who copes with depression (Attwood, 2007; Beebe & Risi, 2003). As a relationship-based therapist, I, following Attwood, often employ techniques countering negative beliefs and self-talk, even within our larger treatments. I've witnessed several teenagers graduate from therapy who, feeling more secure in their ability to express themselves, wish to pursue cognitive-behavioral treatments and strategies that they previously felt unprepared for. These have been more behavioral treatments that involve being with peers and confronting fears, neither of which my clients had felt ready to confront. As I say over and over, when facing such a long-term and potentially handicapping condition, children and teenagers should be exposed to every intervention and strategy that can help in any way.

Therapies that specifically target anger management (Attwood, 2004a; Sofronoff, Attwood, Hinton, & Levin, 2007) can also play a critical role in alleviating the depression that's so commonly associated with Asperger's. Self-hatred often underlies depressive thinking and symptoms. That self-dislike can often arise after the child or teen has had an angry explosion—

perhaps after they've verbally or physically struck out at someone they care for or in a situation like school, where they receive punishment or disapproval. Strategies for managing anger can help children and teenagers to self-regulate their feelings so as not to act so impulsively and destructively, saving themselves from themselves (and from behaviors that bring self-defeating consequences). The *replays* that I spoke of earlier can assist children in resolving, and more so preventing, depression, especially with young and very young children, even if they are not very verbal (Levine & Chedd, 2007). By providing the child with alternative options of handling overwhelming events, circumstances, and feelings, such therapeutic reenactments can powerfully (and quickly) interrupt a vicious cycle that unrelentingly subjects the child to enormous feelings of failure and badness, feelings that if left to harden can accrete into the bedrock of future depressions.

The conception that having a child with any disability, including Asperger's, can stress a family and couple is hardly new or startling. But at least one recent study confirms what our clinical experience tells us, too: The road between the child and family runs in two directions (Kelly, Garnett, Attwood, & Peterson, 2008). Those researchers found that Asperger's symptomatology was related to the child's levels of anxiety and depression, which in turn were related to the degree of family conflict. Children with Asperger's are especially vulnerable to the adverse effects of family conflict. These researchers attributed that susceptibility to the lesser social and emotional resources, including a relative lack of friendships and supports, that can assuage and protect a child against conflict and distress in the home. This also reminds me of what one adult with Asperger's told me: "Just because my mother didn't cause my autism doesn't mean she's a perfect mother, just like I'm not the perfect daughter. My parents and family have as much strife as any other person's." Family therapy can be indicated and helpful for reasons that go far beyond the fact that a child has Asperger's.

Medication also holds a significant place in the overall treatment of these children and teens. There are a wide range of antidepressants and mood stabilizers to choose from. It must be stressed that having Asperger's as a primary diagnosis does not grant children immunity from other problems such as trauma, abuse, loss, neglectful parenting, family dysfunction not related to Asperger's, alcoholism and substance abuse, delinquency and antisocial behavior, and on and on. These children are no less subject to the flukes and vagaries of life that can so trip any other person and that can also contribute to depression.

Imagine what would happen to Jacob, and any children with Asperger's, if they went forever without having their feelings expressed. Imagine the pain they would endure and the frustration they would be left to suffer alone. Without the ability to express their feelings, these children have no means to understand who they are and no signals by which to monitor and guide their behaviors. Without the ability and willingness to share their feelings, they have no means by which to seek help, comfort, and consolation. The sequelae to not expressing oneself, which sounds too clinical and sterile to describe the human hurt involved, are limitless in the degree to which they can add hardship and compromise a child's life, now and as an adult. Our goal as therapists is not to turn these children into touchy-feely bags of unfettered emotion—far from it. Our objective is to help them learn to deal with their feelings in ways that facilitate their living well, ably, and as much as possible, with greater comfort in their own skin, being who, by nature and desire, they are.

9

Social Difficulties

If there is a realm in which the severity and dysfunction of the Asperger's experience is well understood, it is surely in the world of social relations. After recapping the familiar and documented aspects of the social difficulties found with Asperger's, this chapter visits the roles of friendship and one-to-one relationships. I discuss how the basic deficits of Asperger's interfere with social connections and how social anxiety contributes to the child's social avoidance and failure. Throughout, the chapter features the relevance of individual psychotherapy to the child's social life and success, a possibility that challenges the conventional thinking and logic on Asperger's.

ASPERGER'S AND FRIENDSHIPS

In his seminal observations, the children at Hans Asperger's clinic impressed him with their unusual social behaviors. He described their general and consistent inability to derive the unspoken rules of social interaction. Their verbal communication ever strayed from the mark, as they seldom responded in tune with what they heard, instead tenaciously pursuing their own interests or tangents, making inappropriate remarks or asking unwanted questions, speaking private thoughts that discomforted peers, talking too loudly, and so forth. Their nonverbal communication only made matters worse, as when they stood too close, avoided eye contact, or gestured in ways that seemed to contradict what they might actually be feeling or conveying. These children, Asperger wrote, "have a paucity of facial and gestural expression [and] in ordinary two-way interaction they are unable to act as a proper counterpart" (p. 69).

With the empathy and insight that marked his observations and that elevated his maverick case histories to enduring greatness and relevance, Asperger saw that these children's social misery and failure was not due to a social apathy (1944/1991). These children wanted some measure of social connection and friendship; they were just plain awful at it. However much they wished to get it right (i.e., ably process social information), the neurological bases of Asperger's got in the way. In fact, aside from language that's more highly developed, it can be argued that greater social interest is what most distinguishes children with Asperger's from those farther to the left on the autistic spectrum. Asperger himself considered the "limitation of their social relationships" to be the "fundamental disorder of autism" (1944/1991, p. 77). Clinicians who work with Asperger's Syndrome know well the ways, if muted or unique, that these children can appreciate and yearn for people in their lives.

The child's lack of social success is most salient, and potentially most personally discouraging, in the making of friendships. As we saw in Chapter 8, it is during the adolescent years that this hallmark lack of friendships can surface most acutely and take its greatest psychological toll on the developing child. Depending on the child's style, the stress of coping with overtaxing social demands can lead to depression (Barnhill, 2001), aggression (Simpson & Myles, 1998), and "mental and physical exhaustion" (Attwood, 2007, p. 17). In no way overstating it, Tantam wrote that "despite being a milder form of autism . . . [Asperger's] is, clearly, still a highly socially disabling condition" (1991, p. 178). Hans Asperger saw it as potentially devastating.

To best grasp what the lack of friendship implies for the child or teen with Asperger's, we need to remind ourselves what friendship means to the nonautistic child. Friendships can teach social skills, like communicating and cooperating with peers. They teach children about who they themselves are and where they fit into this world. They provide "companionship and fun that relieve the stress of everyday life." They "model . . . helping, caring, and trust." And by providing relationships that are only human, they offer inevitable opportunities to learn how to resolve interpersonal conflict (Hartup, 1992, and Parker & Asher, 1993, as cited in Cole, Cole, & Lightfoot, 2004, p. 556). Friends help to glue a child to the social structure she navigates at school and outside the home. Friends are the buoys and anchors that keep a child afloat and steady through the storms and high seas that childhood and adolescence are sure to throw her way. Friendships foster self-esteem and positive regard and buffers the child against family conflict (Kelly, Garnett, Attwood, & Peterson, 2008). Unfortunately, as clinicians might guess, research documents that teenagers with Asperger's report fewer and a lower quality of friendships, and associated with that, greater depression and loneliness (Bauminger & Kasari, 2000; Bauminger, Shulman, & Agam, 2003; Whitehouse, Durkin, Jaquet, & Ziatas, 2009). For clinicians who work with these children, social functioning has to be a priority.

THE THERAPY OF AN ELEMENTARY SCHOOL-AGE GIRL

Judy Ann, the girl who devoured the *Beacon Street Girls* books, was referred to me in the fourth grade upon the recommendation of her teachers, though her parents said they were close to calling me on their own. They described Judy Ann as a smart girl with many issues creating difficulties in her life at home and school. She was moody and irritable, prone to angry outbursts and long, noisy tantrums. They described Judy Ann as extremely uncooperative with the rules and expectations of the household. She needed to control everything, including her brother and parents. She fought bedtime, waking up, showers, family meals, schedules, transitions—just about every demand of the home. A bright girl, she made homework a nightly battle. School projects led to volcanic and panicked meltdowns.

And yet, for this mighty list, there was a bigger reason for Judy Ann's parents calling me. They were severely worried over her social life. Judy Ann had no real friends, they said. She regularly spent recess and lunch alone on the busy playground, her nose buried in a book. In the classroom, the teacher reported that Judy Ann was a loner who resisted any kind of social or group interaction. When the curriculum forced Judy Ann to work in a cooperative learning group, she tended to go at it alone; that is, when she wasn't openly disagreeing with the other children. When it came to group projects, Judy Ann felt that she was the only child working and that her group-mates failed to recognize her superior efforts. She was seldom invited for play dates or parties, her parents lamented, and when she was, she either refused to go or came home early, unhappy, and full of complaints that the other girls were mean and bossy. "She says everyone hates her," her mother said sadly. That she can feel that way, Judy Ann's parents emphasized, was the main reason for their bringing her for therapy.

But Judy Ann, they said, was not just a victim of mistreatment. She could dish it out in her own way. Judy Ann would mercilessly tease her younger brother and often hit and push him. Sometimes, her parents feared that the two children couldn't be left alone together. Judy Ann could not talk directly with peers about the way she felt excluded by them, but she would say harsh things about one child to another, gossip that usually backfired to Judy Ann's disadvantage.

To say that Judy Ann took to therapy and me like a duck to water would be wishful hyperbole. She found being with me almost as hard as she did other social situations. Judy Ann carried herself in a most serious way. She may have felt anxious or frightened inside, but her facial expressions looked alternately bored, aloof, angry, and annoyed. Her facial and body language could be powerful, in the sense that it made me feel I'd better back off and leave her be.

At first, Judy Ann tended to move around the room. Her activity was not frenetic; it was constant at a slow pitch. She'd draw for a few minutes, then skip, then juggle a ball, and so on. She'd approach me, then retreat. My gentlest queries or comments about anything in her life, social or otherwise, seemed to fall on deaf ears, though the way that her body stiffened and she withdrew said that she listened and heard me. Occasionally, she responded with a curt *no*. She frequently checked the time and asked, "How much longer is this?" At the hour's end and without a word, Judy Ann would make a beeline for the office door, out through the waiting room, and out to the car without waiting for her mother. Judy Ann never said hello or goodbye. I did, believing I should strive to model good social behavior.

Her parents, intelligent and accomplished professionals, were more than eager for me to "fix" things. "How long will it take?" they asked, not in a pushy way but in the way of parents who couldn't bear watching their child suffer one more minute of social rejection and who feared that it might never get better. They described how their daughter's social difficulties also played out at home. Judy Ann was often *incommunicado,* reading or doing artwork or watching television, they reported, and was near impossible to engage in conversation during the day. Late at night was the one time when Judy Ann might chat a little—she didn't like going to sleep. She would usually talk of having no friends, being hated, and being lonely. With a broken heart, Judy Ann's mother would do what any loving mother would do: She'd try to help Judy Ann with her "friend problem." She would gently probe to learn more, offer to make more play dates, try to help her daughter see what might have been going wrong. Judy Ann would have none of it and usually ended the conversation feeling unheard, misunderstood, criticized, and blamed, her abrupt withdrawal saying, *"You just don't get it."* Though, as I continually reminded her mother, Judy Ann's initiating such chats with her mother nightly revealed that she valued them and that she felt some measure of empathy, sympathy, and comfort in their nightly tête-à-têtes.

From early on, I cautioned her parents that Judy Ann's treatment would not be fast. I also knew from experience that Judy Ann's social life would progress even slower. I said that progress would come continually and visibly in tiny steps. Her parents intellectually accepted this, even while they asked questions with impatience. "Why can't she smile at the other girls?" her father asked. "Or say hello?" Why wouldn't she, her parents questioned aloud, prefer playing with peers to reading or drawing, the way Judy Ann's younger brother did? They wondered if urging Judy Ann to try some "fun" social activities might be worthwhile, and I agreed.

They asked whether they should schedule play dates over Judy Ann's reluctance. We recalled how badly her play dates tended to go. Her mother feared that these unsatisfying experiences could make matters worse, lead to more embattled relationships with girls and more mean gossip at school, and leave Judy Ann with a perpetual sense of failure that would fuel a never-ending cycle. I concurred, reframing it: "She'll never desire more social contact until it starts to go well."

Judy Ann's parents had some good ideas in the meanwhile. They signed her up for classes in dance, gymnastics, artwork, and music, activities that built on Judy Ann's interests and talents. Her parents wisely chose classes that met only one to two hours weekly, had lots of structure, required minimal interaction, centered around organized activities, and were supervised by skilled adults. There was a limit as to how badly these endeavors could go. Judy Ann's parents also knew that she would be with a good mix of children.

While her parents moved ahead with their apt plans for social growth, therapy was all about Judy Ann herself. I'd learned to stop bringing up

Judy Ann's social life at school or on the playground. It never got us any-where. By my behaving myself, however—meaning by not forcing Judy Ann to feel what she couldn't yet bear—she gradually and steadily grew to like our meetings. She spent most of every hour standing at my desk do-ing artwork while I sat nearby, mostly watching and admiring. She was an adept young artist who adored creating lovely looking things that were as colorful and cheery as she could be gray and dour. We usually spoke only about her work, its content, her choice of colors, and where in the office she would like to hang it.

Judy Ann colored a poster of the four seasons, which she had titled "Sesions." She stopped coloring to stare at a small piece of ripped paper taped to the wall above the marker box. "Who did that?" she asked with irritation.

"A child who comes here," I answered.

"He can't spell," she said.

I refrained from stating the obvious. Months earlier, her teacher and parents had told me that in spite of her strong intellect, spelling came hard to her and was a source of embarrassment. Though the teacher did not make a big deal out of her spelling, Judy Ann did. She didn't want to go to school the day of vocabulary quizzes. Judy Ann read aloud the list of two- and three-letter words. "He spelled *no* backwards, and what's a 'momanddad?'" she asked with derision. I waited. "Oh," she said, turning red. "Mom and dad." She grabbed her drawing and ripped it up.

"What happened?" I asked.

"It's stupid." Judy Ann withdrew to a glider in the corner. She pinched the skin between her thumb and finger. "How much time?" she asked, and asked again.

When there were just a few minutes left in the hour, I spoke. "I liked your drawing. It was lovely." I looked to the wastebasket where she had thrown the ripped pieces. "But you didn't like it." Judy Ann walked slowly over to the desk and quickly recreated her drawing. Done, she handed it to me. "Where should we hang it?" I asked. Judy Ann pointed right above the other child's list of words.

"They're probably going to feel bad when they see my picture," she said, sort of smiling, sort of looking sad.

That was the first time in her therapy that Judy Ann mentioned another child. From that point on, she grew competitive with the other children I saw. When she'd enter the office, she'd instantly look to try and see what other children had done. If another child made a book, she'd make a larger book with more pages. If a child drew a picture of a house, she would draw a fancier house or an entire landscape that included a house. When she'd found that another child had created something beyond her abilities—as when an older adolescent had built an amazing 20-sided icosahedron, a project that took several sessions—she'd withdraw and forgo any of her own creative efforts that day. Other times, she might grow grouchy and insult me. My steady acceptance of her feelings and reactions led to her growing stiller and teary, though she'd never speak of what she felt.

In many ways Judy Ann's parents were pleased with what they saw. She'd engaged in therapy, something they hadn't thought possible. Her tantrums were smaller and rarer. She'd turned a corner with her spelling. She shared with her mother a new belief that being a bad speller didn't make her dumb, and she prepared more effectively for her vocabulary quizzes. She'd become a more willing participant in her extracurricular activities, though her parents described her as continuing to be isolated and never doing anything after school with classmates. They said she never greeted or said goodbye to the other children at dance or her other extracurricular activities. "She claims the other children dislike her. But when I'm around," her father astutely observed, "they seem to be friendly to her, or at least, a lot friendlier than she is to them." He told a story of their bumping into another parent and classmate at a restaurant. The child and parent lit up to meet them, he said, adding that Judy Ann acted as if they were strangers. "Can't you teach her to say hello?" he asked. "Maybe she doesn't know how to be friendly?" I underscored that as being a significant question that I would pursue.

I eagerly met Judy Ann in the next hour armed with my question. Judy Ann, however, had her own agenda. Over our time together, she'd grown to like me. She rejected and retreated from me less frequently. She occasionally smiled. And she asked personal questions, a curiosity that was particularly unleashed that day. "Who do you live with?" "Are you married?" "Do you have children?" After asking, Judy Ann would spin her chair several times, appearing to ponder the next question. With each revolution of the chair, she stretched her legs out as far as she could to kick my legs with her sneakers. When I pulled my legs back, she stretched further. Her contact was pure connection and not at all aggressive or off-putting. The movement in her relationship to me was so new and positive that I didn't dare risk disturbing it by bringing up her father's question as to what she understood about friendship. I didn't have to wait long though to ask what I wanted to.

Judy Ann arrived to her next hour detached and unfriendly. Shortly before, her mother had left a message that Judy Ann had had a very bad time on the school playground that day. A handful of girls had made "a small island," and when Judy Ann asked if she could join them there, they said it was only for the "popular girls." The school reported that Judy Ann appeared very upset and that, neither crying nor protesting, she'd gone off by herself to read on the far edge of the playground. I tried to bring up the incident by telling her that the school told me that some girls behaved not at all nicely to her. Judy Ann's story pretty much matched what the school had said.

"Did you try to do anything?" I asked.

"I told them they couldn't do that," Judy Ann explained. "I told them that they have to be nice to me and let me on the island."

"And what did they say?"

"They laughed at me."

"Ouch," I said softly. "That is so mean." Judy Ann's eyes welled. I told her that I might have some ideas to help with those girls and asked her if she would like to hear them.

"Not now, but maybe some other time," she said.

"Is there anything I can do to help you feel better?" I asked.

"No," she replied, but she pulled her chair closer to the desk and me and smiled a little.

I took this opportunity, bracing just a bit for Judy Ann's anger that I could ask such a ridiculous question. "Judy Ann, were those girls being friendly?"

"They were *unfriendly,*" she said.

When I asked what friendly girls do, she knew fully, telling me that friendly girls say hello, smile, invite you to join them, give you compliments, don't talk behind your back, and so forth. "You really do know exactly what a friendly girl does, don't you?"

Judy Ann beamed. "Yes, I do."

Taking action to remedy a problem is a human reflex. As one who has renovated two houses, I am ever ready to repair. And loving parents do the same when their children hurt. "What can we do?" her parents asked with greater urgency in our next meeting. I momentarily set that day's question aside and reminded them of our last meeting. I reported to them what Judy Ann had said about the meaning of being a friend. "Well, if she knows what it is, why doesn't she do it?" her father asked, reasonably so, I thought. "That," I replied, "is our $64,000 dollar question—I mean, *questions*." "You mean, like, she knows, but she just can't do it?" he asked. Yes, I nodded. "Figuring out what she can't versus won't do is one of our jobs," I said.

Judy Ann's parents got what I meant. They extended that question of *can't versus don't* to other facets of Judy Ann's life, including her stubborn reaction to household routines, homework, and anything that others wanted her to do. Her parents were beginning to see just how complex their daughter's social difficulties were and how much work lay ahead of us. On the other hand, Judy Ann and her behaviors were coming into a light that made sense and gave them hope.

Originally, Judy Ann felt an aversion to my dog, a standard poodle as large and curly as he was calm and imperturbable. The first time Judy Ann met him in the waiting room, she screamed as if discovering a very large rodent. Basil had sat there placidly, head titled, tail wagging. Judy Ann's screaming and fear, itself atypical for children, was extremely exaggerated. Even after I locked Basil away, she continued to scream. I apologized for my dog's having frightened her and told her that I would never let Basil near her again.

Over many, many months, Judy Ann showed growing interest in Basil. At first, she'd ask where he was and what he might be doing. (*He's behind a locked door. He's probably sleeping.*) Judy Ann asked more and more questions. "Is he afraid of me?" (*No, he looked very relaxed and happy with you.*) "Does he have friends?" (*Kind of. He has dogs he likes to play with.*) "Does he miss me?" (*I think he might.*) "Does he wish he could come see me?" (*Yes.*)

She would ask harder questions, too. "Would he want to be my friend?" (*He would.*) "Why?" (*Because he liked meeting you and would like to get to know you better. That's how friends grow into friends.*) "What would he do if he came to see me now?" (*He would probably walk around you, do some sniffing, and lay his head near your lap. He might stand next to you and lean against your leg.*) Judy Ann was rapt by the answers to her questions and asked further ones that came closer and closer to her real concerns. "Would Basil hate me?" (*I can't think of a reason he would ever hate you.*) "Would Basil play with me?" (*Do you mean, would he not let you play with him?*) Judy Ann nodded that was what she was asking. (*Yes, he would let you play with him. And he would be happy that you would let him play with you.*) "What if he started not to like me?" (*That would feel awful for you.*) Judy Ann looked downcast. (*But I don't think that would happen.*)

At the end of one hour Judy Ann asked that Basil visit us. We did lots of preparing as to how to welcome him, be calm, let him do the approaching, and, as Judy Ann suggested, not scream. She held her breath when I walked Basil into the office. She smiled tentatively, asking within a nanosecond whether Basil seemed to like her. While standing behind me as if a shield, Judy Ann wrapped her arm around my side to gingerly pat Basil's head. "He's soft," she noted.

Over many sessions, Judy Ann grew increasingly comfortable with Basil. She'd share her cookies with him and learned how to get him to sit, go down, and stay. Being able to control Basil delighted her. "He does whatever I tell him!" she crowed. For all of her mastery, Judy Ann would occasionally freak out, imagining that Basil wanted to steal her treats and ruin her things, sentiments that she often felt in relation to peers and her younger brother. She would verbally chastise Basil, even yell at him, while he just sat there like a shaggy log, absorbing the criticism. That Judy Ann could grow so relaxed and competent with a dog surprised and pleased her parents. "Could this," we mused, "possibly generalize to her relationships with children?"

Judy Ann looked at me with a strange smile that looked full of apprehension and sadism. I was in some disbelief as to what I had just seen. She had kicked Basil's rear kind of hard with the sole of her shoe. Basil didn't like it; he made a small cry and ran behind me. Judy Ann watched me closely.

I rubbed Basil where she had kicked him. "You're okay, big fella. I think your feelings are mostly hurt," I told him.

Judy Ann looked very angry. "Why are you patting him?" she asked.

"To comfort him," I replied.

"Why do you have to comfort him?"

"I don't have to," I said. "He's my friend, so I want to comfort him."

"Why does he need comfort?" I looked at her and waited. "Because I hurt him?" she asked, knowing the answer. I nodded. Judy Ann ran from the office, ending the hour early.

For some weeks, Judy Ann continued to provoke Basil. (I had been through enough of this kind of thing to know that he was in no danger of biting a child or in any way being anything but a trusty assistant.) She knew that I didn't like it, because I told her so. With each aggressive act, she would smile with a pained mix of worry and satisfaction. Meanwhile, while girl meets dog was heating up on the inside, news from the outside was encouraging. Judy Ann had initiated a couple of successful play dates, and she was responding more favorably to other children. Though still not the one to say hello, she would say hello back, and she was trying not to say nasty things behind other girls' backs. She was even leaving her books inside at recess, instead trying to join playground games. Her parents caught her practicing these games at home on the weekend.

But most every worthwhile trip has its bumps and stumbles. And so does therapy—a lot of them. That morning I'd gotten a message that a girl who Judy Ann had been making friends with had, in a moment of her own social pressure, turned on Judy Ann, calling her a baby and saying she smelled. Judy Ann was mortified to have been humiliated in front of the popular girls and crushed to have been so betrayed in her first heartfelt attempt to make a good friend. I didn't expect that we would have much of a conversation when Judy Ann showed up, but given how awful her experience had been that day, I had to try. She would have none of it. She got as far away as she could from me and sat in the glider. She called Basil to join her, and he did. He laid at her feet, and she slid to the floor for some much needed warm and affectionate dog comforts child time—just what the child-feelings doctor would have prescribed.

"That's a nice Basil," Judy Ann said. She rubbed Basil's head. "Good Basil." Basil melted into her arms when in an instant, Judy Ann grabbed the hair behind his neck and pulled it hard. Basil let out a pained yelp and ran from her. "Go away, you ugly, stupid dog! I hate you!" Basil stopped and sat to face Judy Ann. She looked straight into his eyes. "No one likes you. I always hated you. You are stupid and ugly and you stink." She struggled not to cry. "I never liked you."

It was one of those therapy moments when I would have preferred to have been the parent who could have given her a big everything is going to be okay kind of hug. One needn't be Freud or even a first-year child psychology trainee to have seen what was going on. Judy Ann stared at me, stuck and seeing no way out of what she'd created and what she felt.

"Do you think Basil could use a hug?" I asked. Judy Ann nodded and ran to Basil's neck. She hugged him and sobbed. "I'm sorry, Basil. I didn't mean what I said."

"He knows that," I said, believing it. "He knows how you really feel about him." Judy Ann smiled through her tears as she kept rubbing and hugging the dog. "He knows you had a rough day," I said.

"How did he know?" Judy Ann asked.

"Your school told me, and I told him." She didn't speak. "I'm sorry that girl treated you that way," I told her.

"I don't think she really meant it," Judy Ann said. "I think I'm going to talk with her."

The next day, Judy Ann did talk with the other girl, and they worked it out. Judy Ann was discovering that relationships are not made of fragile glass but of an organic blend of love and hate and like and dislike and nicety and rudeness, and most of all, that they were something that can be repaired. This led to a totally new phase in which Judy Ann more actively worked on friendships. She began using me as a sort of friendship consultant. She displayed friendlier behavior, even as she grew more able to be overtly unfriendly, confrontational, and assertive in her relationships with both friends and enemies—healthily and adaptively, when circumstances called for it. From that day on, Judy Ann's relationship with Basil and me changed. She started to say hello and goodbye, especially to Basil, asking him how he was and how his day had been. Her fear of him had disappeared, and when in my office, she became his gentle, confident, caring master. "We're best friends!" she announced soon after, as she drew with one hand while massaging Basil with the other.

Over the months since, Judy Ann's social world has expanded. She has made a couple of good friends and has grown more capable and willing to enjoy less deep acquaintances, such as at camp or sports activities. She is more able to compete fully without feeling mean and rejecting herself. She also has grown more aware of ways in which she can put off or mistreat other children. And her relationship with her younger brother has matured to where she can play with and enjoy him, oft times caring for him as might an older sister, teaching him things or sharing in what he likes to do. In therapy, she even comes in and will talk about what's happening socially, allowing us to problem solve together, as she did around her recent first day at camp. Judy Ann spent almost the entire session talking vividly about a much older teenage girl who was condescending, teenage boys who ran around wildly and ruined every game, and another girl who teased her. Judy Ann spoke clearly about each experience, telling how she had dealt with it. (She decided the older teenage girl was unaware of how she sounded, she asked a counselor to slow the boys down, and she let the teasing girl know that she wouldn't tolerate it anymore.) "Wow! You know just how to handle these things," I said. Judy Ann held her arms out in a good-natured *thank you, thank you very much,* her pride as deserved as it was hard earned.

THE THERAPY OF A TEENAGE BOY

Do you recall Martin, who first came to me with his body twisted in tension? He was a textbook example of the child whose strengths and weaknesses are all over the map. His verbal development was superior, with vocabulary and writing skills far beyond his age. He's the one who prior to meeting me had written a long novel about a world of mythological creatures. Martin could write a short story in a night or a 1,000-word blog in minutes, but he never passed a school writing assignment in on time and without torturing himself and his family along the way. He could recall tons of minutiae that interested him, and yet his working memory for academic tasks was inadequate. A deep thinker with mature insights and strong moral fibers, his reflections on life and important subjects could capture others. But then, he could push others away with his monologues on topics that bore little relevance to life. Martin would have been the first to describe himself as clumsy and having neither athletic interest nor aptitude. And while his social relationships were difficult, he forever held romanticized views of what he wished they were. We spent many hours exploring Martin's expectations of the perfect friend and girlfriend. As might be expected, these unrealistic paragons confounded and deterred Martin's pursuit of real (imperfect) relationships with real (imperfect) people. Such high ideals meant that other kids' actual behaviors toward him forever disappointed Martin, not to mention the unbearable pressure they put on him, in his own mind, to be so much more than what he or any other teenager could be. The beginning of Martin's therapy went as gently and slowly as did Judy Ann's. Though Martin explicitly instructed me to tell him like it is, his withdrawal, increased tension, going speechless, and so forth instructed me to proceed with caution and care.

Martin's parents were actually thrilled at how far he'd come. When we'd first met two years earlier, they'd dreamt that one day he could be emotionally expressive, academically engaged and competent, able to independently survive in a regular school, personally responsible, and interested in coming out of his room to be with people. He had become much of that and more, though he still preferred hiding out in his favorite places at home. By both Martin's and his parents' votes, this year would be a year for working on social issues. Martin wanted to make friends, have a girlfriend, and grow away from being the hermit he feared he was headed toward becoming. That Martin could conceptualize, envision, want, and set that goal itself was a landmark heralding much good work in therapy.

Our work on the social scene began centered around Martin's school experience. After all, he mostly hid out at home, so his contact with peers happened near exclusively at school. Martin identified several places where he had troubles. In the classroom, for instance, he said he could be seen as an arrogant know-it-all. When I queried to better understand what this meant, Martin presented it as his classmates' fault. He described them as resentful of his being so smart and knowing all the answers. "So, they're jealous?" I asked. Martin agreed, until some things he heard at school led him to change his mind. One girl had noticed that Martin would raise his hand a lot, like a kid in a much younger grade. Martin felt such shame over this perception that he gave up volunteering in class. This led to Martin's discovering a feeling that he'd never before known—that quiet sense of knowing you know but not having to prove it to everyone else. Our discussions also invoked a memory of an oral speech that he had given years ago. Unlike the encouraging responses that peers had given the other children's presentations, Martin recalled that no one commented on his. At the time, he remembered, he thought his talk was just too advanced and awesome for the other kids to handle.

Martin fidgeted as he was wont to do when stressed. But he looked very sure of what he was about to say. "It wasn't what I thought it was," he said. I waited. "I purposely used words that no one would understand." He looked very sad.

"But you were just trying to do your best job on a paper," I said.

"I'm sick of it," Martin said, awkwardly hammering the chair with his fist. "I want kids to like me. So, why do I do stuff to make myself stand out alone?"

"Maybe because of other stuff you feel," I suggested.

Martin hung his head. "You mean like feeling I suck at the social stuff that all the other kids excel at?"

Just because an adolescent has Asperger's-based processing deficits doesn't mean he doesn't compensate just as might any nonautistic teen. Martin took each insight and with enthusiasm experimented with it the first chance he got. He strove to give a class report using smaller vocabulary and shorter sentences, making it more interesting and using humor. In short, he aimed at giving a talk that kids would like. It worked, and he got high praise from teachers and peers alike. Sitting in class and not offering answers to the teacher's every question also made Martin feel more like the other kids. He felt a sense of belonging by not having to be the perfect pupil. "I never knew that screwing off could feel so good!" he exclaimed.

The bus stop was another source of anguish for Martin. "What," he would ask, "do kids talk about when standing around?" He articulated every pained detail of those 5- to 10-minute periods while waiting for the bus to come. Martin had no idea what to do with his hands, his legs, his face—his body. He, like many children with Asperger's, had enough awareness to feel and see his deficits. "Am I the world's most self-conscious individual?" he asked. "One of them," I replied. Martin chuckled.

We tried role-playing. Martin showed me how he would stand around. He would try leaning on one leg, then the other, his best efforts to appear natural managing to only look more and more wooden. "It's hard to look casual," I said, showing him how I couldn't do it convincingly, either. "You mean I'm stuck being myself?" That wonderful question served as a springboard for many discussions in which we honored who he genuinely was while looking at ways that he himself sought to change and act differently. Martin discovered that trying new ways of being—whether standing, talking, not raising his hand, or expressing himself—felt strange and self-conscious at first. He learned that if he kept at them, these new ways of being grew second nature. "If only we could all be as cool as James Bond," I said. "Totally," Martin agreed.

"I want friends but not that badly!" Martin said, explaining that he was not willing to have a personality transplant or give up what he felt and thought just to be what others wanted or what was demanded for him to have friends. We would break his social interactions down into dyads first, for we agreed that getting along with one person seemed necessary before moving on to bigger groups. Martin laughed that at times, a two-person group could loom too large. When talking to one other person, Martin felt torn between wishes for and fears of intimacy. Yearnings would creep up frequently when he found himself beside a girl. He acutely obsessed over every syllable he spoke, every grimace and stare. "I wish my eyes knew what to do," he said.

Over weeks and weeks, we moved on to explore his being in triads. Conflict, interruptions, attachments, and detachments, there was no end to the dilemma and angst that Martin knew in groups of kids. It was as complex and minutely parsed as if he analyzed what it feels like to be one molecule of oxygen in a flask of chemical reactions—pushed and pulled in every direction. By testing his hypotheses out on me, Martin found he could make clearer decisions socially—to each of which he applied trial and error. His highly invested efforts at group dynamics pushed Martin to come to terms with his true feelings. How do you treat someone you like or don't like? Martin had been so preoccupied—nay, overwhelmed—with what he should be doing that he'd paid little attention to what he really felt. He came to see that his authentic sense of other people carried weight and worth central to how he should interact socially. What he felt and wanted mattered.

Martin had a highly developed moral character that could clash with his wishes for a girlfriend, his growing interest and curiosity in sex, and his discomfort with anything impure. This was a big obstacle when it came to middle school life, for so much of the banter and humor involved bathroom and bedroom jokes, the "cheap laughs" that Martin put down. "I can't help it if it isn't my thing." "Of course you can't," I affirmed. "You've got to be you."

At first, Martin could not even repeat the jokes that had bothered him. Over time, he would, and we'd find out what exactly caused him such distress. He learned that he was a "prude" and that some of his mightier-than-thou morality came as a compensation for his wish to be more virile, robust, and earthy. Witnessing a "delicate and poetic" girl he liked chumming it up with a boy who was telling her "dirty" jokes ignited Martin to get over his "fear of fun." He got to the point where he could listen to such humor without disgust and occasionally with a chuckle. He once tried telling me such a joke, but it was a mess, and we both agreed that it was possible to have a social life without becoming an off-color comedian.

Martin used therapy and me to figure out ways to be with girls, especially girls he liked. He never wanted to repeat past episodes in which, for example, he'd written a note to a girl praising how "nice and bouncy" she looked. He had suffered enough humiliation at school dances and such to last several lifetimes. While girls attracted him physically, Martin dearly wished for a deep relationship full of friendship, love, and understanding—everything that a human wants and that can be so unavailable in the social world of a child with Asperger's. I saw my role as therapist to help Martin learn as much as he could about himself so as to facilitate his finding connections with both friends and romantic interests. How could I not support Martin's wish for love?

How did I do it? I listened a lot to what Martin said and experienced. I helped him to clarify what he saw in a girl and what he might feel about her. For example, I'd listen when he'd tell me how much he loved a girl that he barely knew. However, I'd speak up when he talked of taking a bold and unusual move in her direction.

"How long have you known her, Martin?" I asked.

"Not long, but I know she's just wonderful." I said nothing. "I know what you're thinking. You're thinking I don't even know her," he said.

"I'm thinking that's a big step to take with even a girl you know well," I said.

Martin wanted and benefited from the same kind and patient counsel that any teen can use. He often used my views to alter his actions and would thank me days later after he'd saved himself a heap of red face or backtracking. Martin valued that I took his noble pursuit of love seriously, for that meant I took him seriously. Our sharing helped him to grow less immature and embarrassed over his longings. His previously hidden interests and fantasies could now come into the light during therapy, eradicating the potential for shame and making good decisions more likely. Life and love are full of missteps, for sure. But it's never a bad thing if the child with Asperger's can avoid a fair share of them.

During his therapy, Martin taught me more than any graduate course on psychotherapy, with or without Asperger's. Since that time, Martin taught me something else. Anticipating a tough year in high school and struggling with the increasing demand of schoolwork, Martin chose to end his therapy. For him to assert himself in this way was itself a testimony to his growth. He lives an hour and a half from me now, and among a whole slew of reasons, he no longer wished to devote a good half-day to coming to my office. He also wanted to try it on his own. And why shouldn't a growing teenager who has already put in a yeoman's lot of therapeutic work feel that way? Last, he just recently asked to try a local therapist who specializes in cognitive-behavioral treatment and to see a psychiatrist to be reassessed for medication, something that he had done before and then given up on. His mother reports with pride that in his first sessions with each of those professionals, Martin showed all of the maturity and self-awareness that he had accomplished, in and out of therapy with me. He is now highly motivated and capable, I suspect, of using whatever kinds of help and therapy he chooses.

THERAPY AND FRIENDSHIPS

Children and teens with Asperger's have varying degrees of social difficulty. Because one's social and friendship worlds hold such significant and multilayered relevance and impact, we need to offer the child every form of assistance that can possibly help. Some of these interventions by their very nature seem more certain in their value.

For example, it's hard to imagine how therapeutic groups in which children with Asperger's learn to better communicate, play, and coexist with other children can be anything less than useful. Though social skills treatment is seen as an essential intervention and is prescribed as evidence based, the experimental results have been inconclusive, with some question as to how much learning is generalized (Elder, Caterino, Chao, Shacknai, & DeSimone, 2006). My clinical experience tells me that these children can take much of what they learn—in any caring and attentive context—and run with it, especially when they are motivated to improve their social lives, something probably more common in teens and older children (Attwood, 2000).

The field of *socio-* or *semantic pragmatics* focuses specifically on teaching these children context, content, and processing. It rightly sees the child's social difficulties as a learning disability, not unlike one a child might have for math or reading. The goal of this method is to enable these children to compensate for, catch up with, and even master learning concepts and strategies in social understanding and practice that their Asperger's precludes. (Some children have complained to me that learning scripts lacks relevance when practicing socially with peers that they don't feel a particular connection with, suggesting that the group composition likely plays a factor in its success.) I am ever happy when a child I see participates in such groups, especially when they wish to (though children are not always the best judges of what they developmentally need), just as I am when they are enrolled in therapeutic group activities, such as gymnastics or play groups, where the children are helped to manage peer relations, especially around cooperation, competition, and conflict.

Likewise, several children I've treated have simultaneously or later gone on to cognitive-behavioral treatments that focus on social issues and social anxiety. These treatments, in both individual and group settings, have been extremely helpful—again, especially with motivated teenagers who have gotten to where they can pretty much state that they are sick and tired of living like this and are not going to take it anymore. Over the years, impressed by what I have seen and heard, I have both knowingly and unknowingly incorporated more aspects of cognitive-behavioral treatment into my broader version of relationship-based treatment.

Medication also has increasingly proven to be an invaluable part of the treatment plan. Medication can open a huge window of sunlight and possibility on a childhood and adolescence that has been hindered and tortured by social anxiety and perhaps associated depression. The lifting of inhibitions and newfound courage that follows can reverse chronic and destructive feelings of helplessness, hopelessness, and failure.

That individual therapy in the larger sense also has much to offer the child and teen *socially* may seem an oxymoron. How can working with one adult possibly help a child get along better with children? As I did with Martin, therapists can help the child to think, problem solve, and make better decisions. We can help the child to test reality and to role play, supplying an in vivo laboratory in which to experiment with new ways of gesturing, gazing, talking, and communicating. We can slow the child down and help her see what she is not noticing.

But there are yet other meaningful and effective ways in which this kind of therapy can help the child and teen grow socially, as Judy Ann and Martin demonstrated. To best understand this concept, consider this wise, big, and beautifully put view as to the value of friendship to a child (as if spoken to a parent):

> If you look very closely at one of your children when he finally finds a chum . . . you will discover something very different in the relationship—namely that your child begins to develop a real sensitivity to what matters to another person. And this is not in the sense of "what should I do to get what I want," but instead "what should I do to contribute to the happiness and to support the prestige and feelings of worth-whileness of my chum?"
>
> (Sullivan, 1953, pp. 245–246)

By serving as a child's friend in its deepest and richest sense, the therapist offers a safe and accepting relationship and environment in which to explore and experiment. We as human others provide the child with a real person with real feelings with whom they can learn what they feel and do, just as they watch and learn what we feel and do. The dyad between child and therapist becomes a vital template for growing more connected and communicative, skills and relations that will become part of the child's insides and that he will take with him to all other relationships. There may be some question about how many cognitive social lessons are generalized. There is no question that the lessons of interpersonal dynamics, felt deeply and immediately—experienced affectively at the same moment that they're processed intellectually—grow more internalized and natural. Just as with the nonautistic children I see, the cutting edge of closeness that the child establishes with me is near always followed by correspondingly stronger trust and investment in other people outside of the therapy room.

By helping children to see, understand, and feel more clearly their relationship with peers, along with that trial and error we saw Martin employ, they come to be more eager and competent participants in a potential friendship. Research has shown that, *one best friend* counters loneliness and depression more than sheer popularity can, not just in childhood (Parker & Asher, 1993; Schneider, 2000) but over a lifespan (Hartup & Stevens, 1999), and that the varying states of that friendship can raise and lower a child's esteem (Keefe & Berndt, 1996). Research further demonstrates that preadolescents and adolescents with Asperger's themselves recognize that having one good friendship can protect them against loneliness in a way that having lots of superficial friends cannot (Bauminger, Shulman, & Agam, 2003).

These critical findings compel us as therapists to ever bolster the child's own best efforts at finding, making, and *keeping* good friends. Popularity is not the goal. To that purpose, I take an active interest in following how a child's friendships are going, not like a meddling or monitoring adult but as one who cares about how it is going from the child's point of view. Again, heeding this research, we help the parents keep in mind, too, that the goal is not for a child to become class president or a social butterfly. The goal is not to be more popular but to help children with Asperger's connect with other children with whom they can resonate, enjoy, learn, and do all that nourishing business that friends do with each other.

By getting to know and helping the child to know who she is, we help her to develop a firm identity based on her authentic being. Martin feared that going for friends might require his giving up who he was. That is a worthy worry and one that I take to heart. Carrington, Templeton, and Papincazak (2003) have alerted us that under the pressure to be accepted and nonspecial (in the school and education sense of the word), children with Asperger's can *masquerade,* "pretending" or portraying themselves to be in image something they are not (p. 216). Adults with Asperger's have told us their own heartbreaking renditions of having done the same for much of their lifetimes, adding the happy ending of their finally accepting who they are more fully and freely (Willey, 1999). Their telling lessons are not lost on us. As Frith (1991) poignantly asked (about the child's purposeful efforts to appear typical), "Just how high is the cost, and how much effort is being spent in keeping up appearances?" (p. 22). Even as we nudge the child toward connection to others, *we nurture and preserve her connection to herself.* For without the latter, the former is of little value.

This issue of authenticity reminds us to heed the child's own judgments and wishes, especially when it comes to the social lives of older children and teenagers with Asperger's. We and parents may think we know who their friends should be; maybe, maybe not. Children often know who their souls click with and that kind of thing. It's also consoling to hear that research has found that children with Asperger's profit both from having nonautistic peers as well as those with similar difficulties (Bauminger et al., 2008; Bauminger, Shulman, & Agam, 2003; Solomon, Goodlin-Jones, & Anders, 2004). We don't have to argue for all of one or the other. We remember that whether talking interventions or daily life, for adolescents, "activities with friends are an important part of the daily lives of children" (Mathur & Berndt, 2006, p. 365). Sharing sports, school clubs, volunteer work, skateboarding, or even media like music and video games are all good when it comes to facilitating friendships and can sometimes be a sidetrack toward socializing and maybe a friendship. This research suggests that the type of activity does not matter, meaning that we can try to meet the child where she is, helping her to take the social risk of pursuing her genuine interests (though we, like their parents, also nudge her to try seeing what other kids enjoy, too).

Just as we exploit the child's true interests when it comes to fostering her social skills, we also make the most use of her intellect. We've always known that children with Asperger's can have considerable social interests. They also can have some understanding of friendship (Bauminger, Shulman, & Agam, 2003; Carrington, Templeton, & Papincazak, 2003) that while generally not as full or as strong as their nonautistic peers offers the child and therapist a relatively advanced place from which to build. Most intriguingly, Bauminger, Shulman, and Agam (2003) found in a natural school setting—with "normal," low-functioning, and high-functioning peers—that the higher-functioning children with Asperger's initiated more social interactions that included eye contact, smiling, and social communication. There were for that group, however, fewer social behaviors *to maintain* an interaction. It wasn't clear whether that was due to the children with Asperger's lacking knowledge or motivation to keep their socializing up or alternatively due to the nonautistic children's lack of responding to them. These findings well inform socially directed interventions (e.g., groups and semantic pragmatics), especially when the analysis can occur immediately beside the actual interaction. Individual therapy, however, can offer the child a sense of safety, trust, and connection that may invite self-discovery on these matters to complement those in group-oriented interventions. The therapeutic relationship offers the child "a secure base" from which to safely "observe the world," that "experience of [her] own position in the world [being] the point of departure for [her] being able to see how other people move in relation to one another and toward [herself]" (Blomberg, 2005, p. 41).

Because children with Asperger's use their intellectual gifts to compensate for their social deficits (Kasari, Chamberlain, & Bauminger, 2001), their individual therapists can help them, in depth and breadth, to better understand and promote those adaptive efforts. I've found that children with Asperger's are adept at learning about social situations and experience and how to deal with them by self-study. For example, Judy Ann studied her *Beacon Street Girls* books, partly, it seemed, to learn about what girls her age feel and do socially. Likewise, Martin learned a lot when watching good television shows and movies that featured the social (and love) lives of teenagers. I've worked with many other children with Asperger's who have felt they get a lot from good children and young adult novels and from adult nonfiction and self-help books. Whatever the form and format of the intervention, it seems that employing the child's intellectual and verbal strengths should be a golden rule. Way back in 1944, Hans Asperger wrote that clinicians can be sure that each child will present "full of surprising contradictions which [can] make social adaptation extremely hard to achieve" (p. 83). The children with Asperger's I have personally known have taught me, however, that it is achievable.

BULLIES AND MEAN GIRLS

As most clinicians, educators, and parents recognize, bullying and peer victimization can wreak serious emotional and behavioral damage (Juvonen, Graham, & Schuster, 2003), contributing even to suicide (Kim, Koh, & Leventhal, 2005). Research finds just what we would expect—that the social difficulties of children with Asperger's make them more vulnerable to social bullying and its effects (Shtayermman, 2007), with more than 90 percent of mothers reporting that their children and teens with Asperger's were teased or bullied (Little, 2002). Most every child and teen with Asperger's that I've known has described various degrees of having been bullied, put down, humiliated, estranged, and shunned.

Like much else that I address in therapy, with or without Asperger's, I seek to flesh out exactly what is happening for children in terms of their experience. Some children can tell me; others cannot, and I must look to teachers and parents to fill in the blanks. Of course, I want to hear how bad it is from all sources. I tend to probe, to ask more for the specifics rather than depend on sweeping judgments as to how severe or negligible the bullying or teasing has been. *Where does it happen? How often? With whom—the same kid(s) or different? How does my client deal with it—does she try to defend herself, does she look to peers for help, does she run to school staff?* And equally critical, I ask of adults, *what, in your opinion, does the child do, if anything, to contribute to his being mistreated?* Sometimes it is black and white. A child who ever minds his own business is bullied by a jerk who picks on anybody weaker or more vulnerable. More often, teachers and parents paint a muddier picture in which all agents bear some responsibility.

As with any other matter in therapy, I try to address this on many levels. I urge and support the school in monitoring the situation so as to get a better handle on what is going on. (Usually, in our first discussions, school staff will tell me that so much is going on at the playground that the details are not apparent.) Our talking tends to bring greater awareness on the part of school staff, and that alone can lead to more responsive intervening that helps to cut down on the problem itself. I also encourage school staff to be open with me about the ways that they think my child client is provoking other children. Being kind and caring people, teachers are sometimes reluctant to tell me, feeling that they are being critical or unfair to a "handicapped" child. Through a casual attitude, my own candor, and humor, I quickly make clear that such revelations are invaluable to my helping the child get through these social mishaps more quickly. Supporting the school's assessment of what is going on with the child's being bullied also will serve as a baseline of data that they and I can refer to as the situation changes, helping us to fine-tune the child's growth.

With parents, I urge them to do the same. I ask them to ferret out the details when they see their child being teased, or in fact, when they hear about it secondhand. We problem solve ways that they can be better listeners or can help the child to advance in his social interacting. I also regularly ask parents to inform me on the child's relationships with siblings, for those can serve as models of relating, for better or worse, that the child brings to school and the playground. I've found therapeutic efforts that enhance the child's social success at home, especially with siblings, can also enhance it at school. So, I sometimes meet with the child and his siblings.

I try to help children help me to suss out the many components of their being bullied. Foremost, I aspire to empathize with their experience, sharing what it feels like and means to the child. I continually let them know that there are things that can be done to make the situation better—by me, school staff, and the children themselves. I educate children on aspects of friendship and bullying, helping him to better grasp what is going on in the social context. I watch for signs of unjustified self-blame or that somehow reflect the children's sense that they deserve to be mistreated by peers.

Conversely, while attending to the ever wrongness of bullying, I gently herd children toward seeing what they might be adding to the mix. For example, some children with Asperger's do anything they can to provoke reactions and garner attention. I've found that with such children, helping them to socially tone down their act (and learn ways of earning good attention) can do more than any intervening outside the treatment office. I also try to empower children to be their own best advocates when possible, either by helping to prepare their working it out with the bully or by assisting their best attempts at enlisting the aid of school staff. For many children with Asperger's, this can involve a labored examination of how constructively using adults in one's environment differs from being a tattletale or playing school-yard cop.

Though we often work directly on the problem of bullying, we can also help children work on it indirectly. Every intervention that enhances communication, self-understanding, and so on decreases the likelihood that they will become social victims. Any interventions that help them acquire and maintain a best friend, in particular, can lower the chances for social mistreatment. Any endeavors that lend them competency (in sports, music, art, martial arts, even video games) can foster self-esteem and confidence, raise their social standing, and beef up their immunity to teasing and bullying. Attwood wisely reminds therapists (and parents) that "changing schools [or environments] may have little effect on reducing the likelihood that a child will be a target of teasing and bullying" (2007, p. 111). My experience has shown me that even in cases where bullying is so extreme as to need grown-ups to step in and stop it, it is worth our pushing children to use therapy to better see, understand, and manage the ways that their beings and behaviors impact others. And though it may sound trivial, I also work to help them see ways in which practicing better hygiene, not cutting their own hair, wearing up-to-date clothes, and such might help them to fit in better. (Readers wanting more on this topic are referred to Attwood's chapter on teasing and bullying [2007], Iland's chapter on friendships and bullying in girls with Asperger's [2006], and Dubin and Carley's book on Asperger's and bullying [2007].)

10

Theory of Mind and Other So-Called Impediments to Therapy

A good number of children with Asperger's can use and profit from talk and play therapy. That, you know, is my belief and the leitmotif of this book. I hope that by now, the children and teenagers you've met have begun to draw you to this perspective or perhaps have further cemented your own similar view. Now, above all, is the best time to take on the most basic controversies when it comes to the treatment of children with Asperger's—particularly, the long-held and can I say mythical tenet that they are incapable of psychotherapeutic work and progress that's based on concepts such as relationship, affect, inner worlds, creative play, interpersonal understanding, empathy, and so forth. The research and learned opinions and judgments to that effect are addressed in this chapter.

However, the most illustrative route to fleshing out these concepts and dilemmas implied, I think, is to share a long-term therapy case in detail that touches on most every relevant piece of Asperger's and therapy through the most amazing work and being of a real child who effectively used therapy to go from a disorganized child to an accomplishing adolescent to a self-sufficient adult. The child and therapy speak for themselves, and then I take over, placing this clinical work into (and beside) the existing literature.

THE THERAPY

Timothy was referred to me while I was a predoctoral student in a psychology internship at the Massachusetts Mental Health Center, a Harvard Medical School training site for social workers, psychiatrists, and psychologists. As part of his transitioning from a therapeutic day program to a public school special education classroom, Timothy was assigned to me as an outpatient case. He had originally been referred for severe social avoidance and difficulties, extremely odd and sparse language, perpetual autistic motor movements, and an inability to tolerate frustration of most any source. Above all else, it was Timothy's aggressive and sexualized outbursts that precipitated his coming to our hospital-based day program for children.

Timothy was born from an uneventful pregnancy (Apgar of 10), and there were no psychological or medical issues in his infancy or early childhood. His kindly and devoted mother reported that Timothy, their only child, had never shown an interest in her affection or attention. Although developmental milestones, as then assessed, were grossly intact and attained on time, his innate inclination to not respond to people only grew more visible and obstructive. By the age of 3, Timothy showed all of the signs of autism: peculiar speech, odd movements and mannerisms, an insistence on sameness, lack of eye contact, poor visuomotor skills, an inability to express himself—especially feelings—and great distractibility.

A psychoeducational testing done just when he turned 6 had revealed remarkably variable skills, with his overall functioning at the 37th percentile and some individual skills at the borderline level. The tester saw the assessment as validly reflecting his current state of functioning. Given how untestable she found Timothy, she qualified her results as a probable underestimate to an unknown degree of what he might intellectually be capable of. By the time Timothy got to me, he had been evaluated by some of the most prominent child clinicians in Boston and had been definitively diagnosed with Infantile Autism. These evaluators judged Timothy as too inaccessible and uncommunicative for psychotherapy to be of help. They consistently recommended that his parents seek residential treatment, predicting without doubt that Timothy would never ride a bike or succeed in school, never have social connections, and never acquire any kind of independent skills, such that he would need to be sheltered and cared for by others the rest of his life.

These authorities gave their pronouncements, I imagine, out of their sense of professional caring and responsibility. Parents with such a disabled child, I suspect they would have said, needed to face and come to terms with the reality of their child's diagnosis and prognosis. However crushed they felt, Timothy's mother and father refused to accept this discouraging news for their one and only child. "Maybe we're in denial," his mother told me, "but we're going to keep believing that Timothy can have a life like every other child."

The First Year

Upon our meeting, I couldn't avoid seeing Timothy's autism. He spun his body and flapped his hands excitedly while walking on his toes and never looking at me. I said hello and started to tell him who I was. Timothy covered his ears and hummed loudly. I stopped talking. Timothy ran to the far corner of my office and crouched behind a chair. He smelled the chair and every toy and object he could reach from there. Whenever I spoke, he shut me out. Given how extraordinarily stressed his meeting me appeared to be, I ended our first several meetings after 15 minutes or so. Given how slow the treatment was heading to be, my supervisor, a senior psychiatrist, suggested that I meet with Timothy twice weekly. His parents were thrilled that I felt hopeful enough to recommend such a commitment.

Timothy spent many hours playing a simple board game in which horses raced around a track. He seldom bothered to throw the dice. He just kept the horses running and running, his activity driven and with no sign that it brought him any pleasure. Though he wouldn't look at me, he watched me closely when I looked elsewhere (which I tried to ever do). With the same ear covering and humming, Timothy rejected all of my remarks—remarks that asked him about his feelings, interests, and being with me. But when I lowered my sights, something else occurred.

> "You are smelling the game," I took the risk of noting. Timothy looked panicked. He ran his horses faster and faster about the oval while he studied my grabbing a dog puppet. I put the puppet's nose to the board and sniffed loudly.

"You smell stuff," Timothy said to the dog.

"Yes, I do smell stuff," my puppet replied.

Weeks later, I told Timothy that my dog puppet smelled the world to learn more about it. Timothy replied that he, too, "smells the things that happen" to him. He eventually used his own puppet that he spontaneously grabbed after I had set a limit on his spitting. "Please shut up!" he yelled, in a little, strained, and frightened voice, giving notice that he could take in, process, and respond to what I was saying and doing, albeit more slowly and unusually than might most other children in therapy.

For months, Timothy lived in that corner of the room. I stayed put, occasionally observing aloud that he played in his "own corner of the room." Timothy's lack of strong reaction told me, I thought, that what I had said was both tolerable and had hit home. Over many months, this play evolved to where we each had a house, bordered by a wall of cardboard bricks that we religiously stayed behind. Gradually and on his own, Timothy built himself a mailbox and instructed me to build myself one. His checking for mail told me to send him a letter. I would send simple messages.

"It is raining outside," I wrote.

"Yes, it is raining," Timothy wrote back.

"Rain is wet," I wrote.

"How do you know it is raining?" Timothy wrote.

"I see it out the window."

"How do you know rain is wet?"

"Because I have felt rain on my hands," I wrote.

"And you wrote me to tell me it is raining," Timothy replied.

"Yes, I wrote you to tell you that."

While this communication might appear barren or simple, what it meant to Timothy, I believe, is attested to by the dozens and dozens of such letters I have saved in his record; letters scrawled in large and awkward writing—written on pink slips, phone book pages, construction paper, and take-out menus—every one signed "Timothy." Soon, in Timothy time, he gave us telephones, too. Our calls went much like our correspondence. As long as I kept it concrete and impersonal, he stayed on the line. If I strayed and implied a feeling, he would slam the phone down or feign an operator's voice saying, "The line has been disconnected."

Timothy extended his play to the puppets. At first, he smelled and rubbed and licked them, but then he put them on his hands and made them talk to my puppets. He employed a vast cast of puppet characters that kept him at a safe distance from me and my dog puppet. He might have a cow tell a dragon to ask a lion to write a letter to my dog—which he would actually do on his lion's behalf. If I dared to cut through this protocol and responded directly to the cow, Timothy would angrily pull his puppets back to his lap and not make further contact with me for many minutes or until the next hour. "My dog was supposed to write lion back. Not cow," I wrote. "Yes, he was," Timothy wrote back.

Timothy formed a strong relationship with my puppet whom I named *Schnauzer,* a basset hound with a Sherlock Holmes deerstalker cap, the only puppet that I ever would use with Timothy over many years. He would write to Schnauzer, call him, and even come to visit him. Timothy seemed to believe that my dog puppet lived apart from me, as when asking it to guess behind which door a prize was hidden. My asking Timothy if he wanted me to guess right or wrong invoked his sadly and angrily attacking my stupid question, for, he said, Schnauzer knew how to make his own guesses.

In spite of his long and well-documented lack of interest in people, Timothy wanted more and more of me—extra time, extra sessions, gifts, snacks, and on rare occasions, affection. He would lose himself patting Schnauzer's fur for several minutes. When his baby cow puppet wrote me a love letter, I wrote back:

"Dear Baby Cow,

I wonder if the letter you want is Dear Baby Cow, I love you. Is that the letter you want?" (Bromfield, 1989, p. 443)

Tim ripped the letter to shreds and withdrew until, many minutes later, he re-wrote my letter verbatim, crossing out the words to create the letter he'd desired from me, a simple "I love you."

Timothy's attachment for me was evident in so many other ways, too. With a pained look, at the end of every hour he would watch the clock tick to the final minute; then he would run from the office at full speed without a goodbye. He drew his feelings about the clock with faces that were happy (at onset), worried (in the middle), sad and angry (toward the end), and distorted and fragmented (for the final minute). His odd comment that "Japan blew up" and that he "hates Japan" baffled me, until one day, noticing him staring at my digital clock, I saw a "Japan" label (signifying where the clock was manufactured) stuck to the rotating "50," the number that reliably told Timothy that the end of his hour was near.

The theme of television game shows preoccupied the final months of Timothy's first year with me. His play consisted mostly of his making books that listed facts about actual game shows that he and his parents liked to watch together. My attempts to nudge this play outward (to other children or people) or inward (to what he felt) went nowhere. "Just answer the question," he as show host would state over and over with varying degrees of annoyance and anxiety. The actual death of a game show host that he liked brought an unexpected show of grief. Pretending to be the show's new host, Timothy revealed that audience members felt that the dead host was "mean" for abandoning the loyal viewers he was expected to visit in their homes every week at "the same time on the same channel." Once, when not knowing that I was in the office already, I overheard Timothy in the waiting room: "Wherever could he be . . . he knows I am here waiting . . . this worries me . . . it does" (Bromfield, 1989, p. 446).

Throughout that year, autistic features were ever present. Timothy's eye contact was fleeting. He occasionally stared at me longingly, then would turn away quickly, once stating that my eyes "hurt" his eyes. When so much as a pencil moved, Timothy tried to restore the sameness. "Why did the pencil move?" he would ask sadly. "You want everything to stay the same?" I would ask gently. Timothy would nod his head that he did. My occasional momentary lateness caused Timothy to be sad and, unable to confront me, to ask what was wrong with the clocks. Timothy talked more, though he seldom directly expressed feeling states. When stressed by apparent feeling, Timothy would look more autistic, twisting his body, his shoulder dipping down to then ascend in a fast swoop toward the ceiling, as if the momentum might help him to get the stammering words out. He often echoed what he said many times until it faded out, and he typically referred to himself in the third person: "Timothy is hungry, he is."

The end of my internship year meant that Timothy couldn't continue seeing me (until I got licensed, which was a year off). Learning that we would be ending, Timothy withdrew. He had taken his puppets into a cupboard where he had closed himself in. I overheard his small voice comforting all the other friends who I learned were sad, scared, and already missing me. "Don't be afraid, Wolfie. We have each other," he said. For several weeks prior to our stopping, Timothy spent his hours replicating scripts from *Mr. Rogers' Neighborhood.* "Mr. Rogers is there every day," Timothy said. "He *never* goes away?" I asked. "No, never. Just never," Timothy answered.

Timothy's first year of therapy pleased me and persuaded me that talk and play could indeed help. It had helped Timothy to accomplish more than anything else had to that point. But the gains were not just in my office and by my eyes and ears. Timothy's parents and school staff saw gains of their own. He had stopped hitting and biting other children. He was using his words more to seek the teacher's assistance when confused or overwhelmed. His parents said he had become less oppositional at home and would sometimes take pride in being cooperative or doing as they asked him to. Both his parents and school personnel reported that they liked him better and felt more able to reach him at times. His mother especially enjoyed that he now occasionally gave her a real hug. Stereotypical motor behaviors, while still apparent under stress, were markedly reduced also, as was his ability to bear more of the frustration that could fill his school days. Last, an extensive neuropsychological evaluation conducted several months later found him much more testable and at the 65th percentile, much up from his testing a year and a half or so earlier.

The Middle Years

About a year later, Timothy's mother contacted me, asking that he and I resume weekly therapy as soon as I legally was allowed to do so. His interim therapist, a skilled and compassionate trainee named Mark, filled me in that Timothy had had another good year. He had missed me, and upon learning that we would be restarting, I was told he had been reenacting scenes from *Star Wars* in which Han Solo was defrosted to return to the crew. In Timothy's play, this unsettled the crew, who didn't know how it would go, whether he would still like them and whether they would like him. "Sounds like Timothy's worried about his coming back to see you," Mark wisely observed.

As soon as Timothy resumed therapy with me, he set to work on a sequence of play that lasted for about 14 months (*not a typo—14!*). He spent weeks and weeks drawing maps of Boston's Orange Line, the subway line that ran to his house and that was being replaced by a new, slightly displaced line. Each map grew slightly neater and tighter or more informative. While he drew, Timothy spoke mostly just to question me about facts concerning the new line. My right answers delighted him, and my wrong ones led to angry withdrawal. He drew new and larger maps on which he placed the old and new Orange Lines beside each other, showing how each old station corresponded to a new one.

Many months down the road, Timothy began playing this subway dilemma out. He drew and colored complex subway car dashboards with speedometers, emergency buttons, and many other squares labeled things like "coupler," "pan up," "left doors," "horn 2," and "propulsion reset"— controls that I assumed bore some resemblance to what he'd see on the subway that he rode daily. He built stations that Schnauzer and his puppets would stand in to wait for the subway. Timothy directed all of the puppets to anguish over having to choose which line they wanted to ride—the old line or the new one. His eyes would well up as his puppets deliberated over which line to take. Occasionally, overwhelmed with this impossible decision, Timothy's puppets would miss the train going by or would choose instead to walk miles downtown. "What a horrible choice to have to make," I noted. Timothy agreed sadly as he spoke of the puppets' enthusiasm for a new line and their sad guilt over and disloyalty for forsaking the old line. He built bridges and tunnels to connect the two lines, and for a while, his puppets thoroughly enjoyed his play city's plan to maintain a double Orange Line. Reading an article in the *Globe* that spoke of Bostonians' nostalgia for the old Orange Line, Timothy confirmed that he knew just what they felt. "I wonder if he knows about the new Orange Line." "You wonder if Mark knows?" I asked, hearing Timothy mention the name of his last and beloved therapist. "Yes," Timothy affirmed in a shaky voice.

Timothy had spent *all that time* dealing with the loss and grief of having me return and losing Mark. He spent many more months playing and talking more directly about my having left in the first place. Though he intellectually knew the reasons, he wondered why he had been left by me, what I'd done in the meantime, what children I'd seen, and whether I liked them. "Do you still love me?" Timothy wrote in a letter after 3 years of meeting with me. "We missed each other so much," I wrote back. Timothy nodded as he rubbed his eyes and lowered his head to the desk.

For the next couple of years, Timothy's therapy focused on games and play that involved much more connection and communication with me. He would hide puppets, and I would find them. Each week, the play grew slightly more complex and personal, until he hid himself and asked me to find him. "There you are!" I would exclaim, like a parent finding a toddler. "Here I am!" Timothy would yell. "You found me!" Germane to this play, which could transpire as fast as grass growing, Timothy came into closer contact with me and his feelings. He would later talk of being sad when I couldn't find him or worried where I could be. Though he found himself wanting to be nearer to me more often and wanting more communication, he still often made his need for aloneness perfectly clear. When, for example, Timothy would spend 30 minutes making a form for our games, I let him, staying put where he had left me, keeping my words to myself until it was evident that he wanted me to approach. His joyous exclamation one session upon my finding him said it all: "You let me hide from you, and I like that!" That my smiling acknowledgment led to him spontaneously giving me one of the real hugs that his parents had grown to enjoy only underscored what was true gratitude for my having respected his space.

Timothy's growing motivation and capacity for human connection and all that it brought along, while welcome in itself, created other sorts of therapeutic opportunities and advantages. His growing sense of safety, trust, and openness with me gave me increasing leverage to confront him around problems in his life, as well as problem behaviors. When the school informed me that he had a run-in with a teacher or another child, he would listen to what I had heard and would help me to help him figure out a solution. Though he ever wished to get back to his play, he would let me educate him to a bigger perspective and engage in my attempts to show him alternative behaviors or strategies or elicit his doing the same for himself. "Timothy, what can a boy do when other boys are calling him queer?" I asked. This problem solving and education would go in stops and starts; but it went, and it would go better each time.

While his play and our work proceeded at a snail's pace, the steps ahead were ever clear and apparent. He came to be able, when necessary, to step outside of his lengthy and detailed playing to address more straight-ahead upset, as when he missed a teacher who retired or when his parents were ill. Timothy much loved, needed, and worried over the grown-ups in his life, who previously had not always known what they meant to him—at least, not from the way he held back and seemed at times not to care. Timothy cared a lot, and that was growing more evident to all of the people in his life, at home and school.

Though our play may not have suggested what was happening, Timothy's relationships outside of therapy grew. He was participating in Scouts and some sports activities. His aggression had disappeared. His oddities still got in the way greatly with his socializing, and though he had no best friends, he did have kids that he liked to be around. He seldom got into behavioral trouble at school—at least, not the kind that he used to. And he continued to value therapy and his relationship with me. Academically, despite learning issues, his keen intellect was growing more apparent. Even as they dealt with his deficits, teachers were giving him other kinds of work to stimulate and challenge his greater gifts in thinking and reasoning.

We had in no way arrived where we needed to go. Timothy still required much scaffolding and assistance, not to mention patience and prodding, to get his work done, whether in the school setting or when doing homework in his kitchen. He was far from fulfilling his intellectual potential. He was often distracted by his many obsessive interests, such as television and baseball statistics, and he still spoke and looked quite odd, especially under stress. He remained much alone in his life outside of school and had a hard time joining in with group activities. For all of his considerable advances in communication, attachment, and vitality—nothing to sneeze at—the possibility of his one day living independently remained a distant dream.

The Teen Years

The beginning of Timothy's therapy as a teen looked much like that before. He again played out game shows, only this time game shows for children and teens, replicating their scripts almost verbatim. He was having an extremely difficult time of it at a rough inner-city junior high school, but for some time, he could not talk with me about it. He instead escaped into the comfort of his play in which he could count on not being hurt or interfered with. But gradually and with much greater acceleration than his prior therapy, Timothy came to use me differently. He enlisted me much more as another person with whom to cooperate, collaborate, and negotiate conflict. He would assign me tasks to help get the game going. At other times, he and I worked together to make intricate game sheets, and we even occasionally debated our opposing views on how to best play the game. "That's what makes us friends," Timothy observed proudly and accurately with a handshake after we had worked out one such disagreement.

In a couple of months, compared to what would have once taken many months or years, Timothy gave up his obsessive and rote repeating of shows he had seen, instead creating variations on the theme—remarkably complex games that involved losing and finding, going away and returning, growing up and regressing back. Though real television game shows for children often inspired Timothy's own, he soon refashioned them to fit his own talents, needs, and wishes. So as to move the play along and because I and therapy were growing more part of him, Timothy started to work on this play in between sessions. He would come to therapy with a handful of well-drawn templates, often typed, for our shared consideration and editing. Refining his game and play was a constant in Timothy's therapy. Whether redrawing a sign or rewording the rules, Timothy ever applied his high intelligence to making his games play better, an effort that he and I shared great joy and pride in.

When the public school decided that Timothy's intellect required more than they could offer, he had to interview at several private schools known for educating bright children with significant developmental needs. Timothy came to his hour more distressed than I had ever seen. He had tears on his cheeks; I had never seen that. He pounded the desk and then his head, calling himself a jerk and a moron and telling himself to shut up. I asked what happened, and he explained that he had really liked a school and it was all going well—that is, until the director offered to buy him a soda. Timothy told how he had gone into a long, obsessive monologue on vending machines, a topic that had grabbed his interest years earlier. Timothy believed it would keep him out of that school, and it did. They found him "too autistic," so they said, "to handle the demands of their school."

Now, however, Timothy proved willing and able to take charge. He requested that we schedule an extra session before his next interview. On his own, he attributed his monologue to anxiety and to growing excitement that he had been doing well and was going to get a new school where he would

feel safer from bullies and where he would be more intellectually appreciated. Rather than giving my own advice, I asked Timothy what he would
have done differently. He clearly said that he would have controlled his private thoughts. "No one wants to hear me talk about vending machines," he
said, adding that if he had a chance to do it again, he would have first said,
"Thank you for the soda," and then he would have revealed to the director
that he felt a bit nervous and even excited at the prospect of being accepted.
"They can't blame a guy for that, can they?" Timothy asked. I nodded heart-
ily that he was right.

Timothy came to the next hour bragging about how well his second
interview went. He told me how they complimented his listening and how,
when they gave him a drink, he not only said thanks but added, "That sure
hit the spot." He soon after was accepted into this fine program located outside of Boston in a rural setting.

Timothy made a good transition to this new school. As he had hoped, he
felt safer and better educated. Thus began a many-month sequence of playing
Wile E. Coyote who, as in the venerated cartoon, ever tries in vain to catch the
lightening-quick Roadrunner. This play was not at all ritualistic or repetitive
as his play always once was; it was full of life, humor, surprise, and real feeling.
Pretending to be Coyote, Timothy called Acme Incorporated to complain of
their always fraudulently selling him explosives (that explode only in his own
face) and so forth, leading to actual discussions about Timothy's fears out in
the real world, such as when he bicycled along the streets or took trains to see
the Red Sox or Celtics play. He shared a colossal sense of vulnerability that led
to his constructively coming up with ways to both stay safe and live more fully.
This play reached a crescendo in a sudden and poignant play scene.

Timothy lay across a chair. He told me that he was going to play Wile E.
Coyote having a session with his therapist. Wile E. admitted his great love
for the Roadrunner that he just could never catch. With mocked tears,
Timothy as Coyote spoke of giving up the chase as a lost and unrequited
cause, pretend play that led to real tears as Timothy talked of his mother
having just gone back to school to pursue a career in education, which
meant he would be less frequently comforted, nurtured, fed, and cared for
by her. "I guess me and Wile E. have a lot in common," Timothy said, with
knowing resignation.

Timothy's therapy moved faster and faster. Months of play now took
weeks or *a week*. A real-world train accident led to overt concerns about the

safety of public transportation. The Olympics led to his playing out being a gold medalist and national hero, uncovering confessions related to his being clumsy and a poor athlete, despite his love of sports. Watching reruns of *Get Smart* revealed a crush on Agent 99 and other crushes on girls he knew. These many and assorted themes seemed to add up to something related to identity and growing up, a hunch that soon came to be unmistakable.

After a summer hiatus, Timothy returned much taller and highly discouraged. "It's just not working anymore," he complained, instructing me not to take it personally. My attempts to query angered Timothy. He warned me to back off or I would "be sorry." When I said I wasn't worried, his distress reversed direction and headed inward. "Tim began to pace feverishly, his autistic behaviors suddenly back as intense as ever. He flapped his hands and twisted his head as if to spin a body that was unwilling. Starting to whack the sides of his face, but hearing my urging to let the frustration out of his body he, in a burst, tipped over a chair, knocked a lamp to its side, and fell to the floor, crying and screaming. 'I want to be normal. I just want to be normal. I just want to be like other kids'" (Bromfield, 2000, p. 739).

Timothy eventually explained that his family had befriended another family at a vacation timeshare. This family had a son who was a class president, honor student, and varsity captain, a boy whom Timothy's parents admired and liked much. (In fact, much of what they liked was how respectfully and kindly this boy treated Timothy.) He told how he wished he could be a boy like that—a boy that everyone would love, a son that every parent wished they could have. Timothy came to his next session, acknowledging that he knew he had difficulties and limitations, but "that doesn't mean I can't live a good life," he wisely and rightly determined.

Timothy's coming into his own had taken fire. His arcane obsessions gave way to a mature interest in politics. He read the newspaper, watched C-Span, and actively learned about the government and his representatives. He applied unsuccessfully to be a high school page at the State House, taking the loss in stride, realizing that "fame, fortune, and girls" had been part of the attraction. He got a demanding job at a professional sports stadium vending refreshments, and he did it well. He became an avid cyclist who not only could ably navigate the perils of traffic but also a scary incident when some thugs stole his bike right out from under his body. He resisted his impulses to be heroic and instead sought the police, who apprehended the men and his bike unharmed. In a sure sign of maturity, Timothy spoke less of being a vigilante and more of having felt helpless and frightened. He also could see that the criminals' behavior was a referendum on their defects *and not his.*

Timothy had long given up his play with my toys. He now sat down and talked like anyone else in therapy; that is, any other teen who was capable of using therapy so well and effectively. This young man, whose parents were told that their only child would never ride a bike, explored his fears of driving, and then got his license within days of his 16th birthday; 2 years later, he got his pilot's license. Timothy took up recreational sports and joined mixed clubs of older teens and adults who shared those same games. And his schoolwork became just part of his "job as a teen," as he called it.

Since that day, Timothy—whom professionals had predicted to live a life of dependency and handicap—graduated from high school with good grades and high enough SAT scores for admission to one of the nation's top engineering schools. Now in his late twenties, he has a solid professional career, owns a home, is an active member of his community and church, is an avid sports fan, and is an engaged citizen. Once officially certified to be too autistically defective for any relationship, therapeutic or otherwise, this young man has grown into a man capable of deep and enduring emotion, attachment, concern, and meaningful existence. He's grown into a man who feels deeply for his parents, friends, and country, and a man who, just several months ago, e-mailed his former therapist (a.k.a. me) out of the blue to ask how I was doing and to just say that he was thinking of me and that he was fondly recalling the work we had done together.

SO-CALLED IMPEDIMENTS TO THERAPY

Though little has been explicitly written about the subject, a conventional belief that talk and play psychotherapy is ill suited to children with Asperger's has dominated. That belief arose primarily out of two research findings: one that found children with autism lacking a *theory of mind,* meaning an incapacity to read or understand what went on in other people and their minds (Baron-Cohen, Leslie, & Frith, 1985), and one that found children with autism lacking a capacity for fantasy, imagination, and symbolic play (Ungerer & Sigman, 1981; Wulff, 1985). "Such is the acceptance of this standpoint," it was written in 1993, "that the National Autistic Society itself cites a 'lack of creative pretend play' as one of the features characteristic of the syndrome" (Jarrold, Boucher, & Smith, 1993, p. 281), a position that has since evolved.

Pretend and Symbolic Play

My clinical work does not contradict the extensive findings that children with autism, including Asperger's, display less imaginary spontaneity and symbolic action in their play (Baron-Cohen, 1987; Harris and Leevers, 2000; Hobson, Lee, & Hobson, 2009; Lord et al., 2000; Ungerer & Sigman, 1981; Wulff, 1985); nor do I have any good reason to disbelieve the accompanying explanations that this deficit is based in neurology. *It is.* That fact, however, still begs the critical questions as to whether that deficit is an absolute and whether it's unmovable. Over and over, the children I've seen tell me that this deficit for imagination is both relative and remediable.

Timothy, for example, whose imaginative potential—until we had met, at least—was assessed and documented as nonexistent, showed me all sorts of imaginative play. It may not have looked like some other children's play, but it was pretend all the same. He knew, for example, that the subway we rode together was not the actual Orange Line, just as he knew that our play plastic telephones were not the same technology as the wired telephones in his home and just as he came to use a hammer as a phone (when his own went missing). No one can accuse him of not having put great effort, investment, attention, and so on into his play. Virtually every child with Asperger's I've known has session after session shown me a capacity to play that has in some way been imaginative.

My clinical observations do not undo the research on autism and pretend; far from it. I have not used straightforward traditional talk and play therapy as I might with other children. I have *modified* that basic frame and conception to fit the children and the strengths and weaknesses that Asperger's in large part determines. Could it be that *my modifications* wholly resonate with what the autism researchers have discovered? Though showing less spontaneous pretend play, children with autism, when prompted, eventually go on to show imaginative and symbolic play that goes beyond what they have been trained to do (Charman & Baron-Cohen, 1997; Jarrold, Boucher, & Smith, 1996; Sherratt, 2002).

"Of his own accord, [Timothy] uniquely created a world in which structure and regularity reigned, and in which communication was the prime exercise. By doing so, he spontaneously created the very environment which a more directive therapist might have designed for a child feared to be overwhelmingly lost in the open" (Bromfield, 1989, p. 452). The structure of the play that Timothy so vigorously established under my caring eye provided him with a scaffolding that would be expected to reduce his imaginative rigidity (Jarrold, 2003), and I propose that it, like some tumor-seeking radioisotope, targeted his therapeutic needs more keenly than might have a more formulaic intervention. That a nondirective play experience in itself has been shown to raise the frequency of pretend play acts (Josefi & Ryan, 2004) suggests that a therapist's fostering an accepting, safe, and open place may itself invite greater spontaneity of play and pretend.

Some researchers have dissected symbolic from functional play (Leslie, 1987; Williams, Reddy, & Costall, 2001), finding that children with autism compare favorably when it comes to the mechanics of playing, such as using a ball as a ball. In the actual world of play, however, the line between these distinctions of play grows fuzzy. What is happening when a child uses a play stethoscope as an instrument to play doctor? Likewise, what does it mean that children with autism could play by pouring a pretend fluid onto a toy dog as well as nonautistic controls (Jarrold, Smith, Boucher, & Harris, 1994)? Is there anyone who would not be impressed with Timothy's creative play in dealing with loss and reunion, which aptly sensitizes us clinicians to how difficult loss and grieving can be for the child with Asperger's (Forrester-Jones & Broadhurst, 2007; Marston & Clarke, 1999)?

It's true that Timothy's play was labored and lengthy, but then consider, does anyone care after enjoying a work of good fiction whether the author took 2 or 10 years to write it? While children with Asperger's appear to be built with less or different imaginary capacities (of biologic origin), clinical data suggests that they have plenty enough to use play therapy productively, and the best research does not contradict that. Maybe Jean-Paul Bouvee, a man diagnosed with autism as a child and now a trained historian and library scientist with Asperger's, says it best: "Imagination is something that is different in a person. For me, it was making my lists, creating genealogies of characters, planning imaginary ball games with baseball cards, creating different languages, and the list goes on (Donnelly & Bouvee, 2003, p. 476).

Feelings

The research around feelings and Asperger's has comparably found what appears to be a paucity of emotional awareness (Frith, 2004; Silani et al., 2008). And it's my experience, too, that the children I've seen generally do present with an enduring flatness. Experience has shown me, though, not to read prematurely into that appearance. While many of these children have trouble knowing and expressing what they feel, especially when compared with other children, I've found that many of them feel deeply about people, ideas, and so on that matter to them. This confirms research that's found some children with Asperger's to experience emotional extremes (Capps, Kasari, Yirmiya, & Sigman, 1993).

As with Timothy, in fact, I found one important (therapist) function to be my insulating the child against the feelings that can overly stimulate or overwhelm him. That "quiet, noninvasive posture of 'emotional reserve' seem[s] to lead to fewer and less severe periods of withdrawal" on the child's part (Bromfield, 1989, p. 449; Nagelberg & Feldman, 1953). There's no question here also that neurology is key in the basis of why affect so challenges these children. From a young age, we see that any kind of feeling—be it sadness, anger, even happiness—can overexcite and overtake these children, whose bodies and psyches cannot hold, manage, and process it. A wide array of feelings can lead such a child to the same outcome (e.g., hand flapping, tantrum, or silence). This also includes my insulating Timothy from *my feelings*. As Asperger empathically observed, the children at his clinic learned and grew best with teachers whose own emotions were kept in quiet check (1944/1991).

Just as we who do therapy see daily, researchers have shown that children with Asperger's feel and understand social emotions such as jealousy, pride, embarrassment, and guilt, though they may take longer or not be quite as expressive when articulating it (Bauminger, 2004; Bauminger, Chomsky-Smolkin, Orbach-Caspi, Zachor, & Levy-Shiff, 2008; Kasari, Chamberlain, & Bauminger, 2001). Not only are these basic social emotions felt, but they in turn ever show themselves to play powerful roles in the child's life, revealing dynamics and fallout that much resembles any other child's. To use the language of relationship-based therapy, we as therapists help the child to contain and bear overwhelming bits of affect, helping them to know and name it and then express it. By repeatedly enabling the child to take those steps, we expand the child's repertoire of emotional expression, communication, and contact. And once the child can make her feelings somehow known to us, we can show our understanding and accepting, which confirms the child's own feeling state back to herself. *I feel this, and it is part of who I am.*

Though the child's relative hardship in expressing herself emotionally and symbolically has been viewed as a reason not to attempt the play and talk of therapy, my view is that the deficit *is precisely the reason such intervening works and is called for.* That research demonstrates children with autism can use their strong verbal skills to compensate for their emotional deficits (Hermelin & O'Connor, 1985) seems only to recommend a mode of treatment such as I prescribe in which the child talks and talks about everything—in which her verbal talents are embraced, nurtured, and given full range for any growth, compensatory or primary. I have also learned the hard way that the children I see often feel things that are not at all apparent, such as the way they love to play in therapy (even if their faces do not show the same joy we think should be there). And as to the finding that children with Asperger's seem not to sense the value of knowing their own internal states (Mitchell & O'Keefe, 2008), what better way to acquire it than within a relationship with another human being, a therapist who does appreciate sharing whatever access there is to the children's thoughts and feelings?

Empathy and Theory of Mind

Closely related, and by research thinkers more basic to the deficits of Asperger's, are the issues of empathy and theory of mind. The idea that Asperger's is an indisputable disorder of neurodevelopment (Happé & Frith, 1996) brought an accompanying knowledge that such children biologically lack a basic ability to see, understand, and make sense of what goes on in another person's mind (Baron-Cohen, 1989; Frith, 2001; Frith, Happé, & Siddons, 1994). At its most extreme, the child doesn't even realize that there is another person's mind, or person, to wonder or know about. This discussion, which can get pretty heady and beyond comprehension (mine, at least) and which has many viewpoints well beyond this chapter, has involved teasing cognitive from affective empathy. One recent study found that while lacking the cognitive ability to understand another's perspective, children with Asperger's were as good as nonautistic children in emotionally resonating with another's feeling state (Rogers, Dziobek, Hassenstab, Wolf, & Convit, 2007).

My doing therapy with these children has shown me that they are capable of advancing their empathy, whatever its status when we begin treatment. This growth occurs by all of the social connecting and revealing, to me and themselves, that comes along with the therapy relationship. Empathy cannot be trained behaviorally; it has to involve feelings and caring for the other person, a person who matters deeply to the child and to whom the child feels he matters deeply in return. So-called *empathic failures* serve as the frequent therapeutic vehicles to temporary hurts, grief, and compensation.

For example, if I cut one of Timothy's monologues off abruptly, he would take understandable offense. My noting that I had cut him off and that I had hurt his feelings would confirm what he might not even have fully articulated in himself (though it had registered at some level). The Asperger's experience gives therapists an endless supply of likely places where they unintentionally (and unempathically) step on the child's feelings. My sincere acknowledgment and apology would help Timothy then to get over his hurt, by sharing and being consoled, and to move on, a bit more resilient than he had been before. These miniscule moments of failure (on the therapist's part) add up to something huge, which leads to Timothy's growing a stronger self-esteem. It also models what a person who cares about other people can do when he hurts or somehow lets them down.

And as I have hammered throughout the book, if the child with Asperger's is deprived of anything in life, it is empathy; not because his parents or teachers or others don't love him enough but because his neurological differences and behaviors can make his experiences difficult to empathize with. That is forever his problem. *But it should be ours.* Empathy doesn't equal sympathy, which is feeling sadness, concern, or pity for a child's plight. I can sympathize with a skydiver whose parachute never opened without feeling empathy for either her tragic free fall or her lifelong need for thrills. I can feel sympathetic toward a child for whom I feel little empathy or caring. And empathy is more than merely taking a child's perspective, though that can be important. Therapists' empathy can enable them to accurately sense and respond to the child's needs, whether it's for a hug or to be left alone;

whether to nudge them forward or to sit back quietly and enjoy a monologue on spiders.

As a side note, consider the research on children's abilities to read facial
expressions, again a deficit with Asperger's that appears to be neurological at
both lower brain and higher cortical levels (Ashwin, Wheelwright, & Baron-
Cohen, 2006; Critchley et al., 2000). These children, however compromised
in this basic function, can use their stronger verbal skills to compensate
and help to more ably read facial expressions (Grossman, Klin, Carter, &
Volkmar, 2000; Lindner & Rosén, 2006). In his therapy, Timothy talked
and played, exploiting his strong verbal skills to help him better understand
what went on with me emotionally—something he got better at as therapy
proceeded.

Attachment and Aloneness

If children with Asperger's have taught me one thing, it is their wish to connect and their difficulty doing so. They possess not just a wish to relate to
others; they have deep, deep needs for intimacy and love. If these children
didn't care about other people, their lives would in some ways be easier and
less tormented. They tend to eventually grow well aware of how they differ
and often experience jealousy and envy for the siblings and peers they see
daily who seem to connect with others and their own feelings as easily as
they run and breathe. By sharing a world, play space, language, and so much
else with me, Timothy came to grow more and more connected to me, and
in doing so, he grew connected to himself.

Unfortunately, others, even clinicians, are prone to misread what the
child with Asperger's is thinking, feeling, or wanting. I have supervised
trainees who nonchalantly cancel or change appointments with such a child,
believing that from the looks of it, the child will be relieved. "They hate
coming anyway," they say. Well, maybe they do. But I've found that they do
like coming. I've had such children hide my clock with draperies and try to
hide themselves so as not to have to leave their hour. I've seen several such
children with extreme deficits in language and intellect kiss my things—my
door, my desk, my toys—even as they could not show me any direct affection. Many parents have told me with some surprise that their child, the
ones who walk from the waiting room at a turtle's pace wearing a poker face,
couldn't wait to come to their session. "He woke up so early. He was worried

he'd be late!" "She kept yelling at me to go faster so she wouldn't miss any time." They may look like they don't care, but they do. They want us to be on time, to be present every hour, and to reschedule when we can't be. The advice not to take apparent "aloofness" in these children at face value is wise (Lowery, 1985).

Paradoxically, as is so true of so much that matters in personal psychology, this quest for connection often moves in seemingly contradictory directions. I speak of the wish for aloneness. I have met many children with Asperger's, especially younger ones, who come to treatment fearful and anxious. Their neurologically based deficits and immaturities leave them vulnerable in such new and foreign situations with strangers, and that is what we are, after all. What, though, does it mean to be alone in therapy?

Being alone in therapy for these children is not lonely and not bad. To be left alone under the caring, watchful, and maybe even loving eyes of the therapist can feel good—the way it can feel when we read quietly or maybe pursue a hobby while our spouse or partner does the same across the room. By staying with the child but letting her have her physical and psychic space, putting on her no demands for response or feeling, we give her the utmost respect—for herself and her Asperger's-related vulnerabilities—and all importantly, total control over the closeness (and distance) of the relationship. *To be left alone in that therapeutic sense can make a child with Asperger's feel tightly held and supremely loved,* feelings, not ironically, that will lead her to want to be closer.

But giving the child that type of aloneness isn't easy, especially for therapists who may have been attracted to psychotherapy out of an interest in human connection. Therapists can readily find the child's need for aloneness off-putting, frustrating, stressful, bewildering, boring, rejecting, and angering—and by any measure, that is a heap of hurt for any therapist to feel, manage, and sort through. To feel those ways, of course, is also very human. Therapists who have chronicled relationship-based therapies with such children all know what it feels like (Briggs, 2005; Miller, 2008; Pozzi, 2003; Ruberman, 2002). By keeping in mind that those represent our reactions and not the child's can ever help us as therapists keep clear what the child's confusing and atypical behaviors can mean. Gaining experience with these children tends to augment our database of reference, and living through each misstep and recovery gives us experience-laden knowledge on what these children need and how we can give it with less personal distress.

Therapists also get better at learning how to put the powerful feelings that are evoked in them by the children, that "intersubjective playground," to enlightening and advancing purpose—no small task, given how the Asperger's can interfere with any sense of *us*-ness (Allured, 2006).

Speaking of aloneness in therapy also harkens our attention to the child's being alone in his life outside of the consulting room. Our industrial society has had a tendency to put social connection on a pedestal. That is not to say that human connection doesn't carry the value it does; people need people. But we all need people in our own unique ways. Our goal is not to turn a child with Asperger's into either Ms. or Mr. Popularity. Our goal is to help the child be and feel capable of pursuing whatever kind of social connections he wishes for and needs. One child may need lots of friends, while a second child may be perfectly content and psychologically healthy having a couple of best friends and lots of free time spent in comforting, productive, and peaceful solitude. If, as Uta Frith urged us many years ago, we need to recognize these children's "desire to communicate and be part of the social world" (1991, p. 17), we need to equally recognize when they desire neither.

Timothy's therapy was long. With the experience and understanding I have gained in the past 25 years since first meeting him, I could have helped him to find his way faster and probably better. But our clinical lives, just as life itself, work like this. We can at any one time only do what we can do. And this, meaning the book, is not to say that all children with Asperger's and High-Functioning Autism should undergo this kind of therapy. It wouldn't fit everyone, and everyone wouldn't want it. It can, however, help some children—a lot. Additionally, its underlying principles hold relevance to all sorts of interventional contact with such children, whether therapeutic or evaluative, whether for the long or the short term.

11

Connecting It All

More than 65 years ago, Hans Asperger told us that there are children who have an unmistakably distinct, unusual, and consistent pattern of intellectual, social, and behavioral traits. With painstaking care and his own mix of worry and admiration, he described the contradictory marvels and weaknesses of these children's thinking and being. Ahead of his time, he used thorough testing to reveal their intellectual abilities, cognitive styles, and learning processes. Dr. Asperger told us definitively that this condition, which he termed "autistischen Psychopathen," is neurobiological in its essence and origins; he offered parents support, not blame. And last, he warned us that despite formidable talents and potentials, overriding social difficulties can have devastating consequences for the lives of these children.

While a growing army of stellar researchers ever add insights and details to our understanding, children with Asperger's remain vulnerable in both the short and the long term. What Szatmari said in 1991 is just as true in 2010: Asperger's "profoundly limits a child's participation in this process of growing up" (p. 91). Asperger described that "essential abnormality" as a "disturbance of the lively relationship with the whole environment" (1944/1991, p. 74). As I quoted at the start of the book (Bromfield, 1989, p. 448), "autism represents a syndrome or collection of symptoms originating primarily from a basic (and varied) neurological deficit in social and emotional processing and emotional communication, secondly from 'psychological defenses against states experienced as a result of those deficits, and [thirdly from a] lack of crucial socializing experiences during development as a result of both the deficits and the defenses'" (Bemporad, Ratey, & O'Driscoll, 1987, p. 477). How beautifully and powerfully that conception captures the child's developmental reality and challenge.

More simply put, the child with Asperger's comes into this world neurologically less fit for emotional and social processing and communicating, the primary ingredients for connecting to others—and to oneself. Coping with and compensating for those deficits creates new vulnerabilities and hurts (not unlike the way that people who walk to protect knee problems often create back and hip problems). Because of these differences, as well as due to stigma and prejudice, these children are deprived of the social experiences and interpersonal attention and validation that can fill the nonautistic child's day, thus depriving children with Asperger's of much needed opportunities to practice and get better at life and with people.

Given all this, is it any surprise that life can be so hard for these children and that they may prefer to withdraw and shy away from people and life? Is it any surprise that studying these children and parsing out their cognitive and emotional processes is such a belabored and arduous enterprise? And no less, should we as clinicians be any less overcome when confronting children who present with such enormous hurt, compromise, and complexity? Any of us who would take this lightly or glibly would indeed be missing the reality of what is staring us—or more likely, what is not staring us—in the face. Whether we are clinician, researcher, parent, or child, our work is complicated and will require patience and courage. But challenge offers possibility. While I don't know what directions tomorrow's discoveries will take us, there are some things I can be certain of as we continue to meet new children with Asperger's.

I know that while progress will be steady over the long haul, it will be slow and incremental in the moment, sometimes looking and feeling to be two steps forward, one step backward. But even as there are no sure outcomes, I aspire to proceed with enthusiasm until the child proves that I shouldn't be. I will strive to see the growth in the child's regression, finding the child's gifts and nurturing them with all my might, just as I might tend to the only living plant left on earth. I will look for, recognize, and foster their many intelligences (Gardner, 2006).

Even as I attempt to stretch children's interests, I will respect and preserve what matters to them that day or as they look to find a study or vocation that intrigues and matters to them for a lifetime. I will give that same priority to whatever it is that the child judges worth exploring, ever supporting the child's self-wishes to grow toward something new while realizing the need and value in her holding tightly to what she knows and wants. The concept of assimilation versus accommodation has no dearer relevance than to these children (Piaget, 1954) as we work to "understand [their] perspective, communicate it, [and] work together to bring awareness, solution, or acceptance" (Jacobsen, 2003).

Even as the researchers ferret out what is Asperger's, what is comorbid, and all the clinical reality laying between, I as clinician will work to notice and address any form of hurt or dysfunction that troubles the child, especially the anxiety and depression that so frequently runs alongside Asperger's. As I've repeated, there's no virtue in unnecessary suffering. There is virtue in my seeking the help and expertise of other professionals when I and the therapies I conduct cannot alleviate the child's distress.

I will not shortchange my child clients by believing that they're incapable of growth and opportunities that they themselves seek, and I will support their own good efforts thereto. I will not forget that these children bear it all. Asperger's is no free ticket to bypass the trials and tribulations of childhood, adolescence, and life. Children with Asperger's get cancer, are abused, watch their parents divorce, survive floods and accidents, and on and on. They also face separation, academic challenges, individuation, puberty, and all the developmental tasks and affronts that fall upon every child. The distinction is that the child with Asperger's faces these life issues with one hand tied behind her back while carrying a 40-pound yoke on her shoulders.

Yet, I will not let my cowardice or fear or unhelpful sympathies do less therapeutically than can be done. Just because therapy and growing can be hard or painful is not a reason to avoid it. Looking at oneself is not easy for any child or person, with or without Asperger's. That work, however, can lead to new possibilities and better places. Many teenagers with Asperger's will find that therapy brings excruciatingly painful awareness, as Timothy did when he suddenly felt his wish to "just be normal." That revelation hurt, but Timothy's life was better for it having been brought into the open and expressed. Even children with Asperger's need to see reality in order to make changes that are new, better, or different. For many teens and adults, coming to their own conclusions about and relationship to the term and diagnosis of Asperger's is an enormously and profoundly significant juncture on the road to a more integrated and self-accepting identity.

As the children have taught me, I will search for the meanings in what they try to convey, perhaps while respecting their earlier needs to not communicate so well—just as I'll accept and welcome their approaches toward and away from me. I'll try not to lose sight of the essential fact that what they think, say, do, and act is precious to them, solely because it is theirs. And so, it should be precious to me, their therapist, too. Being misunderstood is a constant experience, rejection, and unavoidable way of life for these boys and girls, which is why their being understood by me and others might be a mixed blessing for them, all at once both threatening and wonderful. I nonetheless will aspire to grasp what they say and appreciate how their being understood can feel as ecstatic and fulfilling as any other form of love and caring. Many children and adults with Asperger's have told me that being understood is the deepest and most connected feeling they know, a revelation that I can wholly relate to.

As a therapist, I will try to walk a balanced line between pathologizing and denial, closely seeking and heeding the child's sentiments in this regard. However much I support the child's efforts to overcome, master, or compensate—fostering competency in the classroom, on the playground, in the world—I never, ever want to dismiss or negate who the child is and who she will ever be. No children, even those with Asperger's, wish to be so many Pygmalions in need of makeovers. For many children with Asperger's, being authentic and sincere is the hallmark of a life well spent. While developing false selves or personae to survive the social scene is a common aspect of Asperger's, it is neither a goal nor a great place to remain or get stuck. As Kenneth Hall (2001) wrote about himself, "I am absolutely determined to be myself and I will not let anyone try to change me. . . . I would really hate if anyone tried to make me into a non-AS kid" (pp. 66–67). But then, he goes on to say that more than anything, he wants to be himself—and better. That could be the motto needlepointed in my office, guiding any therapy I do with a child with Asperger's: Help them to be all that they are and all that they want to and can be.

As a concerned clinician, I'll do my best to keep up to date on new research that sheds light and perspectives on the development, education, and treatment of Asperger's. Just as I will strive to know the basic research, I will trust that researchers will consider the data and insights that I and clinicians like myself discover. Historically, much of what we know about Asperger's has come from close observation and case studies. Hans Asperger arrived at what have proven to be many modern and thorough observations by spending lots of time with a small number of children at his clinic, at the school, on camping trips, and so forth. Other seminal contributions—such as Kanner's early chronicling of "autistic" children (1943), Lorna Wing's clinical account of Asperger's (1981), and Gillberg's small group studies (1989, 1991)—have been based on a limited number of cases. Any who read the leading journals in autism will soon find that even many of the experimental studies are limited by extremely small sample sizes, making them not so different from their cousin, the clinical report.

Doesn't it make sense that the therapist who spends dozens if not hundreds of intimate hours with the child will see aspects of the child and truths that just won't be revealed to the researcher or clinician who alternatively may study dozens, hundreds, or even thousands of children under a much more limited methodology or purview? We each have truths to contribute, and it is foolhardy for either to ignore what the other has to offer. Children with Asperger's and their families deserve all the help that is available from every viewpoint, no matter the continent or discipline.

My openness to learning should not be limited to that produced by mental health professionals. There are a growing number of fascinating books written by adults who have lived with Asperger's and autism and who know firsthand what they are talking about (by authors like Temple Grandin, John Robinson, Daniel Tammet, Donna Williams, Liane Willey, Clare Sainsbury, and many others). As a clinician, I go through my days meeting individuals with whom, near unconsciously, I connect to my own familiar experiences of living without Asperger's. When I work with nonautistic children, I have a frame of reference that I take for granted. Reading these books by adults who have lived with Asperger's and autism inform and enlighten me, giving insights that I would never have gleaned from textbooks or journal articles. And then I've learned, too, from well-done fiction; notably, Mark Haddon's *The Curious Incident of the Dog in the Night-Time* (2004), a wonderful novel told through the eyes and voice of a remarkable 15-year-old boy who it seems is a teenager with Asperger's, though that might be the last of his problems. These authors tell us what matters to them, and that should matter to us.

Last, I stress perhaps the most important thing I have learned while working with Asperger's. Children do not expect me to be perfectly responsive and in tune. I've found that they are most forgiving and understanding of my trip-ups and my errors. What they've let me know is that what they do want and expect is my constant effort to be there for them. They recognize my sincerity and earnest attempt, and that is what they value. They let me know that they need me to care for what, in the best sense of the word, it means therapeutically to never give up on getting to know them and to never give up on them.

It's an exciting time to be working with these children. Research is quickly unraveling parts of the mystery, offering data and insight that may lead to more effective and efficient interventions. We are better appreciating that while the etiology is biological, the remedy doesn't have to be, and worthwhile help can come in all shapes and sizes. The rapidly advancing techniques of neurological investigation are showing in startling fact that behavioral and interpersonal connections can indeed lead to biological changes never before imagined (e.g., new neural connections, more activated mirror neurons for empathy). New science is finding biological correlates to old psychology, even evidence that environment can turn genes on and off, suggesting entirely novel possibilities for our studying and thinking about Asperger's and autism—possibilities that might gel into promising treatments. After all, everything is biological, and in turn, everything coming to embody personal experience and acquiring personal meaning is psychological, too.

As we head out to our clinics and offices—as we head out to these children—we as therapists can be sure of one more thing: No matter how advanced our technology and how sophisticated our research methods, the new science will ever depend on the old psychology. No fMRI or experimental design will ever replace good old-fashioned human connection and understanding. While we expect that research will give us faster and better means of helping these children, it is unlikely that there will ever be a shortcut to what is the Holy Grail: the children's connecting to others and themselves. That the secret weapon might turn out to be found just about everywhere and anywhere in the form of a human being who can provide a presence and connection as profound as it is ordinary should bring us smiles and give us hope. In my own experience with Asperger's, I've yet to meet one child who would disagree.

Appendix: Working with Parents

That children with Asperger's can use and benefit from therapy has not been any part of the conventional thinking. Not wanting to dilute or distract clinicians from my overriding perspective, I purposely relegated my work with parents to a secondary and far distant place in this book. My opening chapter on meeting the parents spoke to many big matters that run through entire therapies. However, at this final juncture, I'm adding some other thoughts on the parents as they relate to their child's treatment. (It's probably obvious to many readers that this book and the following afterword inadequately address the parents' part in a child's therapy and life. The subject deserves a book of its own, authored by someone more experienced in family work than myself.)

GOALS

Goals are an important aspect of any treatment. I explicitly discuss goals with parents at every stage of the therapy. We examine long-term goals, which can also evoke much profound feeling and thinking about their child and the diagnosis, material that is nearly always profitably expressed and dealt with. The discussion of long-term goals usually involves both discouragement and hope and will serve, too, as a kind of baseline of expectation that we'll come to revisit over and over. As parents and their child realize more progress, expectations naturally rise; and that's a good thing. Parents are often surprised when I can point out that some goal, which just a year earlier they had held up as an unlikely dream, has come closer or been attained. This discussion of goals inevitably brings out into the open necessary topics, such as parents' disagreeing on critical goals or methods, unrealistic or overly gloomy goals, or goals that seem to miss the mark for any child's development. I am careful to support and endorse realistic goals and can offer enthusiastic and hopeful support for possible goals whose attainment will only be told in time. I rarely predict anything dire or that denies the parents' goals, unless it is absolutely clear that the parents are wishing and expecting something that just will never, ever be possible.

I help parents to conceptualize their goals in a structure and framework that makes sense for the child's development, therapy, and life. A parent may wish for the child to go to college and have a fulfilling career. Good and fair objective. But how can we help the child actually get there? And so, I help the parents to break the big goal into smaller, intermediary, and short-term goals that can eventually get the child to the ultimate goal. To achieve that long-term educational goal, for example, we might set up middle-term goals for the child to be able to make a smooth transition into fifth grade a year from now. Shorter-term goals might include engaging with her tutor, coming to be willing to read aloud in class, or learning to use the keyboard. And yet even shorter-term goals, the ones that also guide therapy, might be doing 10 minutes of homework without a battle or getting to school on time 2 of 5 days in the following week.

I do not need to delineate every painstaking ounce of planning or deliberation that goes into the therapy. Parents wouldn't want me to. But taking the time and bother to parse out the goals in one or two key areas helps parents to grasp and appreciate how I will work to achieve goals that build into bigger goals, which accrue to both near-future and longer-term life goals. I've found that parents can relate to the concept of way stations that we trek to in order to get to farther and better destinations. As I stressed a few times in the book, I also train parents to seek and revel in baby steps of progress. Many of these parents haven't seen anything hopeful in a long, long time. They need to see my genuine excitement in their child's movement ahead, and they benefit, too, from my explaining intellectually why a particular baby step matters. Parents' learning how goals and baby steps interact and affect each other gives them newfound abilities to think about and reflect on their child's development. We can never afford to underestimate the value of greater understanding to a parent of a child with Asperger's, especially understanding that offers help and hope.

Because assessment and therapy run hand in hand throughout a treatment, we show parents that we are ever interested in new problems, symptoms, and challenges. Asperger's is not a one-time discussion; it is a sequence of discussions that evolves over a childhood, a therapy, and a lifetime. The child's therapy does not fill up on a quota of goals but adaptively revises them and makes room for new ones. If a child with Asperger's develops a new related issue or experiences some event or stress having nothing to do with Asperger's, we want to know, and our goal setting reflects it. A sudden panic disorder or suicidal thinking, for instance, might take precedence over our long-term goal for enhanced academic involvement.

The topic of goals, of course, brings up the most relevant of questions: *Whose goals?* Do we pursue what the parents want for the child or what the teachers want? What we want or what the child wants? It may sound too obvious to state it, but we try our best to listen to and honor all pertinent goals. I often find that they mesh and integrate quite well and easily. Going through this exercise, however, is always useful for parents, children, and myself.

TRUSTING EXPERIENCE

The old and mistaken idea that children with Asperger's are victims of bad parents offends all of us. But I must confess, the newer theme of parents being victims of these difficult children also bothers me. With that qualification, it is nonetheless true that parenting a child with disabilities is a challenge, and so it is with Asperger's. This challenge can take its toll on parents' trust in their own vision, understanding, and abilities. From the day we meet, I see one of my roles as replenishing and restoring that confidence that they as parents have what it takes to raise their child. I do so not with false assurance or glib platitudes. That does nothing good for parents. As with a child, it is true competency that ultimately endows a person with esteem. Helping parents recognize their own skills with their child is itself restorative and enormously therapeutic. I can only see their child one or two sessions a week. The parents are with the child all the time and so have much more opportunity and power to wield. Each time that parents can overcome a misstep or learn to manage a situation, even a tiny one, they grow more able, stronger, and more resilient, ready and willing to take on the next phase or challenge.

TRIAL AND ERROR

Having a child with Asperger's is not a sudden or urgent matter. The bad news is that you have a childhood to deal with it; the good news is the same—that you have a childhood to deal with it. Parents seldom have to worry about having made a mistake that will forever mess up or deter their child's growth. The child offers opportunities to deal with issues 24/7. I work hard to defuse parental expectations of perfection. All kids just need their parents to be good enough, and that goes for kids with Asperger's, too. Images of perfection can doom good enough parents to ever feel inadequate, shortchanged, and even self-hating. These negative and harsh feelings only stress parents further and make it harder for them. Likewise, I try to cultivate in parents a sense that home life is a perpetual experiment in vivo. Buckshot parenting is not good, but using trial and error to learn what works and what doesn't is brilliant. Parents who accept that parenting is a skill and who embrace the notion that mistakes are for learning are guaranteed to grow stronger and more capable.

NEGATIVITY

I stressed throughout the book what it can feel like for parents to get slammed with gloomy predictions and a diagnosis that can hit hard. As clinicians know well, such feelings can get in the way. I leave room in every parent meeting for feelings of despair, discouragement, regret, and so forth. These feelings in themselves are human (and felt by all parents, even those with non-Asperger's children). But when they go unexpressed or suppressed, they can wreak havoc. Parents need to have a place to complain, if they want or need to, just as they might need a place to vent about work or their marriage or who knows what. I have found that good and loving parents sometimes are reluctant to share what they judge to be negative thoughts, believing it is mean or makes them a bad parent. I am happy and parents are happier when they can come to freely complain and joke about their harder moments and feelings. For some parents, this will involve significant grief work (again, something that can pertain to all parents of all children). To facilitate such openness in what they feel, my personal method is to encourage parents to communicate any way that works for them (in scheduled parent meetings, around their child's hour, by phone, or e-mail.)

REGULAR OLD PARENTING

To simply equate the child with Asperger's with any other child would be developmentally remiss. *But the child with Asperger's is much more like than unlike other children*, and it's negligent to not see that. Parents need to know this so that even while they are customizing their parenting to fit their child's special needs, they don't lose sight that their children need plain old parenting, too. It can be easy in an ocean of Asperger's issues to forget the more everyday stuff that burdens all children and families. When we do overlook such stuff, we risk doing to the child what so many others inadvertently do, meaning that we don't see their wholeness. To that end, I regularly work with parents on their parenting in general, helping them to see where structure and limits are needed and sometimes steering parent meetings to non-Asperger's topics that bear relevance. Sure, maybe a toddler with Asperger's throws tantrums because she cannot express herself well. But the fact that her parents set no limits and spoil her rotten is not helping. In addition to helping the child grow straighter, fortified parenting can sort things out so that the parts of problem behaviors that are due to Asperger's become clearer. I, for instance, often give parents used (and inexpensive) copies of Haim Ginott's 1969 classic, *Between Parent and Child,* a wonderfully simple and effective book on making oneself clear to children and avoiding power struggles (available in a 2003 edition published by Three Rivers Press).

HYPERSENSITIVITIES

I try to help the child better express his sensory sensitivities to his parents. Rather than just moan and get angry or run to their rooms, I encourage the child to learn to state what he's feeling and to ask for whatever accommodation is needed. When possible, we work on the child himself attending to his needs with some civility: "Do you mind if I open a window?" (Of course, we need to practice waiting for the reply before opening the window!) I help the child with parents learn ways to negotiate sensory preferences. This happens with clothes often, when a parent wants the child to dress a certain way, one that's often judged to be more appropriate. Parents and child together learn to debate and compromise. That everyone in school wears a collared shirt may not hold any persuasive value to the child who demands collarless T-shirts. We continually analyze the tug-of-war that exists between the child's need to avoid sensory discomfort and the parents' wish to stretch the child—to help the child grow less sensorily irritable and intolerant. Establishing ever-widening paths to mutual understanding and negotiating cannot be overrated when it comes to an issue as large and relevant as sensory sensitivities. I've found that my support in this area can help parents to sustain their patience and empathy for their child's sensory experiences. Parents may appreciate *Asperger Syndrome and Sensory Issues* (by Myles, Cook, Miller, Rinner, & Robbins, 2000, Autism Asperger Publishing) and *Sensory Integration and the Child* (by Ayres, 2005, Western Psychological Services).

ANXIETY AND FEELINGS

Because anxiety and depression are common in Asperger's, I readily question and look for signs of it. I encourage parents to do the same. When a parent reports some immediate sign of anxiety or depression, I try to address it as soon as possible—for example, if it is showing up as a phobia, fear, or worry. Addressing such anxieties and worries is not a detour in therapy; it actually helps move it along in ways that go beyond alleviating the specific symptom. I work with parents to better recognize the inner and behavioral signals that their child is distressed and overwhelmed. We analyze tantrums, withdrawals, and panics in terms of the anxiety and fear that may lie beneath. Together, we work to try and help the child grow more aware of what she feels, which can facilitate more competent self-regulating.

Recognizing that such growth is huge, I urge parents to give plenty of admiration and confirmation to their child's efforts at expressing their anxiety more directly, at seeking others' help, at managing what they feel, and at controlling their outbursts. It is the effort and process that deserves our notice and validation; not just the outcome. I support parents' making space for the child's feelings, especially the teenager's discouragement and despair. Being depressed is bad; being depressed and keeping it all to yourself is much worse. We work at being good listeners, which is not always easy, particularly when the child is talking about horrid feelings. We together work at becoming feeling detectives who can trace the origins of the child's tantrum or anger with the goal of helping it become more articulated without the need of a meltdown or symptoms of distress.

Though parents do not have to be their child's psychotherapist, they can do much to help their child's emotional intelligence exercise and grow. *Asperger's: What Does It Mean to Me?* (Faherty, 2000) and *Exploring Feelings* (Attwood, 2004a, 2004b) offer parents, as well as teachers and clinicians, complete programs for the child's emotional education and specific issues such as anxiety and anger management. Methods such as *replays* (Levine & Chedd, 2007), *floortime* (Greenspan & Wieder, 2006), and *giggle time* (Sonders, 2003) offer parents doable, enjoyable, and therapeutic strategies for helping their children grow emotionally and socially.

COMMUNICATION

In spite of the enormous breadth, depth, and complexity of this matter, my work with parents can be described rather succinctly. I work to help parent and child communicate more and better. I suggest that the reward is less than a behavioral prize and more the satisfaction that comes when the child's communication works—that is, when it's successfully transmitted and received. For that purpose, I work with parents to become active listeners who are interested in and responsive to the child's communications. I underscore that the child's messages are precious, for they are their own, and I reframe their communications as appeals (for some response). In our joint meetings, I model patience, interest, curiosity, and efforts that work to establish a safe place for communication. While many children save the cutting edge of their growing communication skills for home and the parents, others keep them with me and therapy. For those children, I meet with parents to help demonstrate what the child is capable of and to share tricks that seem to help invite the child's communication and wish to share. Whatever the methods, communication needs to be practiced. It needs to be understood and treated with respect and care. Together we work on ways to gently break into monologues and nudge the child's engaging with activities or topics besides their preoccupations.

Above all, I support anything and all that the parents do that helps their child to feel more communicatively welcome and competent. And as I stressed in previous chapters, I totally support and push for parents to pursue the input and intervention of speech and language therapists and educational specialists who know more about these issues and who have the techniques and skills to actually work on language on every level—from enunciation to grammar to idiomatic expressions, all the way to social semantics and pragmatics. I stress without question to parents that these assessments and services are critical, should be started sooner than later, and should be continued for as long as they help the child make progress.

INTELLIGENCE AND SCHOOL

While a child may seem bright to me, only a standard assessment can reveal the child's intellectual profile. Such data represents an important baseline from which future testing can ascertain progress or regression. I quickly support parents in finding a good tester, especially one with experience with Asperger's and who is an able and willing consultant to the school and the child's educational planning. I may be a good enough therapist, but I do not know enough myself to serve as an educational liaison. Some clinicians do possess the inclination and skills to do so.

I help parents face that enormous and difficult dilemma of how to nurture their child's intense interests while getting them involved in other kinds of learning and matters. The dialectic of assimilation versus accommodation becomes our mantra as we work to simultaneously honor where the child is while we also gently urge and stretch her to new places and challenges. When we are all together, in the office and more so in the waiting room before and after sessions, I model for parents ways of edging into the child's intellectual experiences. This can be a hard thing to accomplish, and I find parents are more than happy for any insights or strategies that work.

I, of course, help parents work on ways to get their children to do homework. As with issues of language, I am not an expert here. I push parents to find both tutors and educational specialists who can facilitate learning at home as well as in school. Some schools have excellent programs and staff for children with Asperger's; some do not. It behooves parents to seek out the right people to assist them in shaping, implementing, and monitoring their child's educational needs and programs. As I wrote earlier, while I support parents in finding specialists to consult about their child's education, I believe foremost in empowering parents to become their child's most effective advocate. Who knows their child better than they do, and who cares more about that child? (Parents will appreciate Silverman and Weinfeld's *School Success for Kids with Asperger's Syndrome*, 2007, a clear, detailed, and thorough guide to the best educational practices.)

SOCIALLY

I find that parents are usually the key players when it comes to the child's social growth. Typically, they are ever asking me about this activity and that play group and this sleepover, on and on. I serve mostly as their consultant, helping the parents deliberate over their many options. We ponder whether a child needs a more sheltered or inclusive experience, and we learn that she usually needs both. I caution against overdoing it or moving too fast. We plan out strategies to optimize the likelihood for success, albeit slow. I encourage parents to exploit every worthy social experience, such as group language treatment, social pragmatics, and group experiences at school, especially when they are led by kindly and patient adults. (Sometimes, with such children, patient and kindly seems to carry at least as much weight as well trained and skilled.) As I mentioned earlier, in this area, I confirm parents' own best judgments when evaluating outside social experiences and interventions. *What do you,* I ask them, *think of the group, its composition, its leaders?*

We together seek to find social experiences that tap the child's natural interests and talents. And I ever remind parents that two people can make a group; that is, a child can also learn socially from a one-to-one relationship with a mentor, big brother, tutor, or music teacher. I also encourage parents to honor the child's social interests or lack thereof. I help them to reframe how they see the child's relationship to his room, for example, seeing it as a healthy refuge and not as a malignant sign of perpetual isolation. Together, we come to value sociability and solitude as necessary parts of a whole existence.

SUITABILITY OF THERAPY

Seldom do I engage parents in the debates of autism. They have enough to contend with without taking on the whole field or feeling torn between caregivers, experts, or programs, which, though differing, all offer something good and helpful to their child. I keep parents abreast of the small wonders that occur in a child's therapy. I point out those modest advances in attachment, connection, communication, sociability, personal comfort, and so forth, making clear how they happen, what they mean, and how they are adding up to something bigger and promising. Though I never offer empty hope, I am thrilled whenever I can honestly provide data that warrant our reaction of joy, excitement, and hope. I might have to eventually temper parents' overly exuberant expectations, but I much prefer that they have expectations. I make clear from the outset that not only are parents' every question, comment, and disagreement okay but that they are requisite. I and the child's therapy need to be on board with the parents, just as they need to be equally in sync in return.

The literature on Asperger's is accumulating steadily. Following is a list of books that parents might find helpful (some of which I've already cited).

References

Attwood, T. (2004a). *Exploring feelings: Cognitive behavior therapy to manage anger.* Arlington, TX: Future Horizons.

Attwood, T. (2004b). *Exploring feelings: Cognitive behavior therapy to manage anxiety.* Arlington, TX: Future Horizons.

Attwood, T., Grandin, T., Bolick, T., Faherty, C., Iland, L., Myers, J., et al. (2006). *Asperger's and girls.* Arlington, TX: Future Horizons.

Ayres, A. J. (2005). *Sensory integration and the child.* Los Angeles, CA: Western Psychological Services.

Bashe, P., & Kirby, B. (2001). *The OASIS guide to Asperger Syndrome.* New York: Crown.

Boyd, B. (2003). *Parenting a child with Asperger Syndrome.* London: Jessica Kingsley Publishers.

Faherty, C. (2000). *Asperger's: What does it mean to me?* Arlington, TX: Future Horizons.

Ginott, H. (2003). *Between parent and child.* New York: Three Rivers Press.

Grandin, T. (2008). *The way I see it: A personal look at Autism and Asperger's.* Arlington, TX: Future Horizons.

Myles, B., Cook, K., Miller, N., Rinner, L., & Robbins, L. (2000). *Asperger Syndrome and sensory issues.* Shawnee Mission, KS: Autism Asperger Publishing.

Ozonoff, S., Dawson, G., & McPartland, J. (2002). *A parent's guide to Asperger Syndrome and High-Functioning Autism.* New York: Guilford Press.

Powers, M., & Poland, J. (2002). *Asperger Syndrome and your child: A parent's guide.* New York: HarperResource.

Silverman, S., & Weinfeld, R. (2007). *School success for kids with Asperger's Syndrome*. Waco, TX: Prufrock Press.

Sohn, A., & Grayson, C. (2005). P*arenting your Asperger child: Individualized solutions for teaching your child practical skills*. New York: Perigree.

Sonders, S. (2003). *Giggle time—Establishing the social connection: A program to develop the social communication skills of children with Autism, Asperger Syndrome and PDD*. London: Jessica Kingsley Publishers.

Stillman, W. (2005). *The everything parent's guide to children with Asperger's Syndrome*. Avon, MA: Adams Media.

Willey, L. (2001). *Asperger Syndrome in the family*. London: Jessica Kingsley Publishers.

References

Allen, F. (1964). The beginning phase of therapy. In M. Haworth (Ed.), *Child psychotherapy: Practice and theory* (pp. 101–104). New York: Basic.

Allured, E. (2006). Developing the intersubjective playground in the treatment of childhood Asperger's Syndrome. *Journal of Infant, Child and Adolescent Psychotherapy, 5*(4), 397–419.

American Psychiatric Association. (1952). *Diagnostic and statistical manual of mental disorders* (1st ed.). Washington, DC: Author.

American Psychiatric Association. (1968). *Diagnostic and statistical manual of mental disorders* (2nd ed.). Washington, DC: Author.

American Psychiatric Association. (1980). *Diagnostic and statistical manual of mental disorders* (3rd ed.). Washington, DC: Author.

American Psychiatric Association. (1987). *Diagnostic and statistical manual of mental disorders* (3rd ed., rev.). Washington, DC: Author.

American Psychiatric Association. (1994). *Diagnostic and statistical manual of mental disorders* (4th ed.). Washington, DC: Author.

American Psychiatric Association. (2000). *Diagnostic and statistical manual of mental disorders* (4th ed., rev.). Washington, DC: Author.

Ashwin, C., Wheelwright, S., & Baron-Cohen, S. (2006). Attention bias to faces in Asperger Syndrome: A pictorial emotion Stroop study. *Psychological Medicine, 36*(6), 835–843.

Asperger, H. (1991). Autistic Psychopathy in Childhood. In U. Frith (Ed. & Trans.), Autism and Asperger Syndrome (pp. 36–92). Cambridge, UK: Cambridge University Press. (Original work published 1944)

Attwood, T. (2000). Strategies for improving the social integration of children with Asperger Syndrome. *Autism, 4,* 85–100.

Attwood, T. (2003a). Frameworks for behavioural interventions. *Child and Adolescent Psychiatric Clinics, 12,* 65–86.

Attwood, T. (2003b). Understanding and managing circumscribed interests. In M. Prior (Ed.), *Learning and behavior problems in Asperger Syndrome* (pp. 126–147). New York: Guilford.

Attwood, T. (2004a). *Exploring feelings: Cognitive behavior therapy to manage anger.* Arlington, TX: Future Horizons.

Attwood, T. (2004b). *Exploring feelings: Cognitive behavior therapy to manage anxiety.* Arlington, TX: Future Horizons.

Attwood, T. (2007). *The complete guide to Asperger's Syndrome.* Philadelphia: Jessica Kingsley Publishers.

Axline, V. (1969). *Play therapy.* New York: Ballentine.

Ayres, A. (2005). *Sensory integration and the child.* Los Angeles, CA: Western Psychological Services.

Baranek, G., Foster, L., & Berkson, G. (1997). Sensory defensiveness in persons with developmental disabilities. *Occupational Therapy Journal of Research, 17,* 173–185.

Barnhill, G. (2001). Social attributions and depression in adolescents with Asperger Syndrome. *Focus on Autism and Other Developmental Disabilities, 16*(1), 46–53.

Baron-Cohen, S. (1987). Autism and symbolic play. *British Journal of Developmental Psychology, 5,* 139–148.

Baron-Cohen, S. (1989). The autistic child's theory of mind: A case of specific developmental delay. *Journal of Child Psychology and Psychiatry, 30*(2), 285–297.

Baron-Cohen, S. (2007). I cannot tell a lie. *In Character, 3,* 52–59.

Baron-Cohen, S. (2008). *Autism and Asperger Syndrome.* Oxford: Oxford University Press.

Baron-Cohen, S., Leslie, A., & Frith, U. (1985). Does the autistic child have a "theory of mind"? *Cognition, 21,* 37–46.

Bashe, P., & Kirby, B. (2001). *The OASIS guide to Asperger Syndrome.* New York: Crown.

Bauminger, N. (2004). The expression and understanding of jealousy in children with Autism. *Development and Psychopathology, 16,* 157–177.

Bauminger, N., Chomsky-Smolkin, L., Orbach-Caspi, E., Zachor, D., & Levy-Shiff, R. (2008). Jealousy and emotional responsiveness in young children with ASD. *Cognition and Emotion, 22*(4), 595–619.

Bauminger, N., & Kasari, C. (2000). Loneliness and friendship in high-functioning children with Autism. *Child Development, 71,* 447–456.

Bauminger, N., Shulman, C., & Agam, G. (2003). Peer interaction and loneliness in high-functioning children with Autism. *Journal of Autism and Developmental Disorders, 33*(5), 489–507.

Bauminger, N., Solomon, M., Aviezer, A., Heung, K., Brown, J., & Rogers, S. (2008). Friendship in high-functioning children with Autism Spectrum Disorder: Mixed and non-mixed dyads. *Journal of Autism and Developmental Disorders, 38*(7), 1211–1229.

Beebe, D., & Risi, S. (2003). Treatment of adolescents and young adults with High-Functioning Autism or Asperger Syndrome. In M. Reinecke, F. Dattilio, & A. Freeman (Eds.), *Cognitive therapy with children and adolescents: A casebook for clinical practice* (2nd ed., pp. 369–401). New York: Guilford Press.

Bemporad, J., Ratey, J., & O'Driscoll, G. (1987). Autism and emotion: An ethological theory. *American Journal of Orthopsychiatry, 57,* 477–483.

Ben Shalom, D., Mostofsky, S., Hazlett, R., Goldberg, M., Landa, R., Faran, Y., et al. (2006). Normal physiological emotions but differences in expression of conscious feelings in children with High-Functioning Autism. *Journal of Autism and Developmental Disorders, 36*(3), 395–400.

Bettelheim, B. (1967). *The empty fortress.* New York: The Free Press.

Bleuler, E. (1950). *Dementia praecox or the group of Schizophrenias* (J. Zikin, Trans.). New York: International Universities Press. (Original work published 1911)

Blomberg, B. (2005). Time, space, and the mind: Psychotherapy with children with Autism. In D. Houzel & M. Rhode (Eds.), *Invisible boundaries: Psychosis and Autism in children and adolescents* (pp. 25–42). London: Karnac.

Bogdashina, O. (2003). *Sensory perceptual issues in Autism and Asperger Syndrome: Different sensory experiences, different perceptual worlds.* London: Jessica Kingsley Publishers.

Briggs, A. (2005). A little boy's use of his male child psychotherapist to help him understand a painful conundrum? *Journal of Child Psychotherapy, 31*(3), 352–367.

Bromfield, R. (1989). Psychodynamic play therapy with a high-functioning autistic child. *Psychoanalytic Psychology, 4,* 439–453.

Bromfield. R. (2000). It's the tortoise race: Long-term psycho-dynamic therapy with a high-functioning autistic child. *Psychoanalytic Inquiry, 20,* 732–745.

Bromfield, R. (2007). *Doing child and adolescent psychotherapy.* Hoboken, NJ: Wiley.

Bromfield, R. (2004). *Playing for real.* Boston: Basil.

Bromfield, R. (2010). *Precious goods: Nurturing the self of the child with Asperger's.* Philadelphia: Jessica Kingsley Publishers.

Capps, L., Kasari, C., Yirmiya, N., & Sigman, M. (1993). Parental perception of emotional expressiveness in children with Autism. *Journal of Consulting and Clinical Psychology, 61,* 475–484.

Carrington, S., Templeton, E., & Papincazak, T. (2003). Adolescents with Asperger Syndrome and perceptions of friendship. *Focus on Autism and Other Developmental Disabilities, 18*(4), 211–218.

Charman, T., & Baron-Cohen, S. (1997). Brief report: Prompted pretend play in Autism. *Journal of Autism and Developmental Disorders, 27*(3), 325–332.

Cole, M., Cole, S., & Lightfoot, C. (2004). *The development of the child.* New York: Worth.

Critchley, H., Daly, E., Bullmore, E., Williams, S., Van Amelsvoort, T., Robertson, D., et al. (2000). The functional neuroanatomy of social behaviour: Changes in cerebral blood flow when people with autistic disorder process facial expressions. *Brain: A Journal of Neurology, 123*(11), 2203–2212.

Dawson, G., Osterling, J., Melzoff, A., & Kuhl, P. (2000). Case study of the development of an infant with Autism from birth to 2 years of age. *Journal of Applied Developmental Psychology, 21,* 299–313.

de Bruin, E., Ferdinand, R., Meesters, S., de Nijs, P., & Verheij, F. (2007). High rates of psychiatric co-morbidity in PDD-NOS. *Journal for Autism and Developmental Disorders, 37,* 877–886.

Dinklage, D. (n.d.). Asperger's disorder and non-verbal learning disability: How are these two disorders related to each other? Retrieved September 10, 2009, from Asperger Association of New England Web site: http://www.aane.org/asperger_resources/articles/miscellaneous/asperger_nonverbal_learning.html.

Donnelly, J., & Bouvee, J. (2003). Reflections on play: Recollections from a mother and her son with Asperger Syndrome. *Autism, 7*(4), 471–476.

Dubin, N., & Carley, M. (2007). *Asperger's and bullying: Strategies and solutions.* London: Jessica Kingsley Publishers.

Dumitrescu, C. (2006). Neuropsychological profile differences between children with Asperger's Syndrome and nonverbal learning disabilities. *Dissertation Abstracts International: The Sciences and Engineering, 66*(7-B), 3945.

Elder, L., Caterino, L., Chao, J., Shacknai, D., & DeSimone, G. (2006). The efficacy of social skills treatment for children with Asperger Syndrome. *Education and treatment of children, 29*(4), 635–663.

Elkis-Abuhoff, D. (2008). Art therapy applied to an adolescent with Asperger's Syndrome. *Arts in Psychotherapy, 35*(4), 262–270.

Faherty, C. (2000). *Asperger's: What does it mean to me?* Arlington, TX: Future Horizons.

Feinstein, A. (2001). Interview with Gary Mesibov. *Looking Up, 2.*

Fitzgerald, M., & Molyneux. S. (2004). Overlap between alexithymia and Asperger's Syndrome. *American Journal of Psychiatry, 161,* 2134–2135.

Fombonne, E. (2003). The prevalence of Autism. *Journal of the American Medical Association, 289,* 87–89.

Fombonne, E., Heavey, L., Smeeth, L., Rodrigues, L., Cook, C., Smith, P., et al. (2004). Validity of the diagnosis of Autism in general practice records. *BMC Public Health, 4*(5), 1–9.

Forrester-Jones, R., & Broadhurst, S. (2007). *Autism and loss.* London: Jessica Kingsley Publishers.

Frith, U. (Ed.). (1991). *Autism and Asperger Syndrome.* Cambridge, UK: Cambridge University Press.

Frith, U. (2001). Mind blindness and the brain in Autism. *Neuron, 32,* 969–979.

Frith, U. (2004). Emanuel Miller lecture: Confusions and controversies about Asperger Syndrome. *Journal of Child Psychology and Psychiatry, 45*(4), 672–686.

Frith, U., Happé, F., & Siddons, F. (1994). Autism and theory of mind in everyday life. *Social Development, 3,* 108–124.

Gardner, H. (2006). *Multiple intelligences: New horizons in theory and practice.* New York: Basic.

Ghaziuddin, M., & Mountain-Kimchi, K. (2004). Defining the intellectual profile of Asperger Syndrome: Comparison with High-Functioning Autism. *Journal of Autism and Developmental Disorders, 34*(3), 279–284.

Ghaziuddin, M., Weidmer-Mikhail, E., & Ghaziuddin, N. (1998). Comorbity of Asperger Syndrome: A preliminary report. *Journal of Intellectual Disability Records, 42,* 279–283.

Gillberg, C. (1989). Asperger Syndrome in 23 Swedish children. *Developmental Medicine and Child Neurology, 31,* 520–531.

Gillberg, C. (1991). Clinical and neurobiological aspects of Asperger Syndrome in six family studies. In U. Frith (Ed.), *Autism and Asperger Syndrome* (pp. 122–146). Cambridge, UK: Cambridge University Press.

Gillberg, I., & Gillberg, C. (1989). Asperger Syndrome—Some epidemiological considerations: A research note. *Journal of Child Psychology and Psychiatry, 30,* 631–638.

Gillis, J., Natof, T., Lockshin, S., & Romanczyk, R. (2009). Fear of routine physician exams in children with Autism spectrum disorders. *Focus on Autism and Other Developmental Disabilities, 24*(3), 156–168.

Ginott, H. (2003). *Between parent and child.* New York: Three Rivers Press.

Grandin, T. (2008). *The way I see it.* Arlington, TX: Future Horizons.

Grandin, T., & Scariano, M. (1986). *Emergence.* New York: Grand Central Publishing.

Greenspan, S., & Wieder, S. (2006). *Engaging Autism: Using the floortime approach to help children relate, communicate, and think.* New York: Da Capo.

Grossman, J., Klin, A., Carter, A., & Volkmar, F. (2000). Verbal bias in recognition of facial emotions in children with Asperger Syndrome. *Journal of Child Psychology and Psychiatry, 41*(3), 369–379.

Haddon, M. (2004). *The curious incident of the dog in the night-time.* New York: Vintage.

Hall, K. (2001). *Asperger Syndrome, the universe and everything.* London: Jessica Kingsley Publishers.

Happé, F., & Frith, U. (1996). The neuropsychology of Autism. *Brain, 119,* 1377–1400.

Happé, F., & Frith, U. (2009). The beautiful otherness of the autistic mind. *Philosophical Transactions of the Royal Society, 364,* 1345–1350.

Harris, P., & Leevers, H. (2000). Pretending, imagery and self-awareness in Autism. In S. Baron-Cohen, H. Tager-Flusberg, & D. Cohen (Eds.), *Understanding other minds: Perspectives from Autism and developmental cognitive neuroscience* (pp. 182–202). Oxford: Oxford University Press.

Hartup, W. (1992). Friendships and their developmental significance. In H. McGurk (Ed.), *Childhood social development: Contemporary perspectives* (pp. 175–205). Hillsdale, NJ: Lawrence Erlbaum.

Hartup, W., & Stevens, N. (1997). Friendships and adaptation in the life course. *Psychological Bulletin, 121*(3), 355–370.

Heaton, P., Hermelin, B., & Pring, L. (1999). Can children with autistic spectrum disorders perceive affect in music? An experimental investigation. *Psychological Medicine, 29*(6), 1405–1410.

Henley. D. (2000). Blessings in disguise: Idiomatic expression as a stimulus in group art therapy with children. *Art Therapy, 17*(4), 270–275.

Henley, D. (2001). Annihilation anxiety and fantasy in the art of children with Asperger's Syndrome and others on the autistic spectrum. *American Journal of Art Therapy, 39,* 113–121.

Hermelin, B., & O'Connor, N. (1985). Logico-affective states and nonverbal language. In E. Schopler & G. Mesibov (Eds.), *Communication problems in Autism* (pp. 283–309). New York: Plenum.

Hertz-Picciotto, I., & Delwiche, L. (2009). The rise in Autism and the role of age at diagnosis. *Epidemiology, 20*(1), 84–90.

Hobson, R., Lee, A., & Hobson, J. (2009). Qualities of symbolic play among children with Autism: A social-developmental perspective. *Journal of Autism and Developmental Disorders, 39*(1), 12–22.

Holaday, M., Moak, J., & Shipley, M. (2001). Rorschach protocols from children and adolescents with Asperger's Syndrome. *Journal of Personality Assessment, 76*(3), 482–495.

Howe, S. (1996, September 5). Getting smart about gifted kids. *Boston College Chronicle, 5.* Retrieved September 11, 2009, from http://www.bc.edu/bc_org/rvp/pubaf/chronicle/v5/S5/winner.html.

Iland, L. (2006). Girl to girl: Advice on friendship, bullying, and fitting in. In *Asperger's and girls* (pp. 33–64). Arlington, TX: Future Horizons.

Jacobsen, P. (2003). *Asperger Syndrome and psychotherapy.* Philadelphia: Jessica Kingsley Publishers.

Jarrold, C. (2003). A review of research into pretend play in Autism. *Autism, 7*(4), 379–390.

Jarrold, C., Boucher, J., & Smith, P. (1993). Symbolic play in Autism: A review. *Journal of Autism and Developmental Disorders, 23*(2), 281–307.

Jarrold, C., Boucher, J., & Smith, P. (1996). Generativity deficits in pretend play in Autism. *British Journal of Developmental Psychology, 14,* 275–300.

Jarrold, C., Smith, P., Boucher, J., & Harris, P. (1994). Comprehension of pretense in children with Autism. *Journal of Autism and Developmental Disorders, 24*(4), 433–455.

Josefi, O., & Ryan, V. (2004). Non-directive play therapy for young children with Autism: A case study. *Clinical Child Psychology and Psychiatry, 9*(4), 533–551.

Juvonen, J., Graham, S., & Schuster, M. (2003). Bullying among young adolescents: The strong, the weak, and the troubled. *Pediatrics, 112,* 1231–1237.

Kanner, L. (1943). Autistic disturbances of affective contact. *Nervous Child, 2,* 217–250.

Kasari, C., Chamberlain, B., & Bauminger, N. (2001). Social emotions and social relationships in Autism: Can children with Autism compensate? In J. Burack, T. Charman, N. Yirmiya, & P. Zelazo (Eds.), *Development and Autism: Perspectives from theory and research* (pp. 309–333). Mahwah, NJ: Erlbaum.

Keefe, K., & Berndt, T. (1996). Relations of friendship quality to self-esteem in early adolescence. *Journal of Early Adolescence, 16,* 110–129.

Kelly, A., Garnett, M., Attwood, T., & Peterson, C. (2008). Autism spectrum disorders in children: The impact of family and peer relationships. *Journal of Abnormal Child Psychology, 36,* 1069–1081.

Kim, Y., Koh, Y., & Leventhal, B. (2005). School bullying and suicidal risk in Korean middle school students. *Pediatrics, 115,* 357–363.

Kim, J., Szatmari, P., Bryson, S., Streimer, D., & Wilson, F. (2000). The prevalence of anxiety and mood problems among children with Autism and Asperger Syndrome. *Autism, 4,* 117–132.

Klauber, T. (2004). A child psychotherapist's commentary on Hans Asperger's 1944 paper, "Autistic psychopathy in childhood." In M. Rhode & T. Klauber (Eds.), *The many faces of Asperger's Syndrome* (pp. 54–69). London: Karnac Books.

Klin, A., Saulnier, C., Sparrow, S., Cicchetti, D., Volkmar, F., & Lord, C. (2007). Social and communication abilities and disabilities in higher functioning individuals with Autism spectrum disorders: The Vineland and the ADOS. *Journal of Autism and Developmental Disabilities, 37*(4), 748–759.

Klin, A., Volkmar, F., Sparrow, S., Cichetti, D., & Bourke, B. (1995). Validity and neurological characterization of Asperger Syndrome:

Convergence with nonverbal learning disability syndrome. *Journal of Child Psychology and Psychiatry, 36*(7), 1127–1140.

Leslie, A. (1987). Pretence and representation: The origins of "Theory of mind." *Psychological Review, 94*, 412–426.

Levine, K., & Chedd, N. (2007). *Replays.* Philadelphia: Jessica Kingsley Publishers.

Leyfer, O., Folstein, S., Bacalman, S., Davis, N., Dinh, E., Morgan, J., et al. (2006). Comorbid psychiatric disorders with children with Autism: Interview development rates of disorders. *Journal of Autism and Developmental Disorders, 36*, 849–861.

Lindner, J., & Rosén, L. (2006). Decoding of emotion through facial expression, prosody and verbal content in children and adolescents with Asperger's Syndrome. *Journal of Autism and Developmental Disorders, 36*(6), 769–777.

Little, L. (2002). Middle-class mothers' perceptions of peer and sibling victimization among children with Asperger Syndrome and non-verbal learning disorders. *Issues in Comprehensive Pediatric Nursing, 25*, 43–57.

Lord, C., Risi, S., Lambrecht, L., Cook, E. Jr., Leventhal, B., DiLavore, P., et al. (2000). The Autism Diagnostic Observation Schedule—Generic: A standard measure of social and communication deficits associated with the spectrum of Autism. *Journal of Autism and Developmental Disorders, 30*(3), 205–223.

Lowery, E. (1985). Autistic aloofness reconsidered: Case reports of two children in play therapy. *Bulletin of the Menninger Clinic, 49*(2), 135–150.

Lyons, V., & Fitzgerald, M. (2004). Humor in Autism and Asperger Syndrome. *Journal of Autism and Developmental Disorders, 34*, 521–531.

Lyons, V., & Fitzgerald, M. (2007). Asperger (1906–1980) and Kanner (1894–1981), the two pioneers of Autism. *Journal of Autism and Developmental Disorders, 37*, 2022–2023.

Marston, G., & Clarke, D. (1999). Making contact: Bereavement and Asperger's Syndrome. *Irish Journal of Psychological Medicine, 16*(1), 29–31.

Martinovich, J. (2005). *Creative expressive activities and Asperger's Syndrome.* London: Jessica Kingsley Publishers.

Mathur, R., & Berndt, T. (2006). Relations of friends' activities to friendship quality. *Journal of Early Adolescence, 26*(3), 365–388.

Merriam Webster's Collegiate Dictionary (10th ed.). (1998). Springfield, MA: Merriam-Webster.

Mesibov, G., Adams, L., & Klinger, L. (1998). *Autism: Understanding the disorder*. New York: Springer.

Meyerowitz-Katz, J. (2008). "Other people have a secret that I do not know": Art psychotherapy in private practice with an adolescent girl with Asperger's Syndrome. In C. Case & T. Dalley (Eds.), *Art therapy with children: From infancy to adolescence* (pp. 232–250). New York: Routledge.

Miller, B. (2008). "A kaleidoscope of themes": Intensive psychotherapy with a girl on the autistic spectrum. *Journal of Child Psychotherapy, 34*(3), 384–399.

Minio-Paluello, I., Baron-Cohen, S., Avenanti, A., Walsh, V., & Aglioti, S. (2009). Absence of embodied empathy during pain observation in Asperger Syndrome. *Biological Psychiatry, 65*(1), 55–62.

Mitchell, P., & O'Keefe, K. (2008). Brief report: Do individuals with Autism spectrum disorder think they know their own minds? *Journal of Autism and Developmental Disorders, 38*, 1591–1597.

Myles, B., Cook, K., Miller, N., Rinner, L., & Robbins, L. (2000). *Asperger Syndrome and sensory issues*. Shawnee Mission, KS: Autism Asperger Publishing.

Nagelberg, L., & Feldman, Y. (1953). The attempt at healthy insulation in the withdrawn child. *American Journal of Orthopsychiatry, 3*, 238–251.

Parker, J., & Asher, S. (1993). Friendship and friendship quality in middle childhood: Links with peer group acceptance and feelings of loneliness and social dissatisfaction. *Developmental Psychology, 29*, 611–621.

Piaget, J. (1928). *Judgment and reasoning in the child*. New York: Harcourt, Brace.

Piaget, J. (1954). *The construction of reality in the child*. New York: Basic.

Pozzi, M. (2003). The use of observation in the psychoanalytic treatment of a 12-year-old boy with Asperger's Syndrome. *International Journal of Psychoanalysis, 84*(5), 1333–1349.

Reaven, J. (2009). Children with High-Functioning Autism spectrum disorders and co-occurring anxiety symptoms: Implications for assessment and treatment. *Journal for Specialists in Pediatric Nursing, 14*, 192–199.

Rogers, C. (1949). The attitude and orientation of the counselor in client-centered therapy. *Journal of Consulting Psychology, 13*(2), 82–94.

Rogers, K., Dziobek, I., Hassenstab, J., Wolf, O., & Convit, A. (2007). Who cares? Revisiting empathy in Asperger Syndrome. *Journal of Autism and Developmental Disorders, 37*, 709–715.

Row, S. (2005). *Surviving the special needs system: How to be a "velvet bull-dozer."* London: Jessica Kingsley Publishers.

Rowley, G. (2001). Foreword. In K. Hall, *Asperger Syndrome, the universe and everything* (pp. 11–12). London: Jessica Kingsley Publishers.

Ruberman, L. (2002). Psychotherapy of children with pervasive developmental disorders. *American Journal of Psychotherapy, 56*(2), 262–272.

Sainsbury, C. (2000). *Martian in the playground: Understanding the schoolchild with Asperger's Syndrome.* Bristol, UK: Lucky Duck Publishing.

Sanders, R. (2008). *Talking to parents about Autism.* New York: Norton.

Saulnier, C., & Klin, A. (2007). Brief report: Social and communication abilities and disabilities in higher functioning individuals with Autism and Asperger's Syndrome. *Journal of Autism and Developmental Disabilities, 37*(4), 788–793.

Schneider, B. (2000). *Friends and enemies: Peer relations in childhood.* London: Arnold.

Sherratt, D. (2002). Developing pretend play in children with Autism: A case study. *Autism, 6*(2), 169–179.

Shtayermman, O. (2007). Peer victimization in adolescents and young adults diagnosed with Asperger's Syndrome: A link to depressive symptomatology, anxiety symptomatology and suicidal ideation. *Issues in Comprehensive Pediatric Nursing, 30,* 87–107.

Silani, G., Bird, G., Brindley, R., Singer, T., Frith, C., & Frith, U. (2008). Levels of emotional awareness and Autism: An fMRI study. *Social Neuroscience, 3*(2), 97–122.

Silverman, S., & Weinfeld, R. (2007). *School success for kids with Asperger's Syndrome.* Waco, TX: Prufrock Press.

Simpson, R., & Myles, B. (1998). Aggression among children and youth who have Asperger's Syndrome: A different population requiring different strategies. *Preventing School Failure, 42*(4), 149–153.

Sofronoff, K., Attwood, T., & Hinton, S. (2005). A randomised controlled trial of a CBT intervention for anxiety in children with Asperger Syndrome. *Journal of Child Psychology and Psychiatry, 46,* 1152–1160.

Sofronoff, K., Attwood, T., Hinton, S., & Levin, I. (2007). A randomized controlled trial of a cognitive behavioural intervention for anger management in children diagnosed with Asperger Syndrome. *Journal of Autism and Developmental Disorders, 37,* 1203–1214.

Solomon, M., Goodlin-Jones, B., & Anders, T. (2004). A social adjustment enhancement intervention for High Functioning Autism, Asperger's

Syndrome, and pervasive developmental disorder NOS. *Journal of Autism and Developmental Disorders, 34,* 649–668.

Sonders, S. (2003). *Giggle time—Establishing the social connection: A program to develop the social communication skills of children with Autism, Asperger Syndrome and PDD.* London: Jessica Kingsley Publishers.

Sullivan, H. (1953). *The interpersonal theory of psychiatry.* New York: Norton.

Szatmari, P. (1991). Asperger's Syndrome: Diagnosis, treatment, and outcome. *Psychiatric Clinics of North America, 14*(1), 81–92.

Sze, K., & Wood, J. (2007). Cognitive behavioral treatment of comorbid anxiety disorders and social difficulties in children with High-Functioning Autism: A case report. *Journal of Contemporary Psychotherapy, 37*(3), 133–143.

Tan, S. (2007). *The arrival.* New York: Arthur A. Levine Books.

Tantam, D. (1991). Asperger Syndrome in adulthood. In U. Frith (Ed.), *Autism and Asperger Syndrome* (pp. 147–183). New York: Cambridge University Press.

Tantam, D. (2000). Psychological disorders in adolescents and adults with Asperger Syndrome. *Autism, 4*(1), 47–62.

Thede, L., & Coolidge, F. (2007). Psychological and neurobehavioral comparisons of children with Asperger's disorder versus High-Functioning Autism. *Journal of Autism and Developmental Disorders, 37*(5), 847–854.

Towbin, K., Pradella, A., Gorrindo, T., Pine, D., & Liebenluft, E. (2005). Autistic spectrum traits in children with mood and anxiety disorders. *Journal of Child and Adolescent Psychopharmacology, 15*(3), 452–464.

Treffert, D. (1989). *Extraordinary people: Understanding savant syndrome.* New York: Ballentine.

Treffert, D. (2009). The savant syndrome: An extraordinary condition— A synopsis: Past, present, future. *Philosophical Transactions of the Royal Society, 364,* 1351–1357.

Ungerer, J., & Sigman, M. (1981). Symbolic play and language comprehension in autistic children. *Journal of the American Academy of Child Psychiatry, 20,* 318–337.

Volkmar, F., & Klin, A. (2000). Diagnostic issues in Asperger Syndrome. In A. Klin, F. Volkmar, & S. Sparrow (Eds.), *Asperger Syndrome* (pp. 25–71). New York: Guilford Press.

Whitehouse, A., Durkin, K., Jaquet, E., & Ziatas, K. (2009). Friendship, loneliness and depression in adolescents with Asperger's Syndrome. *Journal of Adolescence, 32,* 309–322.

Willemsen-Swinkels, S., Bakermans-Kranenburg, M., van Ijzedorn, M., Buitelaar, J., & van Engeland, H. (2000). Insecure and disorganised attachment in children with a pervasive developmental disorder: Relationship with social interaction and heart rate. *Journal of Child Psychology and Psychiatry, 41,* 759–767.

Willey, L. (1999). *Pretending to be normal.* London: Jessica Kingsley Publishers.

Williams, E., Reddy, V., & Costall, A. (2001). Taking a closer look at functional play in children with Autism. *Journal of Autism and Developmental Disorders, 31*(1), 67–77.

Wimpory, D., Hobson, R., & Nash, S. (2007). What facilitates social engagement in preschool children with Autism? *Journal of Autism and Developmental Disabilities, 37,* 564–573.

Wing, L. (1981). Asperger's Syndrome: A clinical account. *Psychological Medicine, 11*(1), 115–129.

Wing, L. (2000). Past and future research on Asperger Syndrome. In A. Klin, F. Volkmar, & S. Sparrow (Eds.), *Asperger Syndrome* (pp. 418–432). New York: Guilford.

Winner, E. (1996). *Gifted children: Myths and realities.* New York: Basic.

Witwer, A., & Lecavelier, L. (2008). Examining the validity of Autism spectrum disorder subtypes. *Journal of Autism and Developmental Disorders, 38,* 1611–1624.

Wolff, S. (1995). *Loners: The life path of unusual children.* London: Routledge.

Wulff, S. (1985). The symbolic and object play of children with Autism: A review. *Journal of Autism and Developmental Disorders, 15,* 139–148.

Author Index

Agam, G., 123, 141, 142
Aglioti, S., 112
Allen, F., 19
Allured, E., 168
American Psychiatric Association, xii, 3,
    4, 43, 62
Anders, T., 142
Asher, S., 123, 141
Ashwin, C., 166
Asperger, H., 1, 2, 3, 23, 24, 62, 69, 78,
    79–80, 96, 102, 121–122, 143, 163,
    169, 173
Attwood, T., xvii, 3, 29, 34, 54, 56, 57,
    62, 64, 73, 88, 102, 112, 113, 117,
    118, 122, 123, 139, 146, 181
Avenanti, A., 112
Axline, V., 19
Ayres, A., 180

Bakermans-Kranenburg, M., 112
Baranek, G., 29
Barnhill, G., 116, 122
Baron-Cohen, S., 78, 88, 112, 160,
    161, 166
Bashe, P., 88
Bauminger, N., 123, 141, 142, 143,
    163
Beebe, D., 56, 117
Bemporad, J., 8, 170

Ben Shalom, D., 112
Berkson, G., 29
Berndt, T., 141, 142
Bettelheim, B., xiii, 2
Blomberg, B., 143
Bogdashina, O., 40
Boucher, J., 161, 12
Bourke, B., 79
Bovee, J., 162–163
Briggs, A., 167
Broadhurst, S., 162
Bromfield, R., 8, 19, 151, 159, 162,
    163, 169
Bryson, S., 113
Buitelaar, J., 112

Capps, L., 163
Carrington, S., 141, 142
Carley, M., 146
Carter, A., 166
Caterino, L., 139
Chamberlain, B., 143, 163
Chao, J., 139
Charman, T., 161
Chedd, N., xiv, xvii, xviii, 17, 51,
    94, 112, 118, 181
Chomsky-Smolkin, L., 163
Cicchetti, D., 79
Clarke, D., 162

Cole, M., 123
Cole, S., 123
Convit, A., 165
Cook, K., 180
Coolidge, F., 78
Costall, A., 162
Critchley, H., 112, 166

Dawson, G., 29
de Bruin, E., 45
de Nijs, P., 45
Delwiche, L., xv
DeSimone, G., 139
Dinklage, D., 79
Donnelly, J., 163
Dubin, N., 146
Dumitrescu, C., 79
Durkin, K., 116, 123
Dziobek, I., 165

Elder, L., 139
Elkis-Abuhoff, D., 113

Faherty, C., 53, 112, 181
Feldman, Y., 163
Ferdinand, R., 45
Fitzgerald, M., 76, 112
Fombonne, E., 45
Forrester-Jones, R., 162
Foster, L., 29
Frith, U., 1, 2, 97, 99, 141, 160, 164, 168

Gardner, H., 171
Garnett, M., 118, 123
Ghaziuddin, M., xviii, 45, 78, 113
Ghaziuddin, N., 45, 113
Gillberg, C., 3, 4–6, 62, 86, 173
Gillis, J., 53
Ginott, H., 179
Goodlin-Jones, B., 142
Gorrindo, J., 113
Graham, S., 143
Grandin, T., 43–44, 93–94, 99, 173

Greenspan, S., xiv, 112, 181
Grossman, J., 166

Haddon, M., 173
Hall, K., 60, 88, 172
Happé, F., 97, 99, 164
Harris, P., 161, 162
Hartup, W., 122–123, 141
Hassenstab, J., 165
Heaton, P., 98
Henley, D., 113
Hermelin, B., 98, 164
Hertz-Picciotto, I., xv
Hinton, S., 56, 117
Hobson, J., 161
Hobson, R., 161
Howe, S., 98

Iland, I., 146

Jacobsen, P., 171
Jaquet, E., 116, 123
Jarrold, C., 161, 162
Josefi, O., 162
Juvonen, J., 143

Kanner, L., 1, 2, 13, 173
Kasari, C., 123, 143, 163
Keefe, K., 141
Kelly, A., 118, 123
Kim, Y., 113, 143
Kirby, B., 88
Klauber, T., 62
Klin, A., 45, 78, 79, 166
Koh, Y., 143
Kuhl, P., 29

Lecavelier, L., xviii
Lee, A., 161
Leevers, H. 161
Leslie, A., 160, 162
Levanthal, B., 143
Levin, I., 117
Levine, K., xiv, 51, 94, 112, 118, 181
Levy-Shiff, R., 163

Leyfer, O., 45, 53, 113
Liëbenluft, E., 113
Lightfoot, C., 123
Little, L., 143
Lindner, J., 166
Lockshin, S., 53
Lord, C., 161
Lowery, E., 167
Lyons, V., 1, 76

Marston, G., 162
Mathur, R., 142
Martinovich, J., 113
Meesters, S., 45
Melzoff, A., 29
Meyerowitz-Katz, J., 113
Miller, B., 167
Miller, N., 180
Minio-Paluello, I., 112
Mitchell, P., 164
Molyneux, S., 112
Mountain-Kimchi, K., xviii, 78
Myles, B., 122, 180

Nagelberg, L., 163
Natof, T., 53

O'Connor, N., 164
O'Driscoll, G., 8, 170
O'Keefe, K., 164
Orbach-Caspi, E., 163
Osterling, J., 29

Papincazak, T., 142
Parker, J., 123, 141
Peterson, C., 118, 123
Piaget, J., 62, 171
Pine, D., 113
Pozzi, M., 167
Pradella, A., 113
Pring, L., 98

Ratey, J., 8, 170
Reaven, J., 56, 94
Reddy, V., 162

Rinner, L., 180
Risi, S., 56, 117
Robbins, L., 180
Rogers, C., 17
Rogers, S., 165
Romanczyk, R., 53
Rosén, L., 166
Row, S., 95
Rowley, G., 98
Ruberman, L., 167
Ryan, V., 162

Sainsbury, C., 34–35
Sanders, R., 13
Saulnier, C., 78
Schneider, B., 141
Schopler, E., x–xi
Schuster, M., 143
Shacknai, D., 139
Sherratt, D., 161
Shtayermann, O., 143
Shulman, C., 123, 141, 142
Siddons, F., 164
Sigman, M., 160, 161, 163
Silverman, S., 95, 182
Simpson, R., 122
Smith, P., 161, 162
Sofronoff, K., 56, 117
Soloman, M., 142
Sonders, S., 181
Sparrow, S., 79
Stevens, M., 141
Streimer, D., 113
Sullivan, H., 140
Szatmari, P., 113, 169
Sze, K., 56

Tan, S., 9
Tantam, D., 116, 122
Templeton, E., 142
Thede, L., 78
Treffert, D., 97
Towbin, K., 113

Ungerer, J., 160, 161

van Engeland, H., 112
van Ijzedorn, N., 112
Verheij, F., 45
Volkmar, F., 45, 79, 166

Wall, J., 53
Walsh, V., 112
Weidmer-Mikhail, E., 45, 113
Weinfeld, R., 95, 182
Wheelwright, S., 166
Whitehouse, A., 116, 123
Wieder, S., xiv, 112, 181
Willemsen-Swinkels, S., 112
Willey, L., 141

Williams, E., 162
Wilson, F., 113
Wing, L., 1, 3, 45, 113, 116, 173
Winner, E., 97–98
Witwer, A., xviii
Wolf, O., 165
Wolff, S., 113
Wood, J., 56
Wulff, S., 160, 161

Yirmiya, N., 163

Zachor, D., 163
Ziatas, K., 116, 123

Subject Index

ABA. *See* Applied Behavior Analysis

Abuse, x, 14, 20, 21–22, 118, 171

Acceptance, x, xii, 14, 17, 22, 52, 59, 69, 90–94, 104, 108, 127, 140, 158, 162, 164, 167, 171

Accommodation, 171, 182

Action figures. 113–115. *See also* Puppet play

Affect, xiv, 52, 84, 113, 140, 147, 163, 164, 165. *See* also Feelings

Affection. x, xii, 3, 13, 23, 59, 75, 92, 106, 131, 148, 151. *See* also Physical contact

Aggression, 6, 7, 46, 47–49, 50–52, 102–112, 114–115, 117–118, 122, 148, 153

Aggression,
  setting limit in therapy, 102–112

Alexithymia, 112

Alliance with parents. *See* Parents, working with

Aloneness in therapy,
  child's need for, 26, 119, 155, 165, 166–168

Anger, 7, 49, 58, 65, 105, 118, 128, 159, 163, 180. *See* also Feelings

Anger management, 117, 181

"Anxiety-o-meters," 21

Anxiety, ix, xii, xv, 7, 23, 43–60, 88, 124, 157–158, 171
  aggression and impulsive behavior, disguised as, 45–53
  cognitive-behavioral therapy, 56–57
  comfort zone, 55–56
  "decision zone," 53
  diagnosis of Asperger's, with, 43
  Exploring Feelings program, 57
  fear, 52, 53, 65
  gauging in therapy, 20–22, 24, 49–50
  Grandin, Temple, 43–44
  hang time, 59–60
  history, 44–45
  incremental nature, 54
  intellect, appealing to the child's, 53–54, 56
  medication, 57–58
  microexposure, 55–56, 57
  "Mind the Gap," 53
  phobias, 53
  prevalence, 7, 45, 49, 53
  internal conflict, 58–59
  relaxation techniques, 37, 40, 57
  safety, 20, 52
  separation, 52
  stereotypic behaviors, 20, 21, 23, 45–46, 49–50

Anxiety (*continued*)
  therapist sharing child's, 52–53
  therapist's function, 52–53, 60
  tics, 21, 50, 58
  treatment goal, as 45
Applied Behavior Analysis, 16
Art therapy, 112. *See* also Expressive
  therapies
Asperger "journeys," parents', 12–17
Assimilation, 171, 182
Asperger, Hans,
  "autistically psychopathic"
    ("Autistischen psychopathen"),
    62, 169
  intellectual testing and function, 3,
    78
  parents, as described by, 2–3
  language, as described by, 2, 62
  "little professors," 69–70
  feelings, as described by, 102
  social difficulties, as described by,
    121–122
  traits. as described, 1–2, 169
Asthma, x
Attachment, 41, 65–69, 136, 149–160,
  166–168, 183
  sensory sensitivities, 41
Attention deficit, 7, 78, 95, 102
Attwood, Tony, xiv, 55, 57, 62, 102,
  117
Authenticity,
  in therapist, 23
  in child, 73, 136, 141–142, 172
Autism spectrum, xiv, 12, 15, 35, 62,
  122
  Hans Asperger's anticipation of, 3
Autistic motorisms. *See* Stereotypical
  movements
"Autistically psychopathic" ("Autistischen
  psychopathen"), 62, 169
Awkwardness, social. *See* Social
  difficulties

Beginning therapy, 19–27
  functions, 26–27
  referral call, 11–16

safety, 19–22
talking with child, 62–64
testing the therapist, 103–106
with parents, 11–18
Behavioral therapy, xv, 36, 51, 55–56
Bettelheim, Bruno, xiii–xiv, 2
Biological basis. *See* Neurological basis.
Biting. *See* Aggression
Blaming parents, xiv, 2
Blocks and building toys, 86, 97,
  105, 114
Body language. *See* Nonverbal gestures
Boredom, therapist, 20, 22, 63, 64
Brain science, xiii, xiv
Bullying, 48, 143–146

Camp Wediko, viii–x, 35, 97
Cancellations, 86
Can't versus *won't,* 129
Car sickness, 37
Catch-22, 8
Center for Talented Youth (CTY), 98
Chedd, Naomi, xviii
Child-centered therapy, 17, 51, 112
Client-centered therapy. *See* Child–
  Centered
Cognition. *See* Intellectual Functioning
Cognitive-behavioral therapy, 51, 56–57,
  138
  anxiety, 56–57
  depression, 112, 117
  perfectionism, 94
  social difficulties, 138
Cognitive style,
  working within the child's, 81–88
Communication, xv, 61–76. *See*
  also Language; Nonverbal
  communication
Comorbid diagnoses, xv, 7, 43–45, 49,
  53, 113, 116, 171
Compulsive behaviors, 7, 24, 47
Confirming. *See* Validating
Connection, x, xiii, xiv, 6, 8, 9, 41, 64,
  65, 86, 105, 106, 121, 122, 128,
  141, 142, 149, 155, 167, 168, 174,
  183

Control, child's need to, 47–49, 123
CTY. *See* Center for Talented Youth
Creativity, xv, 95–99, 161–163

"Decision Zone," 53
Dependability of therapist. *See* Reliability
  of therapist
Depression, xv, 7, 101, 113–119, 122,
  171
  adolescence, 113, 116
  aggression, 117–118
  anger management, 117
  anxiety, 113
  cognitive-behavioral therapy, 117
  family strife, 118
  friendship, lack of, 116, 118, 122,
    143
  friends, protective value of, 117, 118,
    122–123
  intelligence, 116
  medication, 101, 118
  prevalence, 113, 116
  replays, 112, 118
  self-hatred,94, 115, 117, 178
  sharing, value of, 113–117
  social group therapy, 113
  suicide, 7, 101, 113, 143
  Desensitization. *See Microexposure*
Developmental burden, x, 171
Diagnosis,
  Asperger's versus HFA, xviii
  child coming to terms with, 159,
    171–172
  Gillberg's criteria versus
    DSM-IV-TR, 3–6
  DSM-IV-TR criteria, 4
  evolution of *DSM,* 3
  Gillberg's criteria, 4–5
  incidence, xv, 45
  limitations of diagnosis, 14
  parents' reactions, 12–16
  sharpening, xv, 45
  inadequacy, 44–45
Disorganization, 78, 79, 93, 95, 114
Distractibility, 46, 78, 79, 80, 148
Divorce, 14, 171

Doctors, fear of, 53
Drama therapy, 112. *See* Expressive
  therapies
Drawing. *See* Art in therapy
DSM-I, 3
DSM-II, 3
DSM-III, xii, 3
DSM-III-R, 3
DSM-IV, 3–6, 14, 62
DSM-IV-TR, 3

Early intervention, xv, 61–62
Eating,
  child's fussiness, 33–34
Echolalia, xii, 2, 21, 62, 152. *See* also
  Language
Educational Program for Gifted Youth
  (EPGY), 98
Educational specialists, 78, 95
Educators. *See* Teachers
Embarrassment, 73, 126, 138, 163
"Emotional reserve" of therapist, 163
Emotions. *See* Feelings
Empathic failure, 165
Empathy, xiv
  child's, 147, 164, 165, 174
  children getting less of, 8
  therapist's for child, 24, 117,
    163–164, 164–166
Ending therapy. *See* Termination.
Enrichment, educational, 98–99
Envy, 7, 116, 117
Epidemiology. *See* Incidence
EPGY. *See* Educational Program for
  Gifted Youth.
Errors,
  therapist's, 24–25
Executive dysfunction, 78, 95. *See* also
  Disorganization
Exploring Feelings program, 57, 112,
  181
Exposure therapy. *See* Microexposure
Expressive therapies, 112–113. *See* Art
  therapy
Eye contact, xii, 2, 4, 21, 104, 122, 142,
  148, 152

Facial expression, 2, 4, 62, 103, 122, 124, 166. *See* also Nonverbal Communication
Familial patterns. *See* Genetics
Family strife, 118
Family therapy, 118
Fear, 47, 52, 53–60, 65, 86, 88. *See* also Anxiety
Feedback, giving parents, 12–16
Feelings, xv, 7, 101–119, 163–164
    accepting, 127
    aggression, 7, 102–112, 114–115, 117–118, 148, 153
    alexithymia, 112
    anger, 7, 49, 65, 163
    anger management, 117
    art therapy, 112
    Asperger's description of, Hans, 102
    Attwood, Tony, 102
    awareness, 163
    cognitive-behavioral therapy, 57, 112, 117
    complexity, 101
    confirming. *See* validating
    drama therapy, 112
    depression, xv, 101, 113–119. *See* also Depression
    difficulty processing, 102
    embarrassment, 163
    empathy for child's, 24, 117, 163–166
    envy, 7, 116, 117
    Exploring Feelings program, 57, 112, 181
    expressive therapies, 112–113
    family strife, 118
    family therapy, 118
    floortime, xiv, 112, 181
    goals, 119
    guilt, 14, 58, 59, 70, 117, 154, 163
    helplessness, 116, 139
    insulating the child, 163
    intellect, using to understand, 164
    jealousy, 7, 65, 111, 116, 134, 163, 166
    lack of remorse, 102–106
    medication, 101, 118, 139
    movement therapy, 112
    music, 98
    music therapy, 112
    neurological deficit, xiii, 8, 112
    pride, 41, 55, 84, 95, 98, 108, 133, 153, 157, 163
    relationships, 101
    reading others', 7
    replays, xiv, 50–51, 94, 112, 118
    self-injury, 101
    self-hatred, 94, 115, 117, 178
    storytelling, 112
    stress management, 57
    therapist's emotion, protecting child from, 163
    value of sharing, 113–117
    validating, 8, 163–164
    words, putting into, 112
Floortime, xiv, 112, 181
Friendship,
    lack of, 122,
    protective value, 118
    understanding of, intellectual, 128–129
Frustration, 7, 8, 50, 59, 65, 94, 95, 98, 114, 148

Gender confusion, x
Genetics, 2
    parents's guilt over, 14
Gestures, 4, 5, 62, 66. *See* also Nonverbal Communication
Giftedness,
    nurturing, 97–99, 156
    learning disabilities and, 98
Glass ceilings, xii–xiii
Goals (therapeutic), 33, 176–177
Grandin, Temple, 173
    view of anxiety, 43–44
    view of Asperger label, 93–94, 99
Grief and grieving. *See* Loss
Guilt, 14, 58, 59, 70, 117, 154, 163

Hang time, 59–60
Helplessness, 116, 139

HFA. *See* High-Functioning Autism
High-Functioning Autism (HFA), vii, x,
xi, xv, xviii
and Asperger's, diagnostically, xviii,
78
Hitting. *See* Aggression
HMOs, 68
Holding, therapeutic
anxiety, and, 52–53
Homework, 24, 95, 122, 123, 129, 176
Honesty,
child's, 23, 88–90
therapist's, 21, 23, 25, 63
Hope,
therapist providing child, 27, 52, 53,
59
therapist providing parent, 14, 18
Hostility, *See* Aggression
Hugs. *See* Physical contact
Humanistic therapy. *See* Child-centered
therapy
Humor, 2, 22, 72, 75–76
Hygiene,
and sensory hypersensitivity, 35–37,
38–39
Hyperactivity, 102–112
Hypersensitivity. *See* Sensory sensitivity
Hypervigilance, 103
Hyposensitivity, 40

Imagination and imaginary play, xiii, 20,
147–160, 161–163
Immigrant experience, 9
Impediments to therapy, supposed,
147–168
Impulsivity, 104, 111, 112, 118
Incidence, xv, 45
Infantile Autism, xi–xiii, 3, 11–13, 148
Inhibition, 38, 57
Inner conflict. *See* Internal conflict
Inner world of child, xiii, 69
Internal conflict, 58–59
Insincerity, therapist's, 21, 23
Insulating function of therapy, 163
Intellect, child's, xii, xv, 3, 23. *See* also
Intellectual Functioning

acknowledging, 23
admiring, 90–94
appealing to the child's, 23, 33–34,
36, 53, 54, 46, 81–84, 164
definition, 77
nurturing giftedness, 97–99
uneven, 3
Intellectual functioning, 77–99. *See* also
Intellect
admiring, 90–94
anxiety, 52
Asperger, as described by Hans, 3,
78
attention deficit, 7, 78, 95, 102
changing over time, xii–xiii, 79–80
creativity, xv, 95–99
DSM-IV-TR, 4
disorganization, 78, 79, 93, 95, 114
distractibility, 46, 78, 79, 80, 148
educational specialists, 78, 95
executive dysfunction, 78, 95
Gillberg's criteria, 5
honesty, 88–90
interests, ix, xii, 2, 4, 5, 12, 20–21,
22, 23, 70–72, 78, 86–88,
90–94, 96–97, 98–99, 133
IQ, limits, xii, xiii, 79–80, 98, 148
learning disabilities, 24, 78, 95, 98,
114
monologues, ix, 20–21, 58, 63–64,
70–72, 87–88, 134, 157, 165,
181
multiple intelligences, 93, 98, 171
neurological basis, 82
neuropsychologists, 3, 78, 95
nonverbal, 2, 4, 78
nonverbal learning disability, 79
perfectionism, 94
savant skills, 78, 97, 98
self-acceptance, 90–94
self-taught mastery, 78
social comprehension, 79
splinter skills, 78
testing, difficulty, 80–81, 148
uneven, 3
validity of testing, 80–81

Intelligence, *See* also Intellect; Intellectual functioning
definitions, 77
Intelligence quotients. *See* IQ
IQ, 98. *See* also Intellect; Intellectual functioning
limits of, xii–xiii, 79, 148
Interests, ix, xii, 2, 4, 5, 12, 20–21, 22, 23, 58, 63–64, 65, 70–72, 78, 86–88, 90–94, 96–97, 98–99, 133, 134, 156, 157, 165, 181
Isolation. *See* social isolation
Irritability, 7, 22, 40, 49, 75, 105, 123, 182

Jealousy, 7, 65, 111, 116, 134, 163, 166. *See* also Feelings
Johns Hopkins's Center for Talented Youth (CTY), 98
Journal of Autism and Developmental Disorders, xiv

Kanner, Leo,
child's language, as described by, 2, 62
traits, as described by, 1–2
Kicking. *See* Aggression
Know-it-all attitude, 69–70, 134–135

Label,
awareness, child's, 159, 171–172
limitations, 13, 14, 93–94, 99
Language, 61–76
Asperger, as described by Hans, 2, 62
assessment, 62
atypical language, ix, 2, 45, 50, 62, 78
creating a shared, 63, 74–75
diagnosis, 62
DSM-IV-TR, 4, 62
dictionary definitions, 61–62
direct, 23, 32, 63
early language therapy, value of, 61–62
echolalia, xii, 2, 21, 62
functions, 76

Gillberg's criteria, 5, 62
humor, 2, 22, 72, 75–76, 158
Kanner, as described by, 2
letter writing in therapy, 150–151
"little professors," 69–70
monologues, ix, 20–21, 58, 63–64, 70–72, 87–88, 134, 157, 165, 181
muteness, 2, 52
natural rewards, 65–69
need for sameness, xii, 2, 85–86, 152, 153
neologisms, 2, 62, 74
neurological deficit, xiii, 8
nonverbal communication, 2, 4, 62, 122
parroting, 2
pedantic, 5, 62
playing with language and words, xii, 2
pronoun reversal, xii, 2, 62, 103, 152
pseudo-grownup language as social problem, 2, 62, 69–70
puns, ix, 75–76
responsive, 63
small talk, 72–74
social mediator, 64–65
speech and language evaluation, 61
speech and language therapists as experts, 61–62, 73–74
speech and language therapists as critical team members, 16–17, 62
speech and language therapy, xv, 16, 61–62, 65, 66
tokens and behavioral rewards, limitations of, 65
ways to talk with child, 61–76
Language therapy. *See* Speech and language therapy
Learning disabilities, x, 69, 78, 93, 95, 98, 114
giftedness, coexisting with, 98
parents as advocates for child's, 14, 16, 17, 95
Letter-writing in therapy, 150–151

Life skills, adaptive, xii–xiii, 78
Liking to come to therapy, 65–69
Limitations, coping with intellectual, 90–94
Limits in therapy, setting, 50–51, 104–106
"Little professors," 69–70
Listening, 16, 17, 20–21, 22, 39, 63–64, 69
Loneliness. *See* Social Isolation
Loss, xii, 19, 86, 118, 152–158, 162
Love of learning, 93

Managed care, 68
Martial arts, 40, 57
Math, 84, 94, 98, 99, 111, 139
Mean girls, 128, 143–146
Medication, xv
    anxiety, 57–58 139
    depression, 101, 118
    social anxiety, 44, 139
Meditation, 57
Meeting parents, 11–18
Meltdowns. *See* Tantrums
Memory, 86, 92, 133
Microexposure, 55–56, 57
"Mind the Gap," 53
Mistakes, child managing, 94–95
Mistakes, therapist owning, 24–25
Misunderstanding, 8, 9, 22, 69, 172
Monologues, ix, 20–21, 58, 63–64, 70–72, 87–88, 134, 157, 165, 181. *See also* Interests; Obsessions; Language
Motorisms. *See* Stereotypical movements
Movement therapy, 112
Multiple intelligences, 93, 98, 171
Music and feelings, 98
Music therapy, 112
Muteness, 2, 52

Need for sameness, xii, 2, 85–86, 148, 152
Neglect, x, 22, 118
Neologisms, 2, 62, 74. *See also* Language
Neuropsychologist, as team member, 78, 95

Neuropsychology, 3, 78
Neuropsychology, of Asperger's versus HFA, xviii, 78
Nervousness. *See* Anxiety
Neurological basis, xiii, xv, 2, 8, 22, 41–42, 44
NLD. *See* Nonverbal learning disability
NVLD. *See* Nonverbal learning disability
Nonverbal communication, 2, 4, 5, 21, 62, 63, 64, 122
    compared with verbal, 78
Nonverbal gestures. *See* Nonverbal Communication
Nonverbal learning disability (NLD), compared with Asperger's, 79
Normalcy, 95

Obsessions, xii, 7, 12, 45, 56, 57, 58, 63, 65, 70–72, 78. 86–88, 91, 93, 98, 156, 159
Occupational therapy, 65
Office, setting up,
    to minimize sensory overstimulation, 30–31
One-child families seen by Hans Asperger, 2
Overstimulation, 7, 22, 29, 30–31, 35, 111

Pain,
    hyposensitivity to, 40
Parent-child work. *See* Parents, working with
Parents, Asperger traits of seen by Hans Asperger, 2
Parents, blaming, xiv, 2
Parents, shocked by diagnosis of Autism, 12
Parents, working with, 102–112, 175–185
    advocates for child, xv, 14, 95
    alliance, 17–18, 48
    anxiety and feelings, 180–181
    Asperger traits, with their own, 2, 17
    baby steps, 176
    communication, 181–182
    diagnosis, reactions to, 12–16

Parents, working with (*continued*)
    disagreement, 15
    empathy for child, 180
    experience, trusting their, 177
    frustration, 3, 15, 17
    goals, 175–77
    grieving, 14, 178
    guilt, 14
    hope, 14, 18
    Hans Asperger supporting, 2–3, 169
    input, 3, 14, 17–18
    intellect, nurturing, 182
    intelligence, 182
    learning from, therapists, 17–18
    meeting, 11–18
    negativity, 178
    noting progress, 175–177
    parenting as a skill, 175
    regular parenting, need for, 179
    school, 182
    sensory sensitivities, 179–180
    social growth, 182
    stigma, parents' fear of, 15
    supporting therapy, 17
    therapist's supporting, xv, 2–3, 16–18
    talking about Asperger's, 13–16
    therapy, suitability of, 183–184
    trial and error, 178
    trusting own perceptions, 14
    watching therapists, 27
Parroting, 2
Perfectionism, 94
Pharmacology. *See* Medication
Phobias, 7, 32, 52, 53, 180. *See* also
    Anxiety; Fear
Photophobia, 30, 32, 33
Physical contact between child and
    therapist, xii, 24, 151–152
Precious goods, 69
Predictions, clinical,
    danger in, xii–xiii, 80–81, 148–149,
        160, 176, 178
Preoccupations. *See* Interests; Obsessions;
    Monologues
Pretend play, 69, 152, 158, 161–163

Pride, 41, 55, 84, 95, 98, 108, 133, 153, 157, 163
Problem solving in therapy, 51, 53, 155
Pronoun reversal, xii, 2, 62, 103. *See* also
    Language
Puns. *See* Humor
Puppets in therapy, 47–8, 50–52, 111, 115, 149–155,

Rapport, 22
Reading, 7, 37, 60, 90–92, 124, 125
Referral call from parents, 11–16
Referrals from school, 12, 24, 45–46, 47, 50, 70, 102, 123
Rejection. *See* Social isolation
Relaxation techniques, 37, 40, 57
Reliability of therapist, 89
Replays, xiv, 50–51, 94, 112, 118
Resistance to change. *See* Need for
    sameness
Respect, x, 16, 17, 22, 24, 90, 116
Robinson, John, 173
Romance, wish for, 37–38, 58–59, 73, 74–75, 134
Rules, child's obsession with, 47–49

Safety in therapy, ensuring, 19–22
    anxiety, and, xiii, 52–53
Sainsbury, Claire, 34, 173
Savant skills, 78, 97, 98, 99. *See* also
    Intellectual Functioning
School, referrals from, 12, 24, 45–46, 47, 50, 70, 102, 123
    team approach, 16, 62, 78, 95, 182
    teacher's input and support, xv, 3, 12, 15, 24, 45–46, 47, 48, 50, 51, 56, 70, 85–86, 93, 94, 95, 97, 102–112, 112–113, 114, 116, 118, 123, 126, 128, 132, 134, 135, 143, 144, 153, 155, 156, 163, 181, 182, 183
Schopler, Eric, x–xi
Self-acceptance, 90–94, 172
Self-awareness, 30, 53, 56, 57, 87, 112, 116, 133, 135, 138, 163, 166, 171, 180

Self-consciousness, 7, 53, 55, 135–136
Self-control, 47, 51, 102–112
Self-determination, 34, 55
Self-fulfilling prophecy, 81
Self-hatred, 94, 115, 117, 178
Semantic pragmatics therapy. *See* Social
    Pragmatics Therapy
Sensory-Motor Integration, 40, 180
Sensory sensitivity, xv, 6, 29–42, 141, 152
    hygiene, 35–37, 38–39
    attachment, 41
    body, strange sense of own, 38–40
    clothing, viii, ix, 32, 37, 38, 64,
        179–180
    compulsions, 24, 40, 47, 50
    definitions, 19–20
    detected in babies, 29
    hyposensitivity, 40
    implications of, 34–42
    intellect, appealing to, 33–34, 36,
        53–54, 56
    journal, 37
    light, 30, 32, 34, 35, 38
    noise, 6, 30, 31, 32, 35, 36, 37, 38,
        40, 41, 53, 89, 149, 150, 151 s
    overarousal, 29–34, 35
    photophobia, 30, 32, 33
    protecting child against, in office,
        29–34
    school, 34–35
    self-stimulation, 40
    Sensory–Motor Integration, 40, 180
    smell, 30, 35, 36, 38, 41
    synesthesias, 40
    underarousal, 29
Separation, 52, 66–69, 112, 171
Separation anxiety, 52, 112
Sexuality, 58, 59, 74, 88–89, 136, 148
Shame, 7, 38–40, 58, 59, 117, 134, 138
Short-term therapy, 65, 68
Siblings, 2, 12, 25, 106, 111, 116–117,
    123, 124, 125, 130, 133, 144, 145,
    166
Silence in therapy, 63, 113, 163
Sincerity, in the therapist, 21, 23, 32, 63
Small talk, 72–74. *See* Language

Sociability. *See* Social difficulties
Social anxiety, 7, 44, 55, 57, 88, 121, 139
Social comprehension, 78. *See* also Social
    difficulties
Social difficulties, xv, 121–146
    adolescents, 123, 139
    aggression, 7, 102–112, 122, 148,
        153
    art work, 126
    Asperger, as described by Hans, 2,
        121–122
    authenticity, nurturing, 73, 141–142
    best friend, value of, 141, 145
    bullying, 3, 48, 143–146, 158
    cognitive-behavioral therapy, 139
    conversation, 72–74
    depression, 122, 123, 139
    dog and therapy, 129–132
    DSM-IV-TR,
    esteem, 140
    exhaustion, 122
    experimenting, social, 136–137
    facial expression, 2, 4, 5, 62, 103,
        122
    false self, 141–142, 172
    friends, functions of, 141
    friendships, difficulty making, 122
    friendship, intellectual understanding
        of, 128–129, 143
    friendships, value of, 122–123
    fundamental deficit, as, 122
    Gillberg's criteria, in, 5–6
    group activity, value of, 125, 139,
        142
    helplessness, 139
    hopelessness, 83, 102, 116, 139, 160
    individual therapy and friendship,
        140
    interests, sharing and nurturing,
        22, 23, 63–64, 86–88, 90–94,
        97–97, 142
    learning disability, as a, 139
    Leo Kanner, as described by, 2
    masquerading, 141
    mean girls, 128, 143–146
    medication, 44, 139

Social difficulties (*continued*)
model, Sullivan's view of therapeutic relationship as primary, 140
neurologic deficits, xiii
nonautistic friends, value of, 142
nonverbal gestures, 2, 4, 62, 122–123
processing, impairment in social, 122
relationships, repairing, 128–132
relationship, generalizing of therapeutic, 140, 142–143
scripts, 139
sensory hypersensitivity, 37–38
social anxiety, 44, 139
social group treatment, 138–139
social interest, x, xiii, 122, 142
social pragmatics, xv, 73, 74, 139, 142, 182, 183
social skills, 8, 59, 122, 142
social skills training, 138–139
teasing, ix, 22, 70, 124, 133, 143, 144, 145, 146
video games, 70–72, 142
Social disability. *See* Social difficulties
Social dysfunction. *See* Social difficulties
Social impairment. *See* Social difficulties
Social information processing deficit. *See* Social difficulties
Social isolation, ix, 6, 7, 8, 22, 70–72, 114, 116, 141
Social learning disability. *See* Social difficulties
Social network, 8
Social pragmatics therapy, xv, 73, 74, 139, 142, 182, 183
Social skills, 8, 59, 122, 142
Social skills training, 139
Social world, shrinking, 8
Speech and language therapist. *See* also Speech and Language Therapy; Language
Speech and language therapy, xv, 16, 61–62, 65, 66
speech and language evaluation, need for, 61

speech and language therapists as experts, 61–62, 73–74
speech and language therapists as critical team members, 16, 62
Splinter skills, 78. *See* also Intellectual Functioning.
Stanford University's Educational Program for Gifted Youth (EPGY), 98
Stereotypical movements, 2, 4, 20, 21, 23, 45–46, 47, 49–50, 102, 148, 152, 153
in therapy, signs of anxiety, 21, 49–50
Storytelling, 112
Stress management, 57
Suicide, 7, 101, 113, 143, 177
Supporting parents, xv, 2–3, 16–18
Symbolic play, 160–161, 161–163
Syndrome,
Asperger's as, xiii, 2, 8, 170
Synesthesias, 6, 40

Tact, lack of. *See* Honesty
Talents. *See* Interests.
Talking with child. *See* Language
Tammet, Daniel, 173
Tantrums, 12, 46, 47, 50–51, 53, 85, 94, 117, 123, 127, 163, 179, 180
TEACCH (Treatment and Education of Autistic and related Communication–handicapped Children), x, 53
Teachers, input and support, xv, 3, 12, 15, 24, 45–46, 47, 48, 50, 51, 56, 70, 85–86, 93, 94, 95, 97, 102–112, 112–113, 114, 116, 118, 123, 126, 128, 132, 134, 135, 143, 144, 153, 155, 156, 163, 181, 182, 183
Teasing, ix, 22, 70, 124, 133, 143, 144, 145, 146
Team approach, 16, 62, 78, 95, 182
Tension. *See* Anxiety
Theory of mind, xv, 160–161, 164–166
The Arrival, 9
Tics, 21, 49–50, 58, 103. *See* also Stereotypic movements
Tough love, 21, 86
Trauma, 13, 21–22, 118

Underachievement, 98
Understanding, x, xii, 16, 19. *See* also
   Misunderstanding
University of North Carolina, x

Validating, 8, 14, 16, 39, 52, 73, 107,
   170, 180
"Velvet bulldozers," 95
Video games, 25, 46, 70–72, 142
Voice, 2

Wall, Jack, 53
Wediko. *See* Camp Wediko
White lies, 90. *See also* Honesty
Williams, Donna, 173
Willey, Liane, 173
Winner, Ellen
   views on giftedness, 97–98
Worry. *See* Anxiety

Yoga, 40, 57

About the Author

Richard Bromfield, Ph.D., a graduate of Bowdoin College and the University of North Carolina at Chapel Hill, is on the clinical faculty of Harvard Medical School and maintains a practice outside Boston. He is author of *Doing Child and Adolescent Psychotherapy*, *Teens in Therapy*, *Nurturing the Self of the Child with Asperger's*, and *Playing for Real: Exploring Child Therapy and the Inner Worlds of Children*.